Selected

Mark van Vugt is Professor of Psychology at the VU University Amsterdam, the Netherlands. He is Research Fellow at the Institute for Cognitive and Evolutionary Anthropology at the University of Oxford and Honorary Professor at the University of Kent. He obtained his PhD in 1996 from the University of Maastricht, the Netherlands. His research has been published in all the major science journals in the field and he is a regular contributor to the popular science media. He was chief editor of *Cooperation in Modern Society* (Routledge, 2000) and co-author of *Applying Social Psychology* (Sage, 2007). He is a fellow of the British Academy Centenary Project, 'Lucy to Language', and currently serves as associate editor of the prestigious *Journal of Personality and Social Psychology*. He lives with his family near Amsterdam. To find out more about Mark van Vugt, please visit www.professor-markvanvugt.com – or to contact him about his work, email m.van.vugt@psy.vu.nl

Anjana Ahuja earned a PhD in space physics at Imperial College in London. She then worked at *The Times* for sixteen years as a feature writer and columnist, and first introduced Mark's work to a wider audience through her comment column. She has held advisory posts at the Royal Society, the British Science Association and the British Council. Now freelance, she lives in London.

Selected

Why some people lead, why others follow, and why it matters

Mark van Vugt and Anjana Ahuja

Random House Canada

www.randomhouse.ca

Random House Canada and colophon are registered trademarks.

Quotations at the start of chapters are reproduced by permission as follows:
1: from *The Open Society and Its Enemies* by Karl Popper; by permission of University of Klagenfurt / Karl Popper Library.
2: from Nobel Prize lecture by Robert Aumann; copyright © The Nobel Foundation 2005.
4: from *King of the Mountain* by Arnold Ludwig; by permission of Arnold Ludwig.
5: from *Animal Farm* by George Orwell; copyright © George Orwell, 1945; reprinted by permission of Bill Hamilton as the Literary Executor of the Estate of the Late Sonia Brownell Orwell and Secker & Warburg Ltd.
6: from *The Birth and Death of Meaning* by Ernest Becker; reprinted with the permission of The Free Press, a Division of Simon & Schuster, Inc.
7: from blog by John Mackey; courtesy of Whole Foods Market. 'Whole Foods Market' is a registered trademark of Whole Foods Market IP, L.P.

Every reasonable effort has been made to obtain and acknowledge copyright permission for quoted material where required. In the event of an inadvertent omission or error, please contact the publisher in writing for a correction to be made in future printings.

Library and Archives Canada Cataloguing in Publication

van Vugt, Mark, 1967–
        Selected : why some people lead, why others follow, and why it matters / Mark van Vugt and Anjana Ahuja.

Includes bibliographical references.
Also available in electronic format.

ISBN 978-0-307-35862-2

        1. Leadership. 2. Leadership—History. I. Ahuja, Anjana. II. Title.

HM1261.V35 2010   303.3'4   C2010-902202-5

Text design by Sue Lamble
Typeset by MacGuru Ltd

Printed in the United States of America

10 9 8 7 6 5 4 3 2 1

Contents

Acknowledgements

This book owes so much to so many people that it is impossible to thank them all. They are all leaders in their own ways.

The book came about from discussions with Daniel Crewe, at Profile, who read a *New Scientist* article I'd penned for Kate Douglas, its features editor. Daniel and Kate convinced me that there was a book in it. Daniel and my agent, Peter Tallack, then had the brilliant idea of pairing me up with Anjana Ahuja, one of the best science journalists in Britain, who was able to turn my research into beautifully crafted prose.

I also thank my colleagues Sarah Brosnan, Edward Cartright, Robin Dunbar, Joris Gillet, Robert Hogan, Dominic Johnson, Rob Kaiser, Andrew King, Rob Kurzban, Rick O'Gorman, Pete Richerson and David Sloan Wilson for their intellectual input into this project.

I thank my current and former PhD students, David De Cremer, Claire Hart, Charlie Hardy, Wendy Iredale, Brian Spisak and Chris Stiff for doing much of the excellent research that is discussed in *Selected*.

I would like to thank the University of Kent, the University of Oxford and the VU University Amsterdam for offering stimulating intellectual environments and the time to write the book.

And now the dedications. First, to Charles Darwin, without whom this book could not have been written. I am glad that Darwin's vision that 'Psychology will be based on a new foundation' is finally being realised. Second, to all the good leaders around the world who are trying their best to improve our lives, often without recognition. A special dedication goes to my partner Hannie, who leads the way in every important aspect of my life.

Above all, I dedicate this book to my son Jamie, whose future will be determined by the quality of today's leadership.

Mark van Vugt
Amsterdam, June 2010

One of my prized possessions as a little girl was a pristine, bound set of *The Children's Encyclopaedia*, edited by Arthur Mee. Its 7,000 pages documented, among other treasures, the 'Imperishable Thoughts of Men Enshrined in the Books of the World'. I had the pleasure of rediscovering it recently, during a house move. Choosing a volume at random, I opened it by chance at the following passage: 'Civilised man is the youngest child of ancient parents who were savage and lawless robbers and murderers by nature and practice. The terrible deep-rooted instincts of that untamed ancestry are constantly thrusting through the thin, modern wrappings with which civilization invests us.' This brutal, controversial sentiment is echoed to some degree in *Selected*. We may no longer be immoral savages, but there is certainly evidence to suggest that modern man is not as modern as he likes to think.

I hope you derive as much pleasure from reading *Selected* as I did from helping Mark to write it. He is, of course, the first recipient of my gratitude. It's been an exhilarating and rewarding partnership, and I hope the book's profound ideas can be used for good. Sincere thanks to Daniel Crewe at Profile, and to Peter Tallack for talking me into it. I am grateful to my editors at *The Times* who granted me a sabbatical to finish it.

Most of all, I would like to thank Tom, Rosa and Seth, and my mum Sharon, for their own deep-rooted instincts of love, humour and kindness. Where they lead, I happily follow. Oh, and thanks, Dad, for buying me *The Children's Encyclopedia*, and teaching me the virtue of knowledge.

Anjana Ahuja
London, June 2010

Prologue

There they are, laid out joyously on your kitchen table: two job offers from two different companies. The generous pay packet is the same, although the benefits vary a little, and both demand the skills that you somewhat creatively claimed for yourself on your CV. Unsure about which way to turn, you consult the oracle of the 21st century: Google. You look up information about each company's chief executive officer, as a way of gauging the culture, the heartbeat, of the organisation you might turn your life over to. Your discovery? That, as of last year, one CEO – let's call him John – earns a salary of a dollar a year. This is no tricksy financial illusion: there are no lavish stock options to cushion the miserly blow. Your heart sinks, because you think it could be a sign that the company is in decline.

Then you spot the letter he sent to his employees the previous year, stating, '... The tremendous success of [the company] has provided me with far more money than I ever dreamed I'd have and far more than is necessary for either my financial security or personal happiness ... I am now 53 years old and I have reached a place in my life where I no longer want to work for money, but simply for the joy of the work itself and to better answer the call to service that I feel so clearly in my own heart. Beginning [this year], my salary will be reduced to $1, and I will no longer take any other cash compensation ...' John goes on to say that the company is starting a hardship fund for employees, and that the company board has decreed that nobody, not even the directors, can be paid more than 19 times the average salary earned on the shop floor.[1]

And then there's the other CEO, Lawrence. He is a constant fixture on the list of the world's best-paid CEOs. He has a fleet of private jets and lives in one of the most expensive homes in the world, a 23-acre Japanese-themed extravaganza. And one of the most memorable things you find online about him is a joke: 'What's the difference between Lawrence and God? God doesn't think he's Lawrence.' Then comes the mental maths: with a remuneration of $57 million, Lawrence earns 1,000 times the salary you've been promised.[2]

You might want to be Lawrence, but the likelihood is that you'd feel more comfortable answering to John. Why? It's hard to articulate; the feeling is based more on instinct. You could go out for a beer with John; you'd feel like a serf sipping sake with Lawrence. By the way, these are not mythical CEOs but real ones: John Mackey, of Whole Foods Market, the organic foods company, and Larry Ellison, who runs the software giant Oracle.

Our brand new theory of leadership, grounded in evolutionary science, explains why a potential employee is more likely to plump for John than for Lawrence (unless you're the kind of person who really does want to be Larry Ellison, in which case you'll swallow the short-term inequity for the slim possibility of a spectacular long-term gain). Not only that, but, when viewed in the context of this theory, much of human behaviour – the leadership styles we prefer, and those we abhor – begins to make sense: why we don't like middle managers, why we prefer the political devil we know to the angel we don't, why we bristle at extravagance among leaders, and why there is universal interest in the domestic minutiae of political figures. Our theory accommodates all the familiar features of the leadership landscape – charisma, personality traits, alpha males, the glass ceiling for women, nature versus nurture – but, unlike other leadership theories, brings them together in a way that makes sense.

We have a name for this bigger picture: evolutionary leadership theory (ELT). Its name reflects our contention, backed up by observations and experiment, that leadership and followership emerged during the course of human evolution and that their foundations were laid long before humans evolved. We call them adaptive behaviours. When scientists use the word 'adaptive' to describe a behaviour, they mean that it emerged during the course of evolution in order to enhance an organism's chances of reproduction by enabling it to adapt to the environment. Evolution selected for a combination of leaders and followers in human society; a template for these behaviours eventually became 'hard-wired' into the human brain. As you'll see, there is an abundance of evidence that leadership and followership are automatic and (usually) beneficial. Groups of strangers speedily and spontaneously arrange themselves into a led group when asked to carry out a task, and led groups invariably fare better than groups without leaders. There is, as all of us already know, something instinctive and unforced about human leadership. The ubiquity of leadership and followership in the hierarchy of life – from fish to bees to humans – also suggests that tagging behind a competent leader is a smart way for any species, not just *Homo sapiens*, to prosper.

This brings us to the distinctive and unique feature of evolutionary leadership theory. We tackle leadership by doing something startlingly simple: turning back the clock and revisiting its origins. Human leadership as we know it had to start somewhere, and it began more than two million years ago on the African savannah with the birth of the species *Homo*. Our ancestors teamed up to hunt, to fight, to live, to love – and, because tribes showing strong leadership thrived, leadership and followership came to be part of the fabric of human life. This perspective makes *Selected* very different from most of the other books on leadership psychology, which often start by scrutinising a great leader and then combing through his background to fathom what makes him tick (no apologies for the male bias here; accounts of successful female leaders are rare, and we'll explain why later on). Such biographies, while making compelling reading, rarely provide insight beyond the psychology of the lantern-jawed hero gazing out assertively from the front cover.

Selected, on the other hand, applies to each and every one of us. It goes back to basics. It transports us back to the beginning, to trace how leadership emerged and changed over an evolutionary time period of several million years. If there is any central figure in the book, it is evolution's Everyman. Conceptually, we believe that the psychology of leadership and followership emerged in our species (as well as in many others) as a response to the challenges of survival and reproduction, which are the ultimate aim of any organism. We should note here that we are adopting an evolutionary perspective which applies insights from evolutionary biology and evolutionary psychology to questions concerning leadership.[3] An evolutionary perspective assumes that certain cognitive capacities, such as language, evolved to solve certain problems that would have preoccupied our ancestors, such as finding shelter and food. This book is not about explaining the specifics of evolutionary psychology; rather, we start from the (very reasonable and widely held) assumption that our brains and psychology were sculpted by evolutionary pressures, just as our bodies were. Combining and integrating insights about leadership from psychology, biology, neuroscience, economics, anthropology and primatology, evolutionary leadership theory investigates what those evolutionary pressures may have been, how they might have prompted differing leadership styles throughout human history, and, finally, attempts to cast some light on what this means for us today. So, for example, we'll find out why people are generally happier in smaller companies than industrial behemoths (absenteeism is a good measure of employee satisfaction, and rates are lower in small companies), and why employers should be suspicious of interviewees who change jobs frequently. If you're concerned about the amount of time your underlings spend around the water cooler – don't be. Gossip is an entirely natural and frankly ineradicable method of winkling out unsuitable managers, although you might not be so keen on office hydration if you're an office ogre. In which case, you should hand in your notice now and hope that your new employer doesn't pick up this book.

You'll discover that, when it comes to the workplace, the pinstripes conceal an ancient brain. That statement is not intended as an insult either to you or your ancestors; it's a fact. First, evolution works on such long timescales that all of us have, more or less, the brains that our African ancestors did, even if your entire white-skinned family has blond hair and blue eyes. Second, we are not entitled to disrespect our forebears: it is thanks to their resourcefulness that *Homo sapiens* has risen to become the most successful species on earth. Whether your distant African relatives were despots or peacemakers, you would not exist were it not for their instinct for survival. Still, the fact is that we are ancient brains trying to make our way in an ultra-modern world; when shiny new corporate ideas rub up against our creaking, millennia-old psyches, the clash can make us feel uneasy. This is a recurrent message in *Selected*, and one worth listening to: nobody wants workplaces to become havens of primitivism, but we do seem happiest when our working environments echo facets of ancestral tribal life – a close-knit structure governed loosely by trusted elders, in which every member was valued for his or her unique contribution to group living and survival.

Evolutionary leadership theory is the first scientific theory of leadership that is consistent with evolutionary theory and attempts to integrate knowledge from across the behavioural sciences to make sense of the richness of data and observations about leadership. By 'scientific' we mean, first of all, that our theory generates predictions that we can test. As you'll see, our theory generates a major idea: the Mismatch Hypothesis. This contends that our relatively primitive brains, which prime us for membership of fairly small, egalitarian tribes, find it tough to cope with the mammoth corporate and civic structures of the 21st century. Sure, we can be the conscientious employee in the faceless corporation and the dutiful citizen in the metropolis, but a surprisingly high proportion of us crave more intimacy in the way we interact with our co-workers, bosses and civic leaders. Because of this psychological mismatch, our brains are still wired to seek out leaders who display physical and behavioural traits that our ancestors would have prized on the savannah (which is why we like tall, strong-jawed leaders).

Our theory is also scientific in the sense that it details a wealth of empirical evidence, much of it conducted by one of the authors and published in world-leading, peer-reviewed scientific journals (although, for the purposes of simplicity, we'll use the pronoun 'we' throughout the whole book to refer to both authors, even when discussing research done in Mark's laboratory). Peer review, which is the practice of fellow scientists deciding whether your work is worth publishing, is a treasured form of quality control in scholarly circles. Getting your research into a decent journal means it has passed under the noses of several experts, all of whom think it meets minimum standards of accuracy and integrity. It is a stamp of confidence that the study or project was designed in such a way that the results can be considered reliable and reproducible. This means that much of what you'll read is not balanced precariously on a froth of anecdotes and parable but built on a solid foundation of rigorous observations and experimental data. While we have strived to make *Selected* accessible to everyone, we hope that its intellectual rigour remains uncompromised (you'll find both technical and popular references for each chapter, and this Prologue, at the back of the book).

But *Selected* isn't meant to be dry and humourless – we hope you'll find it an enlightening and enjoyable voyage of self-discovery. Because evolutionary leadership theory is a way of understanding who we are and why we behave the way we do. It is meant to provide us with an account of human behaviour we recognise in ourselves and those around us. In short, it is intended for anyone who is human. For example, cultures and societies all over the world possess a remarkably consistent idea of the qualities they covet in a leader, which suggests to us that a universal concept of leadership is etched deeply in the human psyche, along with other universal human capacities such as language. Why can nobody find a good word to say about middle managers? Is it because ancestral tribes never practised middle management, and we have no idea how to respond appropriately to a person sandwiched between power and serfdom? Why do we like it when the boss asks after our kids or remembers our birthdays? Is it because, for a large part of human evolutionary history, we spent time in close-knit groups of 100–150 people, each of whom knew us and our kids personally? Why do we look up to tall politicians and down on short ones? Is the preference a hangover from a time when conflicts were dealt with by intimidation and force rather than by negotiation, when physical presence really mattered? And why does almost everyone think hard-working male executives are high-flyers but female CEOs are bitches? Is it because, somewhere in that primitive psyche, we secretly think women should be in domestic and maternal servitude, following the long-established pattern of our female ancestors? This last question leads us to an important disclaimer: we aim to explain, not excuse. If we recognise these primitive prejudices – there is no better word to describe some of our instinctive beliefs – we can navigate around them to appoint more competent people at the top, whether they are black, female or under five feet tall (maybe even all three).

In the chapters that follow, we'll be taking a grand tour through the leadership landscape, first in terms of what existing literature tells us, and, later on, in terms of what evolutionary leadership theory reveals. We'll set the scene in Chapter 1 by offering a definition of leadership and revisiting what we already know about those at the top – such as their tendency to be highly intelligent and ambitious – and how they crop up in every walk of life. We mostly encounter leadership in the workplace and in political life but we also find it, and followership, in other social settings: among friends and family, in gangs and in religions. We'll briefly explore some of the major theories in leadership literature.

In Chapter 2, we'll swoop into the animal kingdom, to find out how leadership and followership evolved in ants, bees, fish and non-human primates. We'll also try to answer the basic question of why we have leaders and followers at all. This is where the science really begins, with game theory, a mathematical approach that allows scientists to model the behaviour of individuals as agents interacting with each other over a particular time period. From this, a clear pattern emerges: one leader teamed up with one follower usually gets the best results. Having two leaders is as ineffective as having two squabbling, competing cooks, with neither agreeing to the other's recipe and so neither getting fed; two followers make for a uselessly passive (though perhaps politer) situation where, again, nothing gets done. We'll also take a small detour into the world of Charles Darwin, whose insights on the pressures of evolution have ultimately shaped evolutionary leadership theory.

If leadership is the preserve of the few, we'll discover in Chapter 3 that followership is the choice of the many. In fact, there is plenty of evidence pointing to a default 'follow' setting in the human brain (think back to the last time you heard a fire alarm; it's a good bet that your decision to ignore it or heed it was based on what you saw other people doing). We are, in effect, primed to follow the crowd, which explains the phenomena of Twitter, weird fashion trends and stock market crashes. This instinct to go with the flow can trip us up if our crowd happens to be a gang, a cult or a terrorist organisation. We examine different degrees of followership, from the nonchalant bystanders to the suicidal diehards; we'll also examine their motivations.

In Chapter 4, we'll mingle with ethnographers and anthropologists who have studied hunter-gatherer communities existing today or within the past century. These societies are, perhaps, our most accurate window on how life would have been lived by our ancestors. In this chapter we meet the Big Men, tribesmen of skill and importance, who wore their elevated status lightly. We'll contrast the relative flatness of these small-scale human societies with the dominance hierarchies of other primates. Somewhere along the evolutionary timeline, we broke away from a despotic primate heritage to become a (fairly) democratic ape. We came to accept a society with leaders and followers because a well-led society brings tangible benefits (such as food surpluses and profitable trade), but we didn't want to be dominated. We introduce the strategies used by our ancestors to keep overbearing leaders in their place, from gossip to assassination.

This largely egalitarian approach to communal living, Chapter 5 explains, worked pretty well until about 13,000 years ago, when agriculture arrived and, with it, a life of plenty. For the first time in human history, people became tied to their land, both to till it and to protect the fruits of their labour. Nomads became settlers, and societies expanded to include non-relatives. This social coalescence triggered the need for more formal governance. Settlements acquired chiefs, whose new-found ability to control much of their subordinates' lives was a recipe for corruption and nepotism. In other words, the agrarian life of plenty resulted in a bumper crop of seriously bad leaders, including warlords, despots and tyrants.

After our whirlwind tour of human societies through evolutionary history, Chapter 6 delivers us back into the 21st century, by introducing the Mismatch Hypothesis.[4] Its central tenet is that our environments have modernised much faster than our brains. Industrialisation means we now work in large faceless corporations run by remote figureheads who assume charge of everything. Contrast this with a tribe in which people became leaders only in the pursuits at which they excelled, such as hunting or herbalism, for the benefit of a group in which everyone was on first-name terms. Those tribal leaders were chosen by peers, not interview boards. Could this be why so many chief executives parachuted in by management committees fail?

We survey evidence that voters prize traits such as height, physique, facial structure, oratorical skill – and a Y chromosome. These make little sense from a political theorist's point of view, because none of these traits (except the power of oratory, which is correlated with intelligence) is obviously linked to being able to govern well. They fit neatly, however, with what we would expect from evolutionary leadership theory. We show that our ancestral biases towards tall men with square jawlines, who look like 'one of us', often exclude better-qualified candidates. We yearn for personal information about potential leaders too – in the absence of CVs and job appraisals, this is how our ancestors gauged the quality of potential leaders within their tribes.

Finally, Chapter 7 shows that our antique brains can be accommodated, quite happily, within today's glass-and-concrete corporate empires. Some companies are, unwittingly, heeding the call of the savannah and rediscovering the art of ancestral leadership and followership. Their CEOs, who we call Natural Leaders (a term chosen to emphasise a management style born of our natural, evolutionary history, and to highlight the contrast with Artificial Leaders) make sure their company units don't grow too large, and ask juniors to appoint the executives. They have been rewarded with a happier workforce and healthier profits. We could count John Mackey, who stepped down from the Whole Foods Market empire in December last year, as a Natural Leader. We provide a checklist of ten rules born out of evolutionary leadership theory.

We also introduce, in an appendix, a suite of leadership roles that would have been crucial for ancestral survival, a broad categorisation that we hypothesise might still hold true today, and have added a questionnaire to measure these roles.[5] We won't spoil the fun by revealing any more in the Prologue – we hope that you'll try out our questionnaire, find out your leadership type, and maybe even go online and become part of our ongoing research project.

1

The nature of leadership

It is clear that once the question 'Who should rule?' is asked, it is hard to avoid some such reply as 'the best' or 'the wisest' or 'the born ruler' ... But such a reply, convincing as it may sound – for who would advocate the rule of 'the worst' or 'the greatest fool' or 'the born slave' – is quite useless.

Karl Popper, *The Open Society and Its Enemies*

Cyril Richard Rescorla lived his life according to the principle of the eight Ps: 'Proper prior planning and preparation prevents piss-poor performance.' Rescorla, born in Cornwall, England, and later a naturalised American citizen, learned the maxim in the army, and it would serve him well in active service, first on behalf of the British military in Cyprus and later commanding men from his adopted country in Vietnam. Both stints earned the soldier, nicknamed the Cornish Hawk, decorations for gallantry.

But Rescorla, who preferred to be called Rick, did not earn his place in history through his bravery on the battlefield. It was later in life, as a security officer for Morgan Stanley Dean Witter at the World Trade Center, that he would leave his mark. And he did it by insisting, against the advice of the Port Authority of New York and New Jersey, which managed the WTC, that his employer's 2,700 staff evacuate the building on 11 September 2001, when the first plane hit the Twin Towers.

With a seamlessness that came from six-monthly evacuation drills carried out at his insistence, Rescorla ensured that 2,694 of his charges made it out of the building before the centre collapsed. In a moving interview given to the *New Yorker* in 2002, Rescorla's widow, Susan, revealed that the hardest thing to cope with was knowing that he could have made a decision to save his own skin and didn't: 'I know he would never have left until everyone was safe, until his mission was accomplished. That was his nature.'

Rescorla's closest friend, an army buddy called Dan Hill, recalled the indomitable spirit of the rugged young soldier he fought alongside in Vietnam: 'I knew him as a hundred-and-eighty-pound, six-foot-one piece of human machinery that would not quit, that did not know defeat, that would not back off one inch. In the middle of the greatest battle of Vietnam, he was singing to the troops, saying we're going to rip them a new asshole, when everyone else was worrying about dying. If he had come out of that building and someone died who he hadn't tried to save, he would have had to commit suicide.' In March 2009, Rescorla's two children accepted the Above and Beyond Citizen Medal on behalf of their father. The award is the highest civilian honour that can be bestowed in America; its recipients are chosen by the surviving holders of the Congressional Medal of Honor, the highest military award in the country.[1]

Rescorla embodies, in two distinct ways, what it is to be a leader. If we detach ourselves emotionally, we can see that he fulfilled the textbook definition of a leader, which goes something like this: a leader is someone able to exert social influence on others in order to accomplish a common goal. The Vietnam veteran was able to persuade those employees to leave their desks, despite official advice that it was safe to stay, and goosestep in pairs down through more than 40 storeys. But if we put dry definitions aside and measure his achievement against what we believe, in our hearts, leadership to be about, we also find that he comes up to scratch. He used his considerable security expertise to make a sound judgement call (the minute the first plane hit, he rang a friend saying he was sure the building would fall down), calmly marshalled employees to the exits, sang Cornish songs through a bullhorn to keep morale high on the stairwell, and selflessly kept returning to make sure nobody had been left behind. It was not just what Rescorla did on that particular day which made him a leader; it was something deep in his character. Most of us would say he was made of the 'right stuff', and this helped him to flourish both on the battlefield and, on 11 September 2001, in the truly terrible situation he found himself in.

We often hear about leadership in atrocities like 9/11, in natural disasters, on the battlefield, or in collective civil campaigns, such as that against racial segregation. But, once you start noticing it, you find that leadership is, in fact, everywhere. It appears to be a human universal.[2] The most obvious form is political and national leadership: every nation on earth has a single person at its helm, whether it is a democratically elected politician, a monarch or a tyrant. We have business leaders, such as the Bill Gateses and Jack Welches of this world. But people who influence others to achieve a common goal – who, in fact, conform to our textbook definition of a leader – can be found in every corner of human existence: the schoolchild who seems to set the playground agenda during free play; the can-do manager who motivates his team to set sales records; the football hooligan who recruits fellow thugs to terrorise supporters of rival teams; the exasperated customer in the slow-moving bank queue who starts a mutiny; the gregarious friend who seems to end up as chief architect of your social life; the witty celebrity whose outrage on Twitter prompts 20,000 followers to sign a petition. All lead in the sense of persuading others to assist in the accomplishment of a shared objective. Some, like Rescorla and the can-do sales manager, are made of the right stuff. They lead their subjects towards the realisation of a mutually beneficial goal. But certain types of leadership, as we'll see, are exploitative and malign, and it's worth remembering that people can lead without being morally competent (such as the hooligans' ringleader or the school bully).

Often, the shared objective is the leader's objective. So becoming a leader is a good way of achieving whatever it is you want to achieve, whether it is building a well or building up support for an ideology. Not only that, but leaders reap benefits, both financial (top executives get paid more than middle-ranking ones) and sexual, because (generally male) leaders appear to get their pick of (female) followers. They also enjoy an elevated social status. We will call these perks the three S's – representing salary, status and sex – and we will see, in later chapters, that this triumvirate of factors drives power-seeking behaviour, because they enhance the reproductive potential of the (usually) men who pursue them. Political leaders, for example, have a long and ignoble history of polygamy and infidelity.[3]

In fact, the three S's have a clear relationship to each other, and to ELT: the ultimate evolutionary aim is reproductive success, which must be achieved through sex, which means catching the eye of sexual partners, which means being a man of status. And how is status signified today? Through salary. And so, thanks to evolutionary leadership theory, we have a thread linking money to power to sex.

This has to be one explanation for the preponderance of books about leadership: people buy them in the hope they can achieve leadership positions, and an accompanying helping of the three S's. This would suggest there are hundreds of authors who understand what leadership is about. If this is true, why do we still have so many leaders in business and politics made of the wrong stuff? Why do half of chief executives fail in their jobs? Why do political leaders lead us into unwinnable wars? Why do incompetence and immorality so often come as part of the whole human leadership package?[4]

For the answers, we do something that no other students

of leadership have yet done: travel back in time to explore the origins of human leadership. *Selected* is about how and why leadership evolved in our species. The 'why' of leadership is very rarely addressed: despite the trillions of words on the different forms leadership can take, and whether people are born to lead or can be schooled for greatness, few have paused to ask why we bother with leaders at all. Why is it that almost every social grouping – from countries to companies, councils to cults – has a figurehead out in front? Why don't individuals break from the crowd and do their own thing? This gaping hole must be plugged if we are to truly understand the human instinct to lead and the accompanying instinct to follow.

Selected is that intellectual stopper – by stepping back deep into human history, into the societies inhabited by our ancestors, we can arrive at a deeper, more complete and pleasingly concise understanding of how the twin phenomena of leadership and followership evolved in our own and other species. It allows us to identify the ingredients of good leadership ('good' in the sense of both competent and moral; as we know from the besieged financial world, leadership is frequently amoral, even immoral, and incompetent) – and to understand why bad leadership flourishes. Evolutionary leadership theory proposes a brand-new framework for answering the 'why' question: it contends that, since humans are evolutionarily adapted to live in groups, and since groups with leaders do much better than groups without leaders, it follows that leadership and followership became prerequisites for reproductive success (which is the only kind of success that matters when it comes to evolution). Simply, groups without effective leaders died out. All of us who live today carry the psychological legacy gifted to us by our forebears: we are programmed to live in led groups and, most of the time, be obedient group members. We crave a sense of belonging, and if we don't find it within our own families, we will seek out other collectives, such as cults or gangs, which can offer it. We want to be seen as team players, rather than outcasts; we long to be on the inside, not shivering on the fringes. As John Donne pointed out, no man is an island. We are programmed to follow; and, when the environment suits, to seek out leadership roles.

From the simplicity of this evolutionary perspective, an astonishing array of disparate, bewildering findings on leadership fall into place. We crave in our leaders maturity in a time of uncertainty, and youth and vibrancy when we ourselves yearn for societal change. We want leaders who conform to a certain physical stereotype – because they flick a subconscious switch in our brains that most of us probably don't even know we have. Psychologists have long known about these subconscious switches or instincts: the 'fear' one is triggered every time we spot a big black spider, or grope desperately around in the dark for those candles we shoved in a cupboard in case there was a power cut.[5] We might be sophisticated animals in the primate hierarchy, but we, like every other animal we share this planet with, have taken a long, grinding evolutionary path to get here, and our minds are littered with psychological souvenirs of the journey. When the boss puts you down in front of your colleagues, or you find out that the politician you campaigned for has been cheating on his wife, the feelings of betrayal by someone you looked up to tap into a deep, primal well of emotions first felt by our ancestors.

The other explanation for the ubiquity of books on leadership is that good leadership really, really matters. Leadership has mostly been studied in the context of armies (military leadership), nations (political leadership) and business (corporate leadership), with good reason. Fine leadership – by which we mean competent and moral, since one can be an effective, but morally bankrupt, leader – in these realms can win wars, defeat evil and create lasting prosperity, stability and happiness. Since these are desirable outcomes, it is natural to strive to understand and emulate effective leadership. But trying to capture the essence of leadership in a single theory has so far been a thankless task. The phenomenon seems too diverse, with too many variables (personality, family background, culture, education) to come together in one coherent picture of what makes an effective leader. There are so many flavours of figureheads: autocrats, tyrants, warlords, democrats and kings (and, rarely, queens). There are benevolent leaders and greedy leaders, reluctant leaders who have greatness thrust upon them and others who feel compelled to thrust their own, self-perceived greatness on others. We have charming leaders and Machiavellian leaders (often, the former turn out to be the latter, and it can be most disconcerting when the truth oozes out).

Again, evolutionary leadership theory can find a niche for all comers: for example, men classed as having Machiavellian personalities have more children than, well, nice men (although sometimes nice men end up unwittingly caring for the offspring of the Machiavellians). The truism is really true: the bad guys get the girls (and when they are in the fertile phase of their menstrual cycle women are particularly attracted to baddies, according to research). Tyrants have similarly productive loins.[6] This is why these personalities stick around in the gene pool, and continue to fool us today. It is important to remind ourselves, once again, that evolution does not make a distinction between a behaviour that is morally good or bad: what matters (if anything can be said to 'matter' to evolution) is only that an organism lives long enough to reproduce. (We will, though, see that evolution happens to have instilled in us a well-developed sense of right and wrong, which we use to reward 'good' group members and punish disloyal or self-serving ones, thus sharpening group unity.)

The wide variety of environments in which we find leadership – in workplaces, in social groups, in religions – has also led to various ideas about what makes an effective leader. We have such disparate ideas as trait theory, situational theory, transactional leadership, transformational leadership.[7] Some of these buzzwords relate to theories that purport to explain the ability to lead; others are simply descriptions of leadership styles. We seem especially charmed by charismatic leaders – John F. Kennedy, Jack Welch, Oprah Winfrey – but a lack of charisma is no bar to power (George W. Bush, Bill Gates). And, on top of that, each of us harbours an instinctive idea of a 'leader', a person who we think worthy of following and perhaps emulating, such as our 9/11 hero Rick Rescorla. It is no wonder that in his Pulitzer-prize-winning 1978 book, *Leadership*, James MacGregor Burns describes it as 'one of the most observed and least understood phenomena on earth'.[8] Even thirty years later, it can seem a thoroughly confusing subject, full of conjecture and speculation, anecdote and hearsay, from which it seems impossible to pull out a unifying thread.

Selected changes all that, by introducing a brand-new theory of leadership under whose umbrella all existing theories can be marshalled. Evolutionary leadership theory argues that leadership and followership were crucial to the survival of ancestral humans, and that psychological templates for leadership and followership emerged and evolved during an estimated two million years of human evolution. Some aspects of this psychology stretch back even farther, before the *Homo* genus (which includes us, *Homo sapiens*) appeared on the scene. We know that leadership and followership pre-date our species because they are found in other social animals, such as ants, bees, fish and baboons. It is difficult to date the emergence of these behaviours but, because we shared a common ancestor with each of these species, we can be sure that they originated many millions of years ago.

In the chapters that follow, we will show that psychological adaptations for both leadership and followership became part of our neurological furniture – these adaptations are, in essence, permanent physical changes in the human brain. The behaviours they elicit – leadership and, more commonly, followership – became instinctive and universal in much the same way as language did. Every human society that has ever been observed contains a minority who lead and a majority who follow, which suggests that this time-honoured way of organising human society is driven by an ancient imperative. As Arnold M. Ludwig writes in *King of the Mountain*, his thorough and engaging analysis of every ruler of a recognised country in the twentieth century (the emphases are his): 'As a result of my studies, I have come to the conclusion that the reason people want to rule is the same reason all societies want a ruler: *It is the natural order of things* ... The compelling need for a leader, often *any* leader, is the only way to account for many of the rulers who have emerged during this past century ... there is no rule that a leader will carry out his social role wisely or well; he simply needs to do it.'[9] There is another way to phrase Ludwig's observation: that leadership and followership have become part of human nature. If so, where did that nature come from, and why?

The strength of an evolutionary approach is that it allows us to begin at the beginning, and go back to first principles. If we shake off modern ideas about leadership to walk in the nomadic steps of our ancestors, to see the world through their eyes as it existed before agriculture and urbanisation, all the contradictory, confusing and bewildering data on leadership begin to cohere. In order to survive on the savannah, our ancestors needed to stick together. This survival strategy – group living – has been drummed into our skulls through evolution. We theorise that leadership and followership evolved to help our ancestors solve problems of social coordination that group living presented, such as foraging for enough food to eat and finding somewhere safe to sleep. And from this simple premise, much becomes explicable. All the leader types we are familiar with from politics and management – the showy ones, the shady ones, the greedy ones, the magnanimous ones – have a walk-on part in the script of evolutionary leadership theory. The one thing that connects these types is that they possess a basic desire to lead. Perhaps more importantly, the one thing that unites their subordinates is that they possess a basic desire to be led.

ELT's basic premise is this: at the dawn of human history, more than two million years ago, in the hostile environment of the African savannah, there was safety in numbers. Individuals who possessed the cognitive capacity for followership thrived better than those lacking it. By 'cognitive capacity' we mean a set of inbuilt 'if-then' rules that pushed us to follow a person, or group, when we needed to. This followership brain enabled our ancestors to make quick automatic decisions about who to tail in certain situations – for example, 'if I am hungry, then follow the best hunter' or 'if my group is under attack, then follow the strongest person'. Those with a 'followership brain' – who instinctively understood they were safer with the crowd than going it alone – were more likely to survive until they could reproduce, and so produced more kids than individuals who struck out on their own. If we make the reasonable assumption that behaviour and personality are at least partly heritable, then parents with brains wired for followership bore children with similarly wired brains. The followership brain thus spread through the generations, as herd-shunning individuals died out. And so the cognitive blueprint for followership became a common feature of the human brain. There is, however, no market for followership in a leaderless society; there has to be someone to follow. And so the rise of followership created a demand for leaders, who could act as appropriate focal points for the group to rally around; the result is that evolution has 'selected' for a human society of leaders and followers.

In effect, evolution has fixed the capacity for followership – and the recognition of leadership potential – into our grey matter. It takes minimal effort to coax these facilities to the fore: we have found that, if you throw a group of people together to perform a task, it can take as little as 25 seconds for the group to nominate a leader and fall into line behind him.

The chosen one will usually have some special expertise that will help the group, making him an appropriate focal point for followership (or he'll be the loudest, and we'll see later why good talkers are able to command leadership positions). The naturalness with which leader–follower relations spontaneously emerge within groups of people suggests it is an adaptation. In other words, it is a behaviour that has become instinctive over the course of human evolution, owing to the immense reproductive benefit it afforded our ancestors. Without the ability to pick a good leader, group living was no guarantee of survival. This is why, as we'll discover in Chapter 6, we have developed firm, consistent and instinctive ideas of what our leaders 'should' look like.

Some readers will recognise that this is natural selection as applied to humans: the theory of natural selection, first elucidated by Charles Darwin in the nineteenth century, contends that certain individuals thrive better than others in their environment.[10] These 'fitter' individuals out-reproduce their less fit compatriots. Looking to our own species, this process of genetic fine-tuning has produced a sophisticated, bipedal primate endowed not just with language and culture, but with the instinct to follow and, sometimes, lead.

We will return to this train of thought in Chapter 2, which covers the evolutionary arguments for the emergence of leadership and followership more fully. But let's revisit the subject of this chapter: before we can unveil our new framework, we need to familiarise ourselves with what is known or inferred about leadership already. While there are volumes of leadership research out there, even journals that are dedicated to its study and analysis, there is no basic, underlying theory of how it all works. There is no master recipe for the psychology of a leader, nor universal agreement on the best leadership style to adopt in a given situation. Even defining the phenomenon is not simple. Take the Wikipedia entry on leadership, which gives us a good idea of the contemporary, collective wisdom on the subject. The second paragraph .

notes: 'Leadership remains one of the most relevant aspects of the organizational context. However, defining leadership has been challenging and definitions can vary depending on the situation.' In this book, we'll use a broad definition of leadership as a process of social influence to attain shared goals. And since such objectives, by definition, can only be met with the cooperation of followers, *Selected* will investigate, in the second and third chapters, the complex, accompanying phenomenon of followership, which is often ignored. We will see that humans show a mastery of followership, which includes the ability to subvert and even overthrow leaders if necessary. Shareholder revolts – and the consequent removal of high-handed chief executives – are a modern illustration of why the power of followers should not be underestimated.

So, we might have a working definition of leadership but the psychology literature does not offer a solid unifying framework for explaining all the different guises it comes in. In the chapters that follow, we shall argue that evolutionary leadership theory provides just such a unifying framework. But before we begin unifying in Chapter 2, let's take a step back and survey the various theories of leadership and descriptions of leadership styles that can be found in the literature.

When it comes to analysing leadership, there appear to be several ways of slicing the pie. You can focus on the qualities of the person in charge, the way he behaves, the situation in which he finds himself, or the relationship between leader and followers. Very broadly, these different perspectives give rise to about ten distinct theories of leadership, aspects of which can be mixed and matched to describe a given leader (they are not mutually exclusive). These ten theories are: the Great Man theory (that leaders are born not made, the concept closest to our idea of some people, such as Rick Rescorla, having the 'right stuff'); trait theory (a derivative of Great Man theory, which posits that leaders are distinguished by the traits or attributes they display, such as integrity and trustworthiness); psychoanalytic theory (Freud's idea that all social groups are representations of the family); charismatic leadership (in which a figure attracts followers purely on the basis of personality); behavioural theory (that effective leadership results from certain behaviours); situational theory (that the way leadership is executed depends on the situation); contingency theory (an expansion of situational theory, which, in addition to situation, takes account of variables such as the kind of task for which leadership is required and how much power the leader has); transactional versus transformational leadership theory (which contrasts a fairly conventional style of leadership with a more visionary, inspirational style); distributed leadership theory (which eschews a strict hierarchy for a more fluid model, in which leadership roles are shared naturally rather than being formally assigned); and servant leadership theory, in which leadership is carried out purely for the benefit of the group, often at cost to the leader himself.

A note before we begin our primer: different sources cite different numbers of leadership theories. The buffet table is crowded with competing leadership dishes, and, if we are to avoid cognitive indigestion, we should explain the thinking behind our selection. We could, for example, have absorbed the Great Man theory into trait theory; some analysts also blend the situational and contingency theories into one. We have chosen to maintain the separation between what look like quite similar concepts because, first, there are subtle differences between them, and, second, you might already have read about them elsewhere and we don't want you to think we've ignored them. Similarly, transformational and charismatic leadership look like two sides of the same coin; in reality, transformational leaders want to inspire followers to effect change or transformation in an organisation, whereas charismatic leaders don't necessarily want to change anything. The focus tends to be on them, rather than on the group, and they lead through sheer force of personality and charm rather than expertise. Having said that, charisma is a common trait of effective leaders across various cultures (think JFK, Nelson Mandela and Richard Branson), and while it is easy to spot it remains hard to define. By the way, if you suspect that charisma plays an important role in evolutionary leadership theory, you'll be pleased to know your (ancestral) instinct is correct: as we shall see in Chapter 6, charismatic leaders occupy a hallowed place in our framework. Charismatic leaders, even those with little more to offer than their own gleaming personality, continue to charm us today because they are able to tap into that deep well of emotions that we carry around like an ancestral psychological heirloom.

The study of charisma will have some overlap with trait theory, because charisma is regarded by some researchers as an innate characteristic (the word stems from *kharis*, the Greek word meaning favour, indicating that the quality is bestowed divinely).

You'll also note a chronology to the theories, with later ones tending to supersede earlier ones. It is not, however, an exact timeline; bits and pieces of various theories still hold sway among current thinkers and some older ideas, such as trait theory, have resurfaced with renewed vigour in the light of modern science (genetic studies show that some traits associated with leaders, such as intelligence and extroversion, are highly heritable). One consequence of the chronological approach is that earlier leadership studies tend to focus on political and military figures, whereas the rise of corporate culture in the twentieth century shifts the focus of later theories to leadership in the workplace (which can be termed organisational, management or business psychology). In the corporate sphere, 'leaders' and 'followers' become 'managers' and 'employees' or 'subordinates'.

It is also important to emphasise here that, despite the following ideas being in wide circulation today, none explains the very basic question of why leaders (or followers) exist at all. They serve only as 'proximate' explanations, which is to say that they describe how leadership manifests itself and what forms it can take. Nonetheless, we cannot ignore them, because any theoretical framework that poses as an ultimate explanation of leadership – as evolutionary leadership theory does – will need to address them. We'll give a brief indication, as we go along, of how these disparate but enduring ideas regarding leadership square with ELT.

The Great Man theory

The backbone of this theory, which prevailed until a century ago, is that truly great leaders are born, not made. Leadership is not really a phenomenon in its own right; rather, it seeps out, like a cloud of dry ice, from superior beings who are blessed with exceptional intelligence, energy and moral capacity (or 'virtue', as Aristotle put it). According to its adherents, the chosen few sweep out on to the world stage, to orchestrate some epoch-changing manoeuvre, and thus change the course of history (we defy you not to think of Winston Churchill or Alexander the Great). This theory owes much to Thomas Carlyle, the nineteenth-century Scottish historian and thinker, who gave a series of lectures in 1840 which were later written up in *On Heroes, Hero Worship and the Heroic in History*. In the first lecture, Carlyle announced: 'The History of what men have accomplished in this world is at bottom the History of the Great Men who have worked here.'[11]

He was not the first to advocate a biographical focus for understanding leadership; Plutarch, a learned Grecian who lived in the second century, was a prolific biographer of prominent classical figures, mostly emperors, and also sought to understood the essence of greatness. Plutarch's most celebrated work is *Parallel Lives*, a series of biographical comparisons between famous Greeks and Romans, which tried to trace a common moral thread uniting each pair of subjects.[12]

Not that Plutarch himself necessarily bought into the Great Man ideology: he believed that the virtues associated with fine leaders could be refined by education (he thought a liberal education more important for the formation of character than nobility or wealth) and taught to others.

The Great Man theory of leadership – that a single, outstanding individual can emerge in a time of crisis and steer a nation to victory, or rescue a company from bankruptcy – still lingers today. For example, in his review of *Judgment: How Winning Leaders Make Great Calls*, Stephen Plotkin described the book, by Noel M. Tichy and Warren G. Bennis, as 'a valentine to that savior-leader, especially to the all-deciding CEO'.[13] The book depicts Jack Welch, the former CEO of General Electric, as such a leader. Welch, a thrice-married former engineer, attracted great praise for his time at the GE helm: he was named Manager of the Century by *Fortune* magazine and very much embodies the idea of a corporate hero.[14] Some observers also note that religious figureheads such as Jesus Christ, Mohammed and Buddha fit the Great Man theory. As we'll see in Chapter 4, the theory shows similarities to the Big Man concept in hunter-gatherer tribes. Big Men have an early starring role in evolutionary leadership theory, and, as we will see, their stage presence still persists today.[15]

The flaw in the Great Man theory is that some Great Men turn out to have been quite ordinary for most of their lives (Churchill was a national hero during the Second World War, but a relatively undistinguished politician in the years preceding it). Some show greatness only under certain conditions; this idea, that events make the man rather than the other way round, lies at the heart of situational theory (which we'll come to later). And, as research in the 1940s and 1950s appeared to show, greatness might in fact equate to a constellation of character traits such as integrity, intelligence and self-confidence. Anyone with the requisite number of appropriate traits could be marked out for leadership, not just a preordained few. This led to the idea of trait theory.

Trait theory

The following critique of Great Man theory, made in 1950 by the unfortunately named Professor Edwin Boring, sums up the mood of the times: 'Although the Great-Man theory cannot be wrong, since it is clear that men die having differed from one another in social effectiveness and therefore in greatness, there has been, nevertheless, for more than a century now, a growing suspicion that the theory asserts very little, since it specifies neither the attributes nor the conditions of greatness.'[16]

And so, at about this time, researchers did begin specifying the attributes that appeared to distinguish leaders from the crowd. These included intelligence, extroversion and ambition. The number of traits, however, kept on growing in tandem with the studies undertaken to identify them; and it soon transpired that a lack of some traits did not automatically exclude people from leadership positions. In addition, some attributes were not innate traits at all but could be learned and were therefore more accurately described as skills or competencies.

A systematic analysis of traits and skills conducted in the 1970s winnowed down the number of 'leadership' traits to a core set comprising such attributes as assertiveness, dominance, energy, self-confidence, persistence, alertness and ambition.[17] Ralph Stodgill's skill set for leadership trumpeted competencies such as intelligence, creativity, oral fluency, diplomacy, persuasiveness and social skills (more recent scientific research suggests some of those skills, such as fluency and intelligence, should be moved back into the 'trait' box).[18]

Even this narrower focus, however, proved frustrating to psychologists because trait theory is based on the premise that the same constellation of traits is required of all types of leaders. For trait theory to be credible, an army general should be built from the same 'right stuff' as a headmistress. While some particularly assertive headteachers do indeed appear to take their inspiration from the military, not all successful teachers behave like platoon commanders. And so trait theory would fall out of favour, to be replaced by an analysis of how leaders behaved, rather than their personalities or temperaments. ELT contends that ancestral leaders were dominant in very specific areas, such as peacemaking or scouting out new resources, and it is likely that different areas of expertise were occupied by tribesmen with different traits.

We should note here that personality tests repeatedly show that leaders are generally highly intelligent, ambitious and outgoing, and often lead in a variety of realms (so, a head girl will also captain the cross-country team and often become an achiever in later life; a modern example would be Meg Whitman, the former eBay CEO who is now running for the post of governor of California in the November 2010 election). We know these traits are highly heritable because identical twins, who share 100 per cent of their genes, show more similarity in these traits than non-identical twins, who share 50 per cent.[19] This fits well with evolutionary leadership theory because it suggests leadership and followership are specific behaviours with a heritable component. If certain behaviours are heritable, it increases the likelihood that they have an evolutionary basis. Crudely speaking, ELT suggests that only humans with the capacity for leadership and/or followership survived in order to have children, and that each successive generation – including ours – carried the finely honed psychological imprint of its forebears.

Psychoanalytic theory

Freud, an avowed Darwinist, believed that groups were comparable to families, with the leader taking on the role of father of the 'primitive clan'. He thus becomes the core of the group's identity.[20] His belief was that childhood experience and family dynamics determined leadership behaviour; some leaders, he thought, longed to emulate their impressive fathers, others strove for greatness in order to make up for absent fathers. His ideas were taken up by other psychoanalysts, who suggested that the charisma of a leader arose from the strong emotional bond of love and fear linking follower to leader, mirroring the bond between father and child. With Darwin, Freud believed that family relations are very important in fostering children's growth and survival. Parental investment is also a key factor in determining whether individuals become leaders, according to evolutionary leadership theory.

The theme of fatherhood figures strongly in modern leadership thinking, with some experts theorising that fabulous success comes from striving for paternal approval. Much has been made of the fact that Barack Obama barely knew his father. Larry Ellison, the CEO of Oracle, who we met as Lawrence in the Prologue, does not know the identity of his biological father; it was not until Ellison was twelve that he found out he was adopted. Later on we discuss what ELT has to say about the role of fathers in the development of leadership.

Charismatic leadership theory

Freud's idea that the emotional connection forged between a leader and his followers lay at the heart of leadership would encourage other academics to study the issue of charisma. This quality is fiendish to define but you know it when you see it. This kind of leadership is most often observed in groups that follow an ideology, such as a political party or a religious cult, rather than a group that is assembled to get things done (such as a company that builds and sells cars).[21] Ludwig suggests that this is why politicians must rely on their personality and powers of persuasion to get elected (or appointed): 'Because [politicians] usually have no identifiable work product attributed exclusively to them other than their ability to get others to comply with their wishes, people's reactions to them often depend more on their personal biases, beliefs and vested interests than on any critical appraisal of a specific body of work ... That is why charisma, oratory, manipulation and intimidation are often more important than wisdom, special expertise and administrative experience.'

And so a charismatic leader rises to a position of power not through what he does, but through what he is, and his ascent comes through unwavering self-belief (and sometimes narcissism). He is a human magnet; people feel drawn to him because of his personality and stirring rhetoric. In fact, so tightly enmeshed is the group's identity with his that without him it would probably fall apart. In their scholarly analysis, David Trumbull and Patrick McNamara point out that, among our ancestors, oratorical skills would have been a good indicator of general intelligence and leadership potential. Those with a gift for language could convey meaningful information in a persuasive manner, which could have relevance to the survival of the group. Their argument, which fits naturally into ELT, is that evolution has equipped us with a kind of erudition detector: we instinctively regard good talkers as being good leaders. This, they suggest, explains why gifted speakers, even those with little experience, continue to fare so well in politics today. Evidence backs this up: leaders tend to have high verbal IQ, and the babble effect – in which the chattiest person in a group is regarded informally as the group's leader – further demonstrates the link between talkativeness and the perception of leadership potential (regardless of whether the information conveyed is useful or relevant!).[22]

Of course, history shows that charisma is not always a force for good. There appears to be some correlation between charisma and Machiavellianism (an artful, cunning and manipulative form of power-seeking behaviour). As we'll see in Chapter 6, evolutionary leadership theory claims a special niche for charismatic leaders, who seem adept at emotionally bonding large groups of strangers. Their personalities act like a kind of social glue, which preserves group unity in challenging times.

Behavioural theory

If, in the mid-twentieth century, the secrets of leadership could not be discerned by examining what effective leaders were like, perhaps the key to success was observing what they actually did. This belief would set the research agenda in the 1960s and 1970s, and shape the corporate landscape. Managerial handbooks became fashionable; these advocated different behavioural styles according to what needed to be accomplished. One of the best-known approaches was a managerial grid devised by Robert Blake and Jane Mouton. One axis recorded 'concern for employees'; the other axis 'concern for task'. The best leader, they theorised, was one who scored highly on both.

Another behavioural concept was the Theory X/Theory Y approach, which made (not very flattering) assumptions about the nature of employees.[23] Theory X managers believe their subordinates are lazy, dislike responsibility and need to be coerced into action; these managers therefore practise autocratic leadership. Theory Y managers take a rather more generous view of their workers, believing they have the potential for hard work, creativity and embracing responsibility. Theory Y managers therefore practise so-called participative leadership. Implicit in these analyses was the assumption that Theory Y managers were kings of the workplace, winning employee loyalty and scoring better profit margins.

The idea that effective leadership was a matter of style, not natural ability, was a gift to management consultants, because it implied leadership could be taught. But this approach would soon be found wanting: researchers struggled to show that success depended on leadership style. Rather, it appeared that different leadership styles suited different situations, which led to the rise of situational theory. In Chapter 5, we'll see how evolutionary leadership theory accommodates both autocratic and participative styles, which emerge under different conditions. The autocratic style is reminiscent of the dominance hierarchies of fellow primates, although, unlike in non-human primates, autocracy can benefit the whole of the group in certain situations. What can look like autocracy in peacetime can look like decisiveness when a country is under siege.

Situational theory

This approach is predicated on the assumption that the type of leadership required depends on the situation. So, while a participative style, which brings subordinates into the decision-making fold, might be productive in one setting, it would not be suited to a fast-moving environment such as a hospital emergency ward or on the battlefield. Someone who can handle a crisis might not be a person who can manage during a slow period.[24]

Evolutionary leadership theory predicts that preferred leadership styles vary according to situation, to reflect the range of problems our ancestors faced on the savannah. This is a prediction borne out by experiments, which we'll cover in detail later on (a crude example: national secretaries of defence are nearly always male, whereas peacemaking, diplomatic roles are very often occupied by women, such as Madeleine Albright and now Hillary Clinton. Corporations often show the same gender divide, with more 'aggressive' roles, such as chief financial officer, going to men and 'softer' roles, such as human resources managers, occupied by women). Importantly, this moves us away from the concept of some universal leader prototype, a supreme character, or Great Man, who can parachute into any situation and take the helm.

Situational theory, meanwhile, would later be expanded into contingency theory.

Contingency theory

As its name suggests, this approach maintains that there is no single successful leadership style; instead, effective leadership is contingent on a number of different factors, such as the type of organisation involved and the goal to be achieved. One pioneer of this way of thinking was Fred Fiedler, who suggested that three factors were crucial in deciding which leadership style was appropriate for a task: the relationship between leader and followers; the kind of task that needed doing (e.g. is it routine and structured, or vague and ill defined?); and how much power the leader wields over subordinates.[25] Not only that, but he split leaders into those who were task-oriented (whose prime concern was to get the job done) and those who were relationship-oriented (who cared more for colleagues and customers than, say, increasing sales). A task-oriented leader managing a highly structured task, such as a car assembly line, would prosper; but this kind of prescriptive management in an unstructured environment, such as a university research department, would bomb.

Fiedler's model was seen as a rather black-and-white guide to managerial style – most leaders care both about the work they do and the colleagues under them. Hersey and Blanchard instead posited a continuum of leadership behaviour, with most leaders occupying the middle ground between autocratic management and democratic management. They expanded leadership categories into four types: telling (the autocratic style), selling (explaining decisions and inspiring enthusiasm for the task), participating (conferring on decisions) and delegating (farming out the process of decision-making to subordinates and being a referee, rather than an authority). Other researchers went even farther, expanding the four categories to seven levels; as the freedom of followers wanes, the manager's authority waxes (and vice versa). Again, we'll see that evolutionary leadership theory can provide insights into how different styles of leadership arose at different points in out evolutionary history, in response to distinct, recurrent adaptive problems faced by our ancestors, such as keeping the peace and finding food.

Transactional versus transformational leadership

Most office workers will recognise the first, rather functional style of leadership, described (along with transforming leadership) by James Macgregor Burns in 1978: it is most similar to the 'telling' style defined in the previous section. This is the stance of transactional leaders: 'I am the boss, you are my subordinate, and you are paid to do what I tell you to do. You are wholly responsible for the outcome. Let's get the job done.' There is a transparent chain of command, and there are rewards for success (salary, bonus, praise, reviews) and punishment for failure (no bonus, poor performance rating). If the company you work for has schemes for keeping strict office hours and for disciplining errant workers, then it practises transactional leadership. It is a fairly rigidly structured, short-term approach that concentrates on the bottom line. It's an instrumental, contractual exchange, in which each party knows where they stand. The job gets done, workers get paid – and that's as far as it goes.

If transactional leadership is about nuts and bolts, then its mirror image, transforming leadership, is about hearts and minds. If ordinary transactional leaders are what most of us get, then extraordinary transforming leaders are what most of us want. They are agents of change and empowerment, appealing to a higher instinct; in Burns's words, transforming leadership 'converts followers into leaders and may convert leaders into moral agents'. There is a flow of ideas and ideals between leader and follower to the mutual benefit of both.

This concept was later expanded by Bernard Bass into 'transformational leadership', in which the leader inspires and somehow elevates his followers. Where Burns saw the leader–follower dynamic as a two-way street, Bass regarded the leader as transforming the follower for the better.

You could call this the Martin Luther King style of leadership, offering moral vision, dynamism, originality and hope. In their 1994 book, Bass and Avolio claimed that 'transformational leadership is closer [than transactional leadership] to the prototype of leadership that people have in mind when they describe their ideal leader, and it is more likely to provide a role model with which subordinates want to identify'.[26]

We think that transformational leaders, who we would expect to be charismatic, would have been very effective at keeping ancestral groups together and, particularly, at persuading followers to go the extra mile for the benefit of the group. That is because transformational leaders are not obliged to their followers in quite the same mercenary way as are transactional leaders (who must keep rewarding followers to retain them).

Evolutionary leadership theory predicts that our Stone Age psyches find transformational leaders more attractive than transactional leaders; there was no such thing as payment on the savannah, and tribesmen earned the right to lead through their powers of persuasion.

Distributed (or dispersed/emergent) leadership

This is a relatively modern leadership theory, which suggests that leadership is most effective when it is not concentrated in one pair of hands but spread around, with people of all ranks taking up leadership roles if they have the requisite expertise. This is, if you like, leadership without a leader; here, followers hold the power. Some companies even allow managers to be appointed by employees. This kind of leadership, with a strong input from followers, is close to that which proliferated during the long course of human evolution. The Big Men in tribal societies – the societies that are closest in nature to those formed by our ancestors – do not wield great power. The slight influence they do enjoy is conferred by followers. In companies practising dispersed or emergent leadership, any hierarchy that does exist is softer and more pliable than most corporate hierarchies. There is evidence to suggest that this flexible, egalitarian type of leadership results in happier employees and healthier profits; evolutionary leadership theory contends that this style, in which power rests in many expert hands, echoes the leadership seen among our forebears.[27]

Servant leadership

This philosophy, first articulated in the 1970s, has resurfaced in the past few years in response to the apparent rise of the greedy, self-serving and exploitative leader. This style of leadership is characterised by humility, empathy, a sense of community, a respect for ethics and responsible stewardship of a group's resources; leaders take on their roles at some cost to themselves to serve the group.[28] Unsurprisingly, this style is popular within the Church; Jesus is seen as a model servant leader.

In response to burgeoning corporate interest, psychologists are developing psychometric tests that can pluck out the humble, modest leader from his avaricious competitors; the financial sector recognises that selfless individuals who have the long-term interests of companies and society at heart, will be less prone to the kind of reckless risk-taking that led to the current recession. In a recent study we found that such selfless leaders emerge in anonymous situations in which one individual helps the group achieve a goal at some personal cost.

Although there are ancient Chinese and Indian texts that appear to describe servant leadership, the practice predates our species. When a meerkat pops its head out to scan for predators, so that fellow group members can forage, it is practising the same principle. It is putting itself at risk for the overall good of the group. ELT suggests that this style would have been prevalent in ancestral societies, because leadership would initially have evolved purely as a device for promoting survival of the group (because without group survival there is no individual survival). This called for individuals prepared to put themselves on the line, even if this disadvantaged them. The most extreme example of servant leadership is a martyr-leader, who'll take a bullet for his comrades. Rick Rescorla's actions on the battlefield, and as security officer during 9/11, earn him a place in this category.

This primer shows there are different sorts of leaders and different theories of leadership that purport to explain them, and we have tried to indicate how each is accommodated under the aegis of evolutionary leadership theory. There are brilliant visionaries, bullies, autocrats and democrats. We have clans that are born to rule – why else do some countries tolerate monarchies? There are charismatic leaders, some of them with high morals and others armed with baser motives and Machiavellian tendencies. There are beloved leaders who inspire affection and despised leaders who inspire fear. There is no doubt that all these different types of leader exist (we know from personal experience that they abound!) and that these figureheads seem to attain their positions through an interplay of genes, personality and environment. The challenge for us is to try to slot them all into our single framework of evolutionary leadership theory – and, where possible, to alight on the kind of leaders that help companies and countries to flourish in the long run.

Chapter by chapter, we will introduce concepts and findings that relate to the leadership types and styles we have

already encountered. We will find that different circumstances throughout human history bred different types of
leaders, and that, for better or worse, these leadership types
are still with us, and come charging out of the landscape to
answer the perceived needs of followers. Not that we like all
types of leaders equally – we do seem to have an instinctive
idea of what a leader should be, and it appears to be a fusion
of the transformational and servant types we met earlier. We
like this composite figurehead because he is wise and inspirational, and because he does not place himself too far above
us (this element echoes the emergent or dispersed leadership
model). He is approachable, in the same way that favoured
individuals were in ancestral tribes, earning their status by
improving the welfare of their groups. And his prime concern
is the welfare of the group, not himself.

Remember, several million years of evolution have
moulded in humans a preference for living in well-coordi-
nated groups, because it aids group survival and reproduction.
We are, though, a complex, self-deceiving, even hypocritical,
species: given the chance ourselves, as a primate species, we
aspire to positions of power, status and dominance because
of the perks they bring, in the form of salary, status and sex,
which improve our own reproductive chances relative to
others in the group. We will see that evolutionary leadership
theory can immediately shed light on this apparent contradiction between how we like to lead (in a dominant way) and
how we wish to be led (in a benevolent, egalitarian way): both
strategies maximise our chances of reproduction, one at the
individual level and one at the group level. Egalitarian leadership has group interests at heart: non-alpha males are permitted to mate and have children, and this ensures that many
men, not just the alpha, have a genetic stake in the group's
survival. Dominant leaders have a 'me, me, me' mindset: they
monopolise the women, father enormous broods and run
their groups as personal fiefdoms. When we go globetrotting
in Chapters 4 and 5, we'll see that both kinds of leader – the

harem-loving tyrant and the democrat who enshrines rights for all – have their place in human history. Scientists are still not agreed on whether we are primates first and egalitarian hunter-gatherers second; or vice versa. It is our contention that we are primarily egalitarian and that when the checks and balances of a civilised society break down (during war or after a natural disaster) we revert to our selfish primate tendencies to give our own stock the best shot at survival.

First, however, we need to ask the fundamental question that so far remains unasked in leadership literature: why do we have leadership and followership anyway? Why do we cluster together in a led group? Why doesn't each man strive solely for his own welfare and pleasure? Chapter 2 will attempt to answer this question, initially by heading into the animal kingdom, then seeking the company of Charles Darwin and, finally, by playing a few mathematical games.

2

It's all just a game

The theory of repeated games is able to account for phenomena such as altruism, cooperation, trust, loyalty, revenge, threats – phenomena that may at first seem irrational – in terms of the 'selfish' utility-maximising paradigm of game theory and neoclassical economics. That it 'accounts' for such phenomena does not mean that people deliberately choose to take revenge, or to act generously, out of consciously self-serving, rational motives. Rather, over the millennia, people have evolved norms of behaviour that are, by and large, successful, indeed optimal.

Robert Aumann, game theorist and winner of the 2005 Nobel Prize for Economics, in his acceptance lecture

The mystery was more than a century old, and had confounded beekeepers of all talents. When a honey bee returns to its hive after gathering nectar, why does it perform a dance in front of its peers? The bee skips around, to a rapt audience, in a chaotic figure-of-eight movement, waggling its abdomen as it does so. Does this waggle dance somehow impart a scent, which other hive members can follow?

It was not until 2005 that the impressive answer came: the dancer is indicating, through its nifty moves, the location of a nectar feast. It is, in fact, acting as a leader. The direction the bee is facing is the direction of the food source relative to the sun; the duration of the waggle represents how far away the banquet lies. Enterprising scientists proved it by setting up artificial food sources and monitoring the behaviour of the bees scrutinising a waggle dance (let's call them follower bees). When the hive was moved 250 metres, the follower bees flew to a site that was 250 metres away from the artificial source, proving that the follower bees were following navigational instructions encoded in the waggle dance rather than a scent. It proved a theory first put forward in the 1960s by the Nobel-prizewinning zoologist Karl von Frisch – and also showed that bees are a lot smarter than anyone, von Frisch excepted, gave them credit for.[1]

The bees that scout out resources – the ones that come back and perform the waggle dance – are essentially leaders. The best dancers recruit the most followers – worker bees who follow the scouts to the area that they identified – and this produces a very efficient foraging system.

The waggle dance is one of many leadership and followership displays that take place in the animal kingdom, from the migration patterns of relatively brainless species such as fish and birds, to war and peace negotiations among our primate cousins, the chimpanzees.[2] In this chapter, we'll take a look at why leadership and followership might have emerged in various species, and what forms they take. Charles Darwin makes a guest appearance: we'll discover how evolution created leaders and followers through his rules of natural selection, and examine how these evolutionary arguments applied to our own ancestors. This, we'll find, is the backbone of evolutionary leadership theory.

Our framework rests on the assumption that ours is a social species adapted to group living, and that evolution favoured groups composed of leaders and followers as opposed to uncoordinated crowds. To this end, we'll introduce the concept of game theory, which models what happens when two or more agents behave according to simple mathematical rules. Game theory shows that when a pair of agents comprises one leader and one follower, rather than two leaders or two followers, prosperity prevails.[3]

Leadership is not unique to our own species; a glance at a flock of birds or a shoal of fish shows it is manifest in others too. There seem to be just two simple conditions needed for the evolution of leadership and followership in a species: first, an imperative for organisms to do something, such as eating, sleeping or migrating; and, second, an incentive to perform these actions together with other members of the species. In other words, leadership emerges whenever there is a need for social coordination.

Sometimes, leadership is purely accidental. Some fish swim together in shoals because the group provides more protection against predators, better foraging opportunities and, finally, an ideal place to find a mate. As the shoal shimmies through the ocean, any individual can find itself in front and thus technically is the leader. Such shoals, however, stay together not through centralised leadership but through local leadership and followership. The movement of an individual is determined by what its immediate neighbour does (and the neighbour's movement is determined by what its neighbour does). Thus, the simple rule 'do what the fish next to you does, but don't bang into him' can produce local leadership, in the form of a highly cohesive group moving around in a beautifully synchronised manner. It is also clear that sticking to a simple rule like 'do what your neighbour does' does not require much brainpower.[4]

A more impressive form of leadership is displayed by Temnothorax ants, in a process known as tandem running. This involves two ants making a little road trip to a food source, with one ant leading and the other following. It is like a formic *pas de deux*, with each creature adjusting its running speed according to the other. The leader ant will slow down in order to let his running mate familiarise himself with landmarks along the way; once the follower has learned that stretch of the journey, he taps the hind legs and abdomen of the leader, to signal that running may resume.

This was an astounding discovery, by Nigel Franks at Bristol University in England, because it appeared to constitute the first evidence of formal teaching in a non-human species.[5] Teaching can only really be said to have happened if the instructor (the leader ant) modifies its behaviour in the presence of its pupil, and suffers for its efforts. This is indeed the case: a leader ant takes four times as long to reach the food while tandem running than when undertaking a solo excursion. The pay-off is that followers a) learn where food can be found and b) become tandem leaders themselves, leading to an efficient spread of information through the colony. So, the long-term gains of leadership and followership in ants outweigh the short-term hassles, and produce a beneficial outcome for the whole colony, which gives us one explanation for why leader–follower pairs are a smart move in the animal kingdom.[6]

Sometimes a more stable leader–follower pattern among individuals emerges in social species as a result of individual differences in temperament, personality or motivation. We, in collaboration with primatologists, have found that, as in humans, some species boast a spectrum of personalities. For instance, the so-called Big Five (extraversion*, agreeableness, neuroticism, conscientiousness, and openness to experience), which describe the core dimensions of personality in people, also work very well for individual chimpanzees, horses and dogs (since chimps, horses and dogs can't fill in their own questionnaires, we deduce this from observations by their caretakers). You can even find a range of personality types in fish, with implications for who leads and who follows.[7]

Guppies are a popular aquarium fish used widely in biology experiments because they are prolific breeders. Some are bold and others shy (shyness and boldness are determined by how quickly they swim towards a novel food patch placed at the other end of the tank). In a recent experiment at Cambridge University, researchers placed a bold guppy in a tank with a shy guppy. Unsurprisingly the bolder guppy

---

*We stick to the usual academic spelling of 'extraversion' when discussing personality research, but will use the more common 'extrovert' and 'extroversion' in everyday contexts.

took the lead in the hunt for food, and the shy one followed. Over various trials a stable leadership pattern emerged as a result of this personality difference. Most importantly, when a bold and shy guppy were paired with each other they were quicker to reach their nutrition-filled destination than when two shy or two bold guppies were paired together. This shows the quickest way to a meal, for both fish, was achieved by forming a leader–follower pair.[8] (The bold leading the shy is also found in humans, exemplified by the previously mentioned babble effect – being talkative is a sign of extraversion, and, of the Big Five personality traits, extraversion correlates most strongly with being perceived as a leader. Extraversion probably equates to boldness in species that lack language.)[9]

So, our foray into the animal kingdom shows that leadership can emerge in very primitive species – ones that we do not particularly credit with intelligence – in situations where coordination is a good idea. What happens to the phenomenon of leadership and followership when we introduce a little more complexity?

Suppose, unlike ants, the individuals in a species can recognise each other individually. For example, reptiles such as lizards recognise each other by smell while emperor penguins recognise each other through vocalisations. In many mammals (including humans and non-human primates) individual recognition is based on faces, and the face radiates reliable clues about the organism's sex, age, kinship and even social status (which is why phrases such as 'aristocratic features' are a useful shorthand). This opens up new opportunities for leadership because group members can now identify individuals they want to follow. In this way, some individuals come to exert more influence than others on group decisions; we can think of them as exercising more leadership.

For instance, when elephants move to find waterholes in the African savannah they tend to follow an older female (elephants have a matriarchal social structure). Age indicates experience; a matriarch with a long memory might be able to lead the herd to a long-forgotten waterhole in the desert which has not yet dried up. Leadership studies with people (including our own research) also show that age is prized in certain situations. In professions that rely heavily on specialised knowledge, such as being a university professor, age tends to correlate positively with status and perceived leadership qualities. This correlation between age and leadership is not found in jobs that require a lot of energy and physical strength, such as being an army officer.[10] We'll come to this in more detail later.

So far we have assumed that all individuals in a particular species want to do the same thing at the same time, such as migrate south to flee the winter, or turn nectar into delicious honey. Nature is not always so agreeable, however; conflicts frequently arise. It might be two males fighting over a desirable female, or vying for dominance over the group. Or conflict might be due to a difference of opinion, such as which waterhole to head for. How do groups resolve these conflicts and where does leadership come in? It's time to head to the zoo again.[11]

Many animal species, including chimpanzees, arrange themselves into dominance hierarchies, in which the rank of an individual is determined by its ability to harm and coerce others. The higher an individual is ranked, the freer its access to valuable reproductive resources such as food or mates. This dominance hierarchy is sometimes referred to as the 'pecking order', because one of the earliest observations of dominance hierarchies came in a study of chickens, in which rank is determined by who is pecking whom.[12] The alpha chicken, if you like, may peck any bird; the chicken on the second rung can peck those below it but not the alpha; and so on.

Sometimes the dominant individual in a group takes up what looks very much like a leadership role (dominance and leadership are not the same thing to biologists and psychologists). This seems to happen particularly when a group is under threat. The Dutch primatologist Frans de Waal has studied chimpanzee behaviour in captive colonies such as at Arnhem Zoo in the Netherlands, where he observed the following incident:

A quarrel between Mama and Spin got out of hand and ended in fighting and biting. Numerous apes rushed up to the warring two females and joined in the fray. A huge knot of fighting, screaming apes rolled around in the sand until Luit [the alpha male] leapt in and literally beat them apart. He did not choose sides in the conflict, like others; instead anyone who continued to act received a blow from him.[13]

Thus, the dominant individual (the alpha male in most primates) acts as peacekeeper, breaking up fights and protecting weaklings from stronger rivals. His actions ensure the group doesn't fall apart. The alpha will also often lead group movements and protect the troop from external threats, such as predators or rival groups. American primatologist Christopher Boehm described this act of leadership from the alpha in a wild chimpanzee group at Gombe national park, Tanzania:

Goblin [the alpha] moves forward quickly to a vantage spot to peer across the valley and Mustard now emulates him. As Goblin (number one), Satan (number two) and Evered (number three) scan the valley, they break off several times to look at one another quickly. After nearly 60 seconds Goblin suddenly makes his decision and begins to vocalize and display. The entire group, which includes adolescents Freud and Beethoven, immediately follows suit and the result is the usual one: Both groups vocalize and display ferociously then slowly retreat into their home ranges.[14]

In these species, leadership looks like hard, thankless work. Why would an alpha assume a leadership role when it could get away with doing nothing? One possibility is a vested genetic interest in the group's welfare. Among mountain gorillas, the alpha does all the mating. By protecting the group, he is shielding his own offspring and thus ensuring the survival of his gene pool. To keep his gang together, he rules like a despot, breaking up fights and dictating where the group goes.

Alternatively, a dominant animal that takes on the mantle of leader might simply be making a pragmatic decision: 'I'll be leader because it is less costly for me to lead the group than for anyone else.' Because alphas are physically formidable they can afford to break up a fight or fend off a cobra with little risk to themselves. Importantly, it is also in the interests of the lesser males to defer to this arrangement: if they follow the alpha, they can remain in his protective shadow. Thus, a hierarchy in which animals know their place is a relatively stable arrangement, in the best interests of all.

Put like this, leadership based on dominance seems to be a recipe for success. Animal and human studies show, however, that there is a cost to the group of consistently relying on the same individual to decide the group's fate (let's look to our own species: a handful of leaders, including the American president and the Russian president, can authorise a nuclear attack that will wipe out life on earth, a state of affairs that not everybody is comfortable with). The clearest problem with a sole leader comes when a group must make a collective decision about where to move to find food, water or a safe place, in cases where information is ambiguous or incomplete. One could rely on the alpha male (as in primates) or on the most experienced animal (such as the elephant matriarch) to lead the way. But how can the group be sure that its leader will pick the correct route among the many possibilities on offer, when there is so much at stake? Ending up at a dry waterhole in the Namibian desert spells certain death for the entire troop.

Mathematical models show that, when uncertainty and complexity reign, distributed leadership actually works better than dictatorial leadership (where one individual decides for the whole group). In this picture, information is pooled from many group members and then a decision is made by averaging out, or a majority consensus. By 'distributed leadership', we really mean democracy. Something resembling democracy has been observed in social species such as bees, birds, buffalo and baboons, when they are deciding where to migrate to.[15] Smell (via pheromones), vocalisations or visual cues are employed to 'vote' for a preferred direction. Buffalo literally vote with their feet to decide where to move next.

An ingenious example of democratic, or distributed, leadership is shown by the hamadryas baboons that live on the savannah in Ethiopia. They sleep in large groups on the cliffs and forage in smaller groups, in open areas, during the day. The German primatologist Hans Kummer once described an example of democracy at work. In the morning, the troop starts the complex process by which they decide where to forage: one individual moves forward a few metres and then stops, facing its preferred direction while it sits. Sometimes, a few in the group will follow; then the whole group moves in that direction. Sometimes, however, nobody follows; the individual is forced to retreat to the group and the bidding process starts again with one or more baboons vying to lead.[16]

Another example of distributed leadership occurs in zebra; when the group goes to a waterhole the stallion leads, but when the group departs the dominant mare takes over the lead, with the stallion bringing up the rear. This example of shared leadership ensures that the stallion is always between the group and the waterhole, the prime patch for predators, thus promoting group survival.

So, our trip into the animal kingdom shows that leadership and followership are widespread, and not just in the crude form of the alpha male and his perch at the top of a dominance hierarchy. Their sophisticated version – democratic leadership – is found in primates other than humans. This gives rise to an intriguing possibility: that leadership and followership are ancient phenomena that pre-date the emergence of our own species. The structuring of groups into the leaders and the led, we suggest, is a product of evolution, and happened because these groups showed a reproductive advantage over groups that were leaderless. To explore this concept further, we need to step into the remarkable world of Charles Darwin, who hit upon the groundbreaking theory of evolution by natural selection.

Charles Darwin, in his nineteenth-century voyage on the *Beagle* to the Galapagos Islands, noted that different species were beautifully adapted to their environment. After much study, he came to the heretical conclusion that different species were created not by a divine hand, to an unchangeable recipe, but arose as a consequence of their environment. Members of a species displaying certain features – say, a giraffe boasting a long neck – flourished in their environment better than less well-equipped members (i.e. better than a short-necked giraffe). A long-necked giraffe would have access to more food (leaves high in the treetops) and this advantage would give long-necked members a survival advantage (some academics have recently theorised that longer-necked giraffes can dominate their shorter-necked peers, reinforcing the selection pressure for that trait). This would result in differential reproduction: long necks would out-reproduce short necks, and, given enough time, long necks would become a universal feature of giraffes. This, Darwin reasoned, explained why creatures seemed so perfectly suited to their ecological niches.

Natural selection, Darwin postulated, operates according to three very simple rules: (1) there is variation in traits between individuals within the same species; (2) some of this variation is heritable (which is why offspring resemble parents); (3) some of these trait variations give individuals an edge in the competition for resources. Taken in the round, these three simple rules lead to 'descent with modification', as Darwin described it. These rules form the backbone of evolutionary theory. Darwin's insights have been proved right so many times that evolutionary theory is no longer treated as a hypothetical possibility but as an explanation of a law of nature.[17]

We can see natural selection operating in front of our own eyes in our own back gardens. Take the peppered moth. These moths rest on tree barks; their brown pepper colour protects them from being eaten by birds. Occasionally mutant moths are born – of a slightly different colour – but they are picked off by hungry birds. Over the past century, tree barks have darkened through pollution, allowing a darker variant of the peppered moth to emerge and spread through the population, at the expense of its lighter compatriots (the lighter ones are now visible to predators, and have become dish of the day, thus disappearing from the population). But thanks to environmental crackdowns, tree barks are becoming lighter again and the original pepper-coloured moth is making a comeback. Unlike Darwin, we now know that traits are bequeathed from one generation to the next through genes (we inherit 50 per cent of our genes from each parent, but which ones we get is a matter of luck).

What does natural selection have to do with leadership? Darwin recognised that natural selection operated on organisms in their entirety, from anatomical features to their behaviours and mental traits. He also recognised (although he kept this quiet for a while) that natural selection operated in humans in the same way as in other animals. There is little controversy about the fact that our anatomical traits have been shaped by evolution through natural selection. Take our ability to walk on two legs, which is almost unique among primates (chimpanzees can do it, but only for short periods). This adaptation emerged when our ancestors turned from forest animals to savannah dwellers; walking upright afforded them an advantage in travelling large distances. In turn, this adaptation liberated our hands, which we turned to tool-making; it freed our throats, which we could now use for language (try talking while you are on all fours).

Evolutionary psychologists assume that what applies to

the body also applies to the mind (and while this book does not go into the detail of evolutionary psychology, it certainly uses the discipline as a springboard). As well as physical adaptations, we also show specialised psychological adaptations that have become ingrained over the course of evolution, in order to solve problems posed by our environment (here, environment is a catch-all term that reflects the natural world and, perhaps more importantly for our species, the social world). The idea that our minds have been honed by evolution has been somewhat controversial – mostly outside academic circles – but, if we accept that the brain is part of the body, it is logically inconsistent to argue that the human body has been shaped by our environment but the human brain has not. Evolution does not 'stop at the neck', as Anne Campbell, an evolutionary psychologist, so starkly phrases it.[18]

And so it is the overwhelming belief of psychologists that the hulking biomass we call the human brain – together with the mind it houses – has been through the mill of natural selection, just as our bodies have.

What does it mean for our brains to be subject to the same evolutionary forces as our body? Brains orchestrate, via psychology, a person's behaviour. People with certain psychological traits thrived better than others, and this survival advantage translated into a reproductive advantage. Evolutionary leadership theory suggests that individuals in led groups out-reproduced members of other groups – to the point where leaderless groups disappeared from the population. In the parlance, evolution has selected for specialised psychological mechanisms that make leadership and followership possible. In short, leadership and followership are problem-solving strategies that have arisen as a consequence of our species facing problems requiring coordination, such as group decision-making, collective migration and group defence. The process of natural selection winnowed down the population to what we see today: a society in which human leadership and followership are ubiquitous.

Here, we should note another fact: our brains have ballooned over the past 2 million years. Compared with other mammals, humans have supersized brains relative to their body weight. Your brain constitutes a fiftieth of your body weight but soaks up a fifth of the calories you eat. In biological terms, it is a costly organ to run. It is unlikely to have become larger without reason – the dramatic cerebral expansion must have been driven by a need.[19]

The most likely explanation is that it ballooned to accommodate the complexity of our social environment. While chimpanzee groups typically number about fifty individuals, early humans are thought to have had social circles numbering around 150. This is now known as Dunbar's Number, after Robin Dunbar, the British evolutionary psychologist who believes that, despite social networking sites such as Facebook, the real-life social circle of the average person still numbers 150 or thereabouts (this includes spouses, children, relatives and friends). Bigger brains made it possible for humans to live in these larger groups, reaping the benefits of cooperation with collaborators while avoiding the costs of competition with rivals. Forging cooperative alliances with other individuals to exploit reproductive resources and trying to outwit rivals for those same resources selected for smart individuals who could work out who to trust. Furthermore, maintaining monogamous relationships and friendships over a long time period while living in a large group probably also required a lot of brainpower (our ancestors had to remember who to trust, who to avoid and who to ostracise). Indeed, cooperation, manipulation, cunning and deceit were increasingly necessary to survive in this complex environment, and that is why human intelligence is often referred to as Machiavellian intelligence.

According to the framework of evolutionary psychology, our brains should be particularly good at solving problems that were important for our ability to survive and reproduce in ancestral group environments. Since most of these problems were social in nature, our brains should reflect these cognitive priorities. We should be particularly adept at things like finding a mate (which is why we are obsessed with love and sex); maintaining an exclusive relationship (which explains the strength of romantic jealousy); and parental care (we generally love our children unconditionally). We should be good at protecting ourselves and our families against people who are trying to exploit us (hence a suspicion of strangers and people not like us); forming cooperative relationships (hence the value placed on friendships and alliances); and negotiating status hierarchies in the group (which is why we continually measure ourselves against peers). Furthermore, we should be skilled at coordinating our activities with others and maintaining group unity in the face of external threats – which is why we rally behind leaders when our nation is being attacked. Our brains appear to have been sculpted to handle group dynamics.[20]

Evolutionary scientists usually ask four critical questions when they analyse a particular phenomenon such as leadership and followership from an evolutionary perspective. First, why might the phenomenon have evolved? Why did leadership emerge in humans and other species? The likely answer is because there are important benefits to coordination, such as finding new food resources and security, and leadership was the best way to harness and orchestrate coordination. The importance of leadership is demonstrated by the fact that it has evolved separately in many social species, albeit sometimes for different reasons.[21]

Then there are two 'when' questions. One is about the phylogeny of leadership: when did this trait emerge in a species, and are there parallels in other species? This chapter has already shown that relatively simple species show leadership, suggesting the timeline of leadership started millions of years ago. The other is about the ontogeny of leadership – namely, when does this capacity show itself in the lifespan of an individual and how does it develop? In the next chapter, we'll see that followership emerges almost at birth and that it happens automatically and spontaneously in the right situations, suggesting an evolved response or adaptation. In addition, the heritability of traits associated with leadership suggests that it is to some extent a stable individual difference, which explains why many people hold leadership positions in different spheres throughout their lives.

The fourth question is 'how': how does this capacity to lead or follow manifest itself in organisms? This has been the preserve of social and personality psychologists as well as business and organisational psychologists. Here we ask such questions as who makes an ideal leader or follower and what personality traits distinguish a good from a bad leader or follower. The literature on leadership seems frustratingly incomplete: while there is plenty of the 'how', the 'why' has hardly been asked, let alone answered. That's the fundamental question that evolutionary leadership theory sets out to answer.

And it is possible to answer the 'why' question, using a variety of research tools, from (auto)biographies, surveys and behavioural experiments to ethnographic and cross-cultural studies, from genetics, neuroscience, and mortality/fertility studies to computer simulations and mathematical models. The trick is combining these very disparate pieces of information and evidence into a coherent whole, something that ELT manages to achieve.

Another technique that is often used by evolutionary scientists to model the evolution of social traits such as altruism, cooperation, conformity and leadership and followership is game theory. Game theory was devised during the Second World War to analyse strategic interactions among combatants. These researchers were particularly interested in whether and how peace could be achieved when two individuals (or countries) are in competition. Perhaps the most famous example is the Prisoner's Dilemma game, which describes a situation in which two suspects of a robbery, say Pat and James, are caught by the police.[22] They are interrogated separately and can, in theory, snitch on each other. The outcomes of the game are such that each suspect is best off claiming his own innocence and blaming his partner (the defection scenario), which means he will go free. If both blame each other they both go to jail. If both remain silent – called the cooperation scenario – then, under the rules of the game, both receive a lighter sentence.

If we imagine their partnership as an alliance, the strategy that best preserves the alliance is for both parties to remain silent, and for each man to put up with a short jail term. The problem is that neither knows what the other will do and the safest move – to avoid the risk of being lumbered with all the blame – is to become a grass. Thus, as game theory aficionados would put it, defection dominates cooperation between the suspects. The only way out of this game (and out of prison) is to make a promise in advance to remain silent if caught, but the only way to make each other keep the promise is through the threat of punishment (Pat: 'Once I get out of jail I will come and get you, James!').

Can we also model leadership and followership using game theory? We believe so. Our assumption, as evolutionary scientists, is that the behaviours that lead to the best outcomes (in game theory, the best outcomes equate to the highest scores) gradually spread and become fixed in the population over evolutionary time. This is how game theory relates to evolutionary leadership theory: we play a version called evolutionary game theory. It considers the conditions under which it pays to be either a follower or a leader, and whether these strategies are fixed (someone is always a leader) or conditional (a leader in some situations, a follower in others).

Consider Pat and James again – but let's imagine they exist several hundred thousand years ago, as hunters on the African savannah. They need a rest, having been hunting all morning, and they need to seek out one of the terrain's few waterholes. Because the savannah is well supplied with predators (but not with water) they must stick together for safety.

Additionally, let's assume they can't communicate through language (language probably emerged around 50,000–100,000 years ago).[23] How will they decide where to go? It so happens that Pat is a little thirstier than James; he did most of the running after the deer they eventually caught. In this case, Pat emerges as the leader and James will be the follower. And if Pat is always a little thirstier than James (because of his dehydration-prone metabolism) then a stable leadership–followership relationship emerges. This is the simplest situation in which coordination through leadership benefits both equally.

Things get a little more complicated if the two hunters have different preferences. Pat favours the waterhole to the north (because he knows the territory) whereas James prefers the waterhole in the south (because his girlfriend is waiting there for him). The scene is set for conflict. Despite their opposing opinions, neither can afford to go solo. This scenario therefore requires more strategic leadership.[24]

Pat's water-craving metabolism might drive him to make the first move north, leaving James with no option but to follow. If this happens once James might accept it, but if it happens frequently then James might insist they take turns. If Pat doesn't fancy that idea, James might decide to disband their partnership and team up with a different hunter. So, in order to lead, Pat must 'persuade' James to follow him. If Pat is a persuasive sort (in a non-verbal kind of way, of course) and succeeds frequently with this strategy of grunted influence, then Pat's outcomes will consistently be better than James's, creating inequality (because Pat gets to his preferred waterhole, while James's girlfriend is left fuming). On the other hand, to preserve the partnership, Pat might display a form of self-sacrificial leadership (which charismatic leaders such as Mandela and Gandhi display) and concede to James's request to head south, so that the lovers can be reunited. Readers may recognise that this describes the evolution of servant leadership.

Skilful negotiation and self-sacrifice are not the only solutions to this 'game'. Dominance is another strategy. Suppose

Pat is much stronger and does not need James for protection; Pat can do pretty much what he wants, and James will always have to trail him for safety. This type of leadership is prevalent in gorillas and other animals that have a clear dominance hierarchy. It is much rarer in humans, however, who needed each other to survive on the savannah. It is no coincidence that physical size varies less between humans (especially among males, but also between males and females) than it does among primates operating according to dominance hierarchies, such as the mountain gorilla.

If such coordination games were sufficiently frequent and important to the welfare of our ancestors, we would expect leadership and followership traits to have emerged in our ancestors. If we consider these behavioural strategies to be underpinned by genes (as evolutionary game theory does, with the genes providing the biological link, via the brain's architecture, to the psychological trait) then we can look at how different versions of these genes fare in achieving a successful outcome in these games. It is clear that a 'gene for' going it alone – we do not actually believe that such a trait is underpinned by a single gene, but this is for purposes of simplicity – would not be passed on because when either Pat or James possesses this gene, they do not coordinate over choice of waterhole and thus die of thirst or predation. If individuals with a leadership gene each (or a followership gene each) played the game against similar individuals they would not fare well either. It is probably the case that two leadership genes lead to a worse outcome than two followership genes because individuals with the latter genes would simply stay put and wait for the other to move. In contrast, two individuals with leadership genes would probably leave each other and die. A gene for leadership would lead an individual to prosper, but only when interacting with a gene for followership. Thus, we would expect natural selection to produce a mixed population of individuals: some carrying leadership genes and others followership genes (in what proportion remains to be seen).

If, indeed, a proportion of the population carried leadership genes it would suggest that the Great Man and trait theories are not yet dead. Alternatively it is possible that natural selection has produced individuals who carry both leadership and followership genes and can use them conditionally depending upon who they are interacting with; this would chime with situational and contingency theories of leadership.

Of course, when we say 'a gene for' leadership we do not actually mean that who leads is determined by a single gene. We are referring to a particular constellation of inherited traits that make their owners more likely to emerge as leaders (and these traits are underpinned by genes). As the waterhole example shows, any trait that makes an individual seize the initiative should increase their propensity to lead. What are these traits and are they heritable?

As discussed, psychologists use the Big Five personality scale to indicate the five main dimensions of personality: agreeableness, extraversion, neuroticism, conscientiousness, openness to experience. Some psychologists have also recently identified a sixth trait, which is called honesty/humility and which may be particularly relevant for leadership. Studies of twins show these traits are partly heritable: by this, we mean that identical twins, who share 100 per cent of their genes, show more similarity in these traits than do non-identical (fraternal) twins, who share only 50 per cent of their genes, as regular siblings do. Leadership shows the strongest correlation with extraversion, as would be expected based on the babble effect (the most talkative person in a group is often seen as the leader). Leadership also correlates positively with openness to new experience (e.g. being creative and adventurous) and negatively with neuroticism – who would want to follow an emotionally unbalanced person?[25]

There is no systematic relationship between leadership and being agreeable: being nice does not always lead you to your favoured waterhole. Being ambitious and dominant (yet not openly aggressive) helps and so does being a risk-seeker.

Many prominent men seem inexorably drawn to stupid risks; Bill Clinton, and his adulterous antics at the White House, springs to mind.

As conflicts of interest were common in our ancestral environment (as they are today) we would expect leaders to have particular qualities that might convince individuals to follow them, even if this runs against the follower's direct self-interest. Intelligence is one such factor. James might have a preference for heading south, but if he thinks Pat is clever enough to lead him to a better hole elsewhere, he might be prepared to put aside his own desires. Intelligence is indeed strongly associated with leadership – and it is strongly heritable. The IQs of American presidents are almost always above average; Bill Clinton, a Rhodes scholar, stood out in this regard. It makes sense, in terms of evolutionary leadership theory, that intelligence should be a prerequisite of leaders; a stupid leader – one who led followers into risky territory, or to a barren waterhole – would not do much for group survival. We would expect this attribute to be magnified over evolutionary timescales: as the size and social complexity of groups increased, so did the cerebral requirements for leadership.[26]

It is interesting that the IQ component that most strongly predicts leadership is verbal ability. Persuading people to follow you is easier if you have great oratorical skills or, as in the case of Fidel Castro, a mesmerising delivery. Having the ability to read the minds of others also helps in figuring out what followers want. Sensitivity to non-verbal cues, such as facial expressions and body movements, is a help; canny leaders scan the crowd to size them up and respond appropriately.

Finally, research suggests an important distinction between leadership emergence and leadership effectiveness. Who gets to lead might not be the most effective leader in the long run – although we would expect evolution to have built in mechanisms to protect us from choosing the wrong leaders. It seems that regular leadership changes through elections or rebellions are helpful in correcting for this. Very interestingly, people who score highly on the first two out of the three so-called Dark Triad traits – Machiavellianism and narcissism (but not psychopathy) – often surface as temporary leaders because their charm and enthusiasm attract followers. In the long run, however, their selfishness and exploitative nature bring them, and often their group, down. (The term 'Dark Triad' was coined in a 2002 paper by psychologists Delroy Paulhus and Kevin Williams.[27]) Adolf Hitler and Jim Jones, a cult leader who led a mass suicide, are exponents of this ignoble art.

Thus, it is clear that particular traits associated with initiative-taking and intelligence propel people to leadership positions and that these traits are heritable to a certain degree. This suggests that the Great Man and trait theories of leadership are to be taken seriously; it would be fascinating, and possible, to compare the genomes of great leaders with those of bad leaders and mere mortals. It is also true, however, to some degree, that evolution has selected for those we might call 'generalists': individuals who mainly follow but who can lead if the situation requires it. For instance, any parent, whether bold or shy, will lead their child to safety if it is attacked by a dog. Any individual, whether extroverted or deeply introverted, will raise the alarm if there is a fire in the theatre. We can reconcile these seemingly contradictory positions: someone may have a stronger propensity than others to be a leader but anyone can step up to the leadership plate when the situation demands it.

Before turning to followership we should examine the benefits that accrue to leaders. There are three main perks: salary, status and sex. How did this state of affairs arise in our ancestral environment? Going back to the waterhole example, let us suppose that Pat succeeds repeatedly in going to his preferred waterhole. The benefits of leadership for him are obvious: he gets to do what he wants. But we can envisage additional pay-offs. Valuable knowledge about the waterhole might give Pat prestige and status in the group. Thus, hunters might want to hang out with Pat and share their meat with him. Finally, his status might attract sexual mates. His knowledge in a valued domain might be a highly desirable trait, because, to a potential mate, it signals access to a valued resource (water). Thus showing off your ability to lead might act as a 'peacock's tail' which might attract high-quality females. In a recent study we conducted with Wendy Iredale, at the University of Kent, we found that men show more conspicuous generosity in their interactions with strangers when their actions are being observed by women. The more attractive the female observer, the more generous the subject and the larger his charitable donation. In contrast, women's generosity towards strangers did not alter in the presence of a member of the opposite sex, no matter how handsome. Generosity is widely regarded as a classic leadership trait, and we found, in a separate study, that women rated generous men as more sexually attractive.[28] Indeed, you could think of a man's wallet as his peacock's tail.

Also, in ethnographic studies of the Yanomamo, an Amazonian tribe, warriors who lead their group into battle acquire more status; these warriors have more sexual partners and sire more children. In fact, one anthropologist found a correlation between the number of men a warrior had killed and his tally of sexual partners. The more bloodthirsty the fighter, the more children he fathered.[29] Dispensing with out-group men means easier access to the women left behind; and also the status that comes with being the group's protector.

After his affair with Monica Lewinsky, Bill Clinton responded to the question of why he transgressed with the answer: 'Because I could.' He was alluding to something that we all know is true: that men in power enjoy more sexual opportunities than ordinary folk. A combination of status, sex and – in lieu of salary – extra meat might have made it very attractive for our ancestors to aspire to leadership positions.[30]

So, by strolling into the animal kingdom, we have seen

that leadership and followership are widespread among social species. And, by exploring evolutionary game theory, we can see that the evolution of these behaviours is logical. We have acquainted ourselves with the perks available to leaders, and how some men, like persuasive Pat, manoeuvre themselves into leadership positions. But our discussion raises another interesting question – what is in it for the followers? What about the Jameses of this world, who have to forgo a much-anticipated reunion with their girlfriends in order to traipse north? Why do they fall into line? That's what we will discuss in the next chapter.

3

Born to follow

Sometimes it's good to be a sheep

Billboard advertisement for ING Direct, a UK online savings bank, 2009

H ere's an experiment for the bold among you. Stand still in a busy shopping area and stare silently at the sky. Eventually – hold your nerve – someone will stop and follow your gaze. Soon, others will stop what they are doing and look up at the sky too. Before you know it, you will have unwittingly assembled a crowd, all scrutinising the clouds. Not only have you just performed a classic social psychology experiment, but you have also created your very own cult of temporary followers.[1]

Humans have a natural capacity to follow, just as evolutionary leadership theory would suggest. You could call followership the default setting of the human psyche. Cast your mind back to when the fire alarm in your office last went off; did you make your own decision to stay or leave, or did you copy your colleagues? (This mimicry of inertia is thought to have cost lives in the 9/11 attack on the World Trade Center in New York.) When people don't know which exit to use in a theatre, they tend to follow the crowd. In times of uncertainty, we turn to others who might have the answers. We become followers, and, in a similarly reflexive way, our behaviour makes leaders of those we look up to.

Not that you would know it from perusing the groaning bookshelves devoted to psychology, management and leadership; any information about those who march behind the people in front is remarkably hard to come by. In one way, it's not surprising: followers are many and leaders are few, and it is human nature to concentrate on the outliers. Even the terminology describing leaders and followers is loaded: the former are lions and the latter are sheep. It is always the loudest beast which attracts the most attention.

And so we are naturally inclined to strive to understand, and emulate, those at the top of the power pyramid. After all, it is the leaders, not the followers, who soak up status and monetary and sexual advantages, which explains why self-help and business bookshelves are stuffed with tomes supposedly exposing the secrets of superior leadership but devoid of manuals that trumpet the advantages of hanging back and following the herd. Apart from the odd scholarly book, such as Barbara Kellerman's *Followership*, a similar neglect can be found in academia.[2] Researchers focus on the person in charge without paying much attention to the massed ranks in the lower, broader layers of the pyramid, even though these lowly types far outnumber the apex-huggers. Since it is statistically more likely that you, like most people most of the time, fall into the followership fold, you deserve to be told the other half of the leadership–followership story. That is the purpose of this chapter: to define the different forms of followership and explain how they work. We will also see how they fit within the framework of evolutionary leadership theory.

Given the pay-offs available to leaders – the three S's, salary, status and sex – there is no confusion about why somebody would want to be top dog. Yet what is truly puzzling, at first glance, is why someone would want to be a follower. On the face of it, evolution should select against followership because followers lag behind leaders in spreading their genes. In the previous chapter we looked at a few scenarios that make the evolution of followership likely. Here we delve deeper into the pay-offs for followers.

First of all, what do we mean by followership? A follower is an individual who coordinates his actions with another individual, the leader. And this means setting aside your own goals and adopting the objectives of the leader.[3]

There are many different ways in which you can follow. You become a temporary follower when you follow your friend's directions to the nearest pub. In contrast, a stable follower is someone who, say, supports the monarchy. You can follow reluctantly (when you carry out the orders of your loathsome boss), or passionately (as a member of a religious cult or terrorist organisation). You can be the first follower, or the follower of other followers. First followers are critical, because they turn individuals into leaders. The personalities of these pioneering followers is a current area of research for us.

Being a follower, though, does not necessarily require the presence of a leader. Individuals can be followers of an idea, such as a religion or a political ideology (although we have a strong inclination to attach figureheads to these beliefs, be it God, Allah or Marx), an object (a road sign) or a custom (such as a fashion trend). Regardless of the specific context, a follower is someone who relinquishes his individual autonomy for someone or something else. That's no trivial matter because there are huge potential costs that accompany the decision to follow. These costs are twofold. First, followership sometimes requires that you put your own desires to one side, as James presumably did in the previous chapter, when he made the decision to follow persuasive Pat and thereby abandon his girlfriend. On a night out with friends, you might wish to go to a familiar drinking den, but an insistent member wants to try a new pub that's opened round the corner. Anyone who is reasonably sociable will traipse after their friends rather than nurse a pint alone.

Second, there is always the risk of following the wrong individual and suffering as a result. Think of those who followed the advice of Bernard Madoff, who perpetrated the biggest private investor fraud in history. His followers included such famous names as the film director Steven Spielberg and the developer Mort Zuckerman. Even for these high-flying types, the urge to follow their friends into what turned out to be a pyramid selling scheme was overwhelming. To prospective investors, he sounded like a man of supreme ability and confidence; it is almost as if he led a financial cult.[4]

To understand our enthusiasm for following we must revisit the world of our ancestors. In the hostile environment of the African savannah – an arid, unforgiving terrain which teemed with predators, where water and sustenance were precious commodities that were hard to come by – it paid to be in company. Individuals who wanted to do their own thing, or who failed to pay attention to others, were in danger of becoming isolated from the group. Rather than finding a meal, they ran the risk of becoming one, and thus bringing their genetic lineage to a grisly end. Conversely, individuals who practised the philosophy 'safety in numbers', who were careful to hang on to the coat-tails of their compatriots on the savannah, were more likely to survive (and thus reproduce). Over evolutionary time, this would have selected for brains and behaviours that favoured followership; and natural selection would have weeded out the loners. Interestingly, there is no explicit need for leadership to evolve under this scenario; the only evolutionary driver is the need to stick to the group (leadership behaviour, we theorise, could have emerged after followership, as well-directed groups out-reproduced leaderless clusters). As in a shoal of fish, this simple rule facilitates group movement and action without the need for a central leader.[5]

Charles Darwin made a similar argument in his book *Descent of Man*: 'With those animals which were benefited by living in close association, the individuals which took the greatest pleasure in society would best escape various dangers, while those that cared least for their comrades, and lived solitary, would perish in greater numbers.'[6] Darwin's beautifully phrased observation resonates with the deep human desire to forge comradeship in the most dire of situations.

So, we can see how evolutionary pressures in the ancestral environment set the scene for the emergence of followership in humans. Before we march on, though, it is worth stopping to ponder how leadership would have strode on to the scene.

Evolutionary leadership theory explains it like this: the need to coordinate one's activities with other individuals to escape Darwin's 'various dangers' bred the capacity to follow. Once this happened, a niche opened up for individuals to take on leadership roles that choreographed the group's coordination. It may have happened first by happy accident: out of the tribe emerged an exceptionally intelligent and/or talkative and/or dominant personality, who was picked out by his peers as the focus for the group. These led groups fared better – survived longer and produced more descendants – than the 'leaderless' groups.

We can imagine that humankind would quickly experience the benefits of being led competently, and in time would offer inducements to attract a clever individual to the helm. Thus, leadership traits would benefit both the group (in terms of survival and prosperity) and the leader (perks), resulting in two predictions: first, that people in groups with competent leaders would out-reproduce those in groups lacking them, and so leader–follower relations would become a characteristic feature of society (since leaderless groups would die out), and, second, because of the inducements, individuals would come to aspire to be leaders.

In this subtle progression, leadership starts off as an accidental phenomenon, but the phenomenon brings such large, immediate pay-offs that accident evolves into blueprint. This, we theorise, is why we observe leadership of one form or another in so many species.

Now we come back to how followers fit in – how, exactly, do leaders earn their keep? What do they bring to the table that is absent in leaderless groups, and that brings such pay-offs for followers? In most non-human primates the leader is the dominant male in the troop, the alpha. He acts as the focal point for group activities. In gorillas, for example, lowly individuals are permanently attuned to the actions of the silverback. When he moves, they follow; when he turns his head, they turn theirs. The focus on the alpha serves to foster group cohesion, which is key to the survival of all primate groups (safety in numbers).

The alpha is said to have 'attention-holding power' which keeps the group together. (Think back to the classic experiment in which shoppers were persuaded into staring at the sky, simply by copying the actions of one person.) The same phenomenon exists in humans: the queen is a figure around which (most) Britons unite. At political rallies, the attention of a crowd is usually focused on the speaker; he provides the psychological glue that holds the group of followers together. Thousands hang on his every word, and, without him, followers would disperse. And so one evolutionary explanation for the emergence of leaders is that they bind groups together. Without that human glue, groups are at risk of disintegrating, placing the survival of the entire collective in peril.[7]

In addition, following a leader may have been an effective strategy for our human ancestors to learn new things in an unpredictable environment. Many relatively primitive creatures survive perfectly well on a limited set of instincts. Many spider species, for instance, employ only one technique to gather food: they spin a web to catch small flying insects, and this capacity for web-making is innate. Each spider is born with this skill and there is no learning involved. Now, the reliance on a set of innate capacities is absolutely fine in environments that are stable and predictable, where there are always flies to feed on and nice places to spin webs. But this dependence does not work as well for species such as our own, which inhabits a world that is changing and unpredictable, surrounded by such varied terrain as forests, tundra and savannah. Gathering food here is not straightforward; it comes in many forms, each requiring its own gathering technique. If you are going to eat, and therefore survive, it pays to be versatile and varied in the way you seek out dinner. And so it pays to learn.

One way of learning is through simple trial and error. So, one could learn from scratch how to kill a rabbit or find a mushroom that is safe to eat. Can you spot the obvious problem with this strategy? One mistake – such as confusing a toxic false morel mushroom for a safe variety – means curtains for the taster. In scientific terms, trial and error is potentially a very costly strategy. This is what reportedly happened to Christopher McCandless, a young man whose story was recounted movingly by Jon Krakauer in *Into the Wild*.[8] The book-loving graduate gave his money away and, in search of the inner peace that sometimes comes through isolation and self-sufficiency, trekked deep into the wild to live off the land. He was found dead aged 24, having starved to death. Krakauer speculates he may have eaten some seeds coated with a poisonous fungus. Darwin's observation that 'those that cared least for their comrades, and lived solitary, would perish in greater numbers' seems tragically suited to McCandless, and reinforces the idea that evolution tends to favour followers, not loners.

Instead of trial and error, it seems more sensible to follow the example of others; this is exactly where we excel. When we don't know what to conjure up for dinner, we happily assume the role of follower and line up behind our chosen leader, whether it's Nigella Lawson, Jamie Oliver, Martha Stewart or plain old Mum. We are reassured that these figures have faced similar culinary challenges before, whether it is how to make a béchamel sauce or how to rescue a lumpy custard.[9]

A third reason – following on from the first (group

cohesion) and the second (it's safer to copy others than to go it alone) – why humans are natural followers is that by following a leader, you can note and learn the qualities required if you are to become leader one day. It's like on-the-job training. Following a leader not only raises your chances of survival in a mean world, but it is a tutorial in leadership that you can one day turn to your advantage. Not everyone will go down this route – many people actively shun leadership or management positions, and covet the anonymity of followership. But given the benefits associated with leadership – salary, status and sex – it is unsurprising that so many people harbour leadership ambitions. And what better way to learn than by watching?

The former British prime minister Gordon Brown profited in this way from his long-standing alliance with Tony Blair, his prime ministerial predecessor; their partnership must rank as one of the closest in British political history. The two men were neighbours in Downing Street – Blair as PM, Brown as Chancellor – for almost a decade. Although Brown steered a more separate ideological course towards the end of Blair's premiership, his time in the proximity of power reinforced his image as Blair's natural successor. Indeed, it is doubtful that Brown could have acceded at all without having been close to Blair. When Steve Ballmer became CEO of Microsoft, he had already spent two decades in trusted senior positions in the company.

We see a similar pattern among married political leaders. While she is an adept politician in her own right, Hillary Clinton's political career has undoubtedly profited from her time in the White House as wife of the president. She will have learned from Bill Clinton the dos and – perhaps mostly – the don'ts of top-drawer politics.

And so the avenue of evolutionary reasoning brings us to this conclusion: the three main benefits of followership for our ancestors were group cohesion (safety in numbers), knowledge during a time of uncertainty (not eating the poisonous mushroom) and the opportunity to be groomed for a leadership position. In combination, these three benefits would have made it extremely tempting for individuals to become sheep.

The use of the word 'tempting' is slightly misleading; we are ascribing to our forebears an unwarranted consciousness of action. Your ancestor didn't necessarily choose to become a follower any more than he chose his hair colour; he was born with the traits that made him so. He was a sheep because evolutionary pressures selected his temperament to be sheeplike (because his sheeplike parents survived long enough to reproduce, unlike their reckless, go-it-alone counterparts), and weeded out those who shunned the herd. Solitary individuals are likely to have had their lives shortened, and their genetic spread curtailed, by their wish to remain apart from the group. Through a process of natural selection – descent with modification – we can begin to picture how the unique and ubiquitous psychology of followership in humans was sculpted.

Following this line of reasoning also allows us to make predictions about the circumstances ripe for followership. Because, if our followership psychology emerged in response to ancestral challenges, then we'd expect to see particularly strong evidence of followership whenever individuals or groups face challenges akin to those that our ancestors faced, such as a shortage of resources, or threats from an outside group. We can hypothesise, therefore, that people are more likely to follow a leader when they (a) believe group unity is under threat, (b) don't know what to think or do, and (c) aspire to a leadership position. We'll return to this later in the chapter.

But, first, evolutionary leadership theory assumes that followership is an adaptation. In other words, it is a trait that has developed to solve a specific problem faced by our ancestors. If this is this case, and if followership is instinctive rather than learned, we would expect the trait to appear at an early age, and to look like a spontaneous, automatic behaviour.

What is the evidence for this? Let's scutinise what happens between nursery and adulthood.[10]

The extraordinary human appetite for followership shows itself while we're still in nappies. Research demonstrates that, shortly after birth, an infant starts mimicking the facial expression of her mother (when her mother smiles, the tot will beam back) and from the age of three months will follow the mother's gaze.[11] The mother–infant relationship is the first form of leadership–followership that we encounter in our lives; and when something goes wrong here, it can leave indelible emotional scars. The British psychologist and psychiatrist John Bowlby argued that the mother–baby bond, reinforced by mimicry, was an evolutionary strategy on the baby's part to enhance its chances of survival, since it is utterly dependent on a carer in infancy and early childhood.[12]

Babies do not, of course, follow only their mothers. Sigmund Freud, an enthusiastic Darwinist, stressed the role of the father in the development of followership behaviour. In the book *Moses and Monotheism*, which he wrote in London in 1939 just before the outbreak of the Second World War, he examined why the masses adore and follow leaders such as Hitler so enthusiastically: 'Why the great man should rise to significance at all we have no doubt whatsoever. We know that the great majority of people have a strong need for authority which they can admire, to which they can submit, and which dominates and sometimes even ill-treats them. We have learned from the psychology of the individual whence comes this need of the masses. It is the longing for the father that lives in each of us from his childhood days.'[13]

Both maternal and paternal influences probably shape, in early childhood, that seemingly innate capacity for followership. The mother's main duty is generally one of providing care; it tends to fall to the father to demonstrate authority. It is interesting that many children – especially boys – who grow up fatherless seem to lack the qualities to become good followers (here, 'good' has moral connotations). They often end up treading two radically different paths, one leading to deviancy and downfall, and, more rarely, the other to power. Abraham Lincoln, Bill Clinton and Barack Obama were all reared primarily by their mothers, with their fathers rarely, if ever, on the scene. Meanwhile, any socially deprived area – these neighbourhoods tend to show the highest rates of absent fathers – can provide evidence of deviancy. Young men who grow up without male role models are at a disadvantage when it comes to learning how to conform to societal norms. They have no one to follow. One can speculate that, having been reared in the presence of fewer behavioural boundaries, they feel less bothered about violating certain codes of behaviour.

This could be why the children reared by lone mothers generally fare worse – educationally, financially and socially – than children raised by both parents. The Prince's Trust, a charity founded by the Prince of Wales that works with disadvantaged teenagers, published a 2008 report claiming that teenagers joined gangs because they had no parental role models.[14] This, we think, is evidence of a mismatch at work: the human desire to follow is so strong that if a parent is not around to provide leadership, a child will frequently turn to other, less positive, role models. We discuss the Mismatch Hypothesis more fully in Chapter 6.

On the other hand, we know from such figures as Barack Obama that fatherlessness does not inevitably lead to failure. Carlo Strenger and Jacob Burak have noted that many successful entrepreneurs have been brought up with little or no positive fathering; the academics suggest that, in these cases, the child seeks to become the father he never had, which is reminiscent of Freud's psychoanalytical reasoning.[15] The psychological traits that develop are the same strong characteristics required to make a success of business. They term this the Leonardo effect, after Leonardo da Vinci, who had no contact with his father for the first five years of his life (contact resumed when his Florentine nobleman father finally admitted paternity and took the prodigiously clever boy into his home).

A similar thesis was put forward in 1970 by Lucille Iremonger in *The Fiery Chariot*, an analysis of the backgrounds of British prime ministers over a 130-year period. Iremonger noted they were more likely than the general population to have lost a parent (and, she theorised, less likely to have developed an Oedipus complex).[16] It is tempting to speculate that, if an intelligent child never learns the art of followership, he is less intimidated about practising the art of leadership.

Outside the family home, children also pick up the followership habit pretty early, quickly engaging in such games as 'follow my leader'. They soon grasp that following the group and sticking together is important, even if they are unable to articulate why. In so doing, they are acting out behaviours shaped in the ancestral environments, when being in a group enhanced the chances of survival. Children's culture is filled with stories of characters who stick together, such as the following rhyme from *Peter Pan*, which begins:

We're following the leader wherever he may go
We won't be home till morning, till morning
We won't be home till morning
Because he told us so …

And there are also fairy tales that warn of what happens when a character strikes out on his or her own, such as Little Red Riding Hood and Hansel and Gretel. Such fables also convey a useful warning about not trusting strangers (who are, of course, not one of the tribe and therefore a figure of suspicion).

Children, in the absence of parents, tend to follow each other. In the classic novel *Lord of the Flies* the boys stranded on a desert island swiftly organise themselves into two factions, each with their own leadership and followership structure.[17] By doing so, they attempt to create some stability in the chaos of their parentless world. In his classic 1960s studies of summer camp, the Turkish-American social psychologist Muzhafar Sherif observed something similar among its schoolboy attendees.[18] One of the first things these newly formed groups did was to appoint a team leader to organise their activities, which included a sports match. (Interestingly, while it tends to be the most dominant pre-schoolers who lead group activities, these bullies lose their status later in their schooling. In infant school, for example, children will often ignore the overtly dominant child, aka the braying bully, and instead trail the most popular kid in the class.)[19]

So, followership emerges quite spontaneously in children. What about when they grow older? As most exasperated parents will know, teenagers are less keen to follow their parents and sometimes even openly rebel against them. Evolutionarily speaking this makes a lot of sense since, as a child gains independence, there is less need for her to stay close to her parents to ensure safety and security. But our teenager is not abandoning her innate tendency to follow; merely switching allegiance. Her parents can probably no longer provide her with relevant or accurate information on how to progress in life – such as finding a mate, and choosing clothes to attract them – because of the generation gap. This is the window during which their peers, or individuals who are slightly older than them (who might have realised similar aspirations), become more influential as role models. These characters become the new teen leaders, providing inspiration and guidance as to how life should be lived. This is also the point at which a leadership vacuum becomes dangerous; the last thing parents want is to see their own steadying influence being usurped by antisocial or violent gangs.

You might assume that adults, capable of thinking for themselves, are less prone to slavish followership because they don't rely on others as heavily as children for the fulfilment of their needs and goals. This is only partly true. There are many situations which prompt people to follow automatically, especially when these situations mirror ancestral situations that have traditionally elicited followership. In these cases, our evolved instincts respond like puppets to the cues (which are: group cohesion coming under threat; an uncertainty about what to think or do; and a desire to become a leader one day).

We, together with Edward Cartwright and Joris Gillet at the University of Kent, performed an experiment to gauge how quickly leadership and followership emerge spontaneously among adults.[20] We invited four undergraduate students, all strangers to each other, to come to the laboratory and play a coordination game in which they could earn money. They were ushered into different cubicles and could interact with each other only via computers (these experiments often prohibit face-to-face interactions because good-looking people tend to exert a disproportionately large influence on the group). The coordination game involved individuals choosing between two options, say between cheese and wine, each with a particular payout for him or her. So, you might get £7 for choosing cheese but only £5 for choosing wine. Unless you really hated cheese, you'd probably plump for it on financial grounds.

But what if you could see that options for your fellow players were different from yours, and that another player was better off choosing wine? And what if, to add a layer of complexity, you could see that if you and he chose the same thing, then you would both get a bonus? You might not mind giving up on cheese so much, if the bonus from choosing wine was sufficient.

The concepts of self-interest and trade-offs can be illustrated like this: picture yourself walking into a shop to buy a game console. Imagine you have to choose between a Wii or an Xbox. You might prefer a Wii because it has cooler games. But what if all your friends – who also have an extraordinary amount of time on their hands – own Xboxes? You would reap some benefit from having an Xbox too, because you can swap games. So, despite your preference for the Wii, you might make a judicious decision to follow your friends. You shell out for the Xbox. Your bonus payout, so to speak, is an enhanced circle of idle friends all willing to come round and waste an evening in front of a computer screen with you.

Back in our experiment, instead of cheese and wine, we played it with Xs and Ys, with each letter being assigned a value, e.g. X = £5 and Y = £7 – our guinea pigs had to make similar decisions with defined trade-offs. And we looked for two things: the speed with which a decision was made, and the actual decision (X or Y) itself. We defined the quickest on the keyboard as the leader; the others, who seemed to be waiting for someone else to choose first, were labelled followers.

Our results showed very clearly that people did what was best for their pocket. They led the group when they had a strong preference for X over Y in scenarios when the coordination payout was low (and therefore there was little incentive to take the same option as fellow players). In cases when players were ambivalent about choosing X over Y, the coordination payouts were key to what happened. With a large coordination payout – this is the bonus that accrues from everyone plumping for the same option – people became followers. They looked to see what other guinea pigs were selecting, and jumped into line behind them in order to pocket the bonus. In other words, they followed when it was prudent – and profitable – to do so.

Back to our analogy: if only a handful of your acquaintances have an Xbox then you might stick to getting a Wii. In the parlance, the coordination payout – the benefit gained from doing the same as someone else – is miserly. And so you should choose the console that you'd prefer to have, rather than follow what others are doing.

Despite the complexity of the game, it took an average of 25 seconds for the groups to reach a consensus, and most groups achieved the best possible coordination solution. This means that all the members of the group maximised their payouts. This result echoes other studies in which ad hoc groups come together to complete a particular task, such as assembling a radio. Even in groups of strangers, people are very quick to recognise each other's expertise and follow the person most able to tackle the task at hand. A group of strangers can very easily and instinctively work together to produce an outcome that is beneficial to the collective; this clearly shows the pay-offs of followership. Fascinatingly, in terms of actual pay-outs, leaders tended to fare worse than followers. This suggests that instinctive leadership leans towards servant leadership.

The instinct to fall into line behind others, however, can lead us astray. The Yale University psychologist Stanley Milgram showed that our willingness to follow can take us on a path that is very different from that mapped out by our moral compass.[21] Milgram's famous obedience experiment, conducted in the 1960s, saw participants asked to play the role of teacher to a learner. The teaching technique involved delivering electric shocks to the learner, if he failed to answer questions correctly. Participants were told that the learner, housed in another room, had been treated for a heart condition but that the shock would be harmless. The teacher would then administer a memory task; each time the learner answered incorrectly, the teacher was instructed to deliver a shock. The shock delivery machine contained a series of levers delivering shocks ranging from 15 to 450 volts; the teacher was told by the experimenter, always attired in a white laboratory coat, that the shock level had to increase with each error.

It was clear that the participants were torn between two motives, gaining social approval from the authority figure (the white-coated experimenter) versus doing the (morally) right thing and refusing to flick the levers. The teachers often implored the experimenter to stop the task – but, when it came to the crunch, they were still prepared to deliver the shocks. Their desire to follow orders trumped their desire not to inflict suffering. Astonishingly, around 65 per cent of participants were willing, albeit reluctantly, to deliver a potentially lethal shock level of 450 volts. This shows how strong our follower-ship tendency is, when we are being corralled by an authority figure. It is worryingly easy for our followership instincts to override our moral values.

This is clearly a legacy of our ancestral past, in which following authority figures and gaining their social approval would have been important for our survival, even if it involved harming others. Indeed, some gangs require new members to carry out initiation ceremonies that involve seriously harming, or even murdering, members of rival gangs. Only by committing such an extreme act can a gang leader be sure of his initiate's loyalty. It is hard to imagine a more dangerous form of followership than that forged in blood.

This evolved 'follow the authority' rule has also been easily exploited by malicious leaders throughout history. Our past, from Nero to Mao, suggests that ardent followers of brutal leaders can be much more dangerous than people who stand apart from society. These figures were able to command others to do their murderous work, which shows how far we are willing to go to prove an allegiance.

This instinct to follow authority often plays tricks with us when we are confronted with shrewd advertisers. For instance, when a new washing powder appears on the market it is usually launched by a middle-aged white male, in a white laboratory coat in an attempt to convey scientific credibility (despite Stanley Milgram's revelations about our slavish obedience to authority, those white laboratory coats remain a disturbingly powerful cue).

In fact, advertising is a $400 billion industry built on followership.[22] And the use of attractive or successful people – usually both – to sell products taps into our evolutionary mindset. In ancestral times beauty and facial attractiveness were probably signs of physical health, which in turn was a reliable indicator of success at surviving in a hostile environment. Our latent thinking goes like this: if he's handsome, I'll do whatever he's doing (which means buying whatever he's endorsing). Ditto for successful people: if there's the slightest chance that David Beckham's designer underwear or newest fragrance is the secret of his success, we will willingly buy into it in the hope that it will bring us success too.

Not only have we evolved to follow authority, but we have also developed an innate 'follow the majority' rule. On the savannah, when a person was stuck as to what to do, they would either turn to an expert for advice or copy the crowd. When most of the tribe fancies trekking to waterhole A, it's safer to follow them than side with a minority making tracks in the opposite direction. This makes perfect sense. Information pooled from many group members, as opposed to fewer, leads to better decision-making (except when a collective is under time pressure and led by a forceful leader, when we get a disastrous decision-making process known as groupthink). Furthermore, following the majority also makes sense from a self-defence point of view. There is safety in numbers – and everyone sticking together promotes group unity, which is needed for group survival.[23]

What happens when we want to follow the majority, but the group's opinion clashes with our own? Amazingly, we would rather follow the crowd, even when it's wrong, than stand apart, simply because of our unwillingness to undermine group cohesion.

This has been demonstrated in so-called conformity experiments. One of the earliest was conducted by an enterprising but little-known American psychologist called Arthur Jenness, in 1962. Jenness, who spent much of his career researching hypnosis, invited a succession of people, one by one, into a room to estimate the number of beans in a glass jar. Then participants were brought together in the room, and asked to make a group estimate. Afterwards, Jenness repeated his initial experiment, giving each individual the chance to change his estimate. Almost all seized the opportunity to modify their original estimates, to make them closer to the group estimate.[24]

The most famous conformity experiments, however, were conducted in the 1950s by Solomon Asch. His work shed particular light on followership, because it showed that social pressure could make people say something they knew to be untrue.[25] Let's do the experiment with Anne, Bronwen, Charles and David, all strangers.

Each of them in turn is shown a picture featuring three lines of varying lengths, and then a picture of a single line. Their very easy task is to match the single line to one of the other three lines, and announce their answer in front of other participants. It's an unbelievably easy task: they all pick out the same line, give the same answer, and David inwardly congratulates himself on finding such an easy way to make money (because participants in psychology experiments usually get a token payment).

But, when the experiment is repeated, what if Anne, Bronwen and Charles pick out the wrong line? Not only that, but the same wrong line? What does David do? Asch found that David – who doesn't know that his three new friends are stooges, in on the study – was very likely to conform by also choosing the wrong line. Indeed, through these ingenious tests, Asch uncovered a remarkable human desire to conform: only a quarter of participants followed the courage of their convictions to announce the correct answer in the face of others announcing the same wrong answer. The desire to conform overwhelms the desire to be correct, which is a startling fact in the science of followership.

Asch also found, however, that conformity rates dropped when a dissenter was introduced. If Anne and Bronwen had picked the wrong line, followed by Charles announcing the correct line, David would be more likely to pipe up with the correct answer too. It shows that even a small dissenting minority can have an important effect on group (dis)unity. It takes only a small ripple to rock the boat – and illustrates that disgruntled or dissenting followers can easily destabilise a leader. It can therefore pay for a company to be alert to employee gripes, and give workers a way of venting their dissatisfaction (such as a suggestions box, in which criticisms can be aired anonymously). We'll look at this balance of power between leaders and followers in a later chapter.

The 'follow the majority' rule can thus lead to some bizarre situations; we can think of these situations as mismatches, where our evolved psychology (which is trained to regard 'follow the majority' as a lifesaving rule, as our ancestors did) clashes with modern life. Take the example of the Heaven's Gate community, a Californian cult that fused some elements of Christianity with a belief in UFOs.[26] They lavished several thousand dollars on a high-powered telescope because they had heard rumours about a small object that appeared to be trailing the Hale-Bopp comet. They maintained it was a spaceship that was coming to earth to save them, before the planet was destroyed. Unfortunately, the telescope did not testify to the existence of such a vessel. They took the telescope back and complained; the salesman explained that there was no trailing object and that their assumption was based on a flawed picture in the newspaper. At this point, members of the community could have ditched their leader in annoyance at being misled. But they didn't: remarkably, the followers remained steadfast in their beliefs. The leaders, meanwhile, maintained that there was indeed a spaceship hot on the comet's trail, and that the telescope was simply not sensitive enough to detect it. And so the cult members consumed a last meal of pudding, vodka and phenobarbital, in order to save their souls before the earth came to an apocalyptic end.

Those cult members prized loyalty over life. Being a contrarian is not easy, even when you know you're right. Evidence from social psychological research shows that a person who takes up a minority position will be actively discriminated against. First, the group will mount a campaign of persuasion; if that falls on deaf ears, the contrarian is ostracised. In ancestral times, ostracism could spell death; it is not surprising, then, that individuals try their best to fit in, including on occasions when it goes against their better judgement (although consenting to group suicide is, admittedly, an extreme example).

The urge to follow the majority is powerful even when being in a majority or a minority is a matter of opinion, such as when choosing what shoes to wear or what car to drive. There is no factually correct answer to the question of whether a Nike running shoe is better or worse than an Adidas shoe (except if you are a Nike executive), or whether Christianity is more or less valid than Islam or Judaism. All that matters from the viewpoint of group unity is that you believe what your group believes in. Either you are in with the in-crowd, or you are out. And in a social species such as our own, 'out' is a very lonely place to be.

Paradoxically, the costlier the rituals associated with a belief system, the more enduring it is. One study of religious communes in nineteenth-century America showed that those making the most extreme demands on their followers – giving up worldly goods, celibacy, shunning contact with outsiders, relinquishing certain foods and alcohol – were the most enduring.[27] Such sacrifices ensure that only the most loyal and committed adherents become followers. After that, the follower remains tied to his leader through the wish to be consistent with his previous, group-oriented actions.

So, up to this point we have argued that our innate propensity to follow (shown by infants towards their parents) is ramped up whenever we want to be a 'good' group member (such as when David chose the wrong line, to fit in with his three new friends), or whenever we are mired in uncertainty (which explains why we might choose an aftershave promoted by David Beckham). What about the third rationale: following as a strategy to learn how to become a leader? There is little doubt that this is an important motive for some of the herd, although it won't necessarily be a conscious strategy. To become a leader one day, it pays to follow first. If an individual aspired to become a good hunter in ancestral times, what better training was there than shadowing the most accomplished hunter in the group and following his actions closely? The same applies to any form of expertise, including leadership skills. For instance, by staying close to a leader one can note how he uses his verbal and non-verbal skills to convince people, mediate in conflicts and deal with hostile rivals.

There is, though, an unstated quid pro quo: in return for an apprenticeship at the feet of a master, the disciple must show a deferential allegiance. Only on these terms will a leader share his hard-won wisdom. After all, it reflects well on a leader to have followers. As evolutionary leadership theory reminds us, the acquisition of a leadership role is a status symbol, a sign of prestige, and there is a major benefit that comes with it: reproductive success. Prestigious individuals in hunter-gatherer societies, such as the best hunter or warrior, are feted. As a result, they enjoy the pick of the best sexual mates in the neighbourhood.

A modern manifestation of this prestige-based system is today's celebrity culture. Think of a famous person – whether it's a rock star, a politician or a footballer; he is trailed by a crowd of followers who model themselves on him and want to be like him (or, in the case of female fans, want to marry him and have his babies). Consequently, these talented people gain prestige, which can have pay-offs in many ways. Some celebrities always snare the best tables in smart restaurants and don't have to queue at airports; they are richer than their followers (not only do they make money in their day jobs, but they can also enjoy sponsorship deals and lucrative media tie-ups for exclusive coverage of weddings and births) and have access to high-quality (or, at least, good-looking) reproductive partners. Followers (or fans, as we usually call them) will do almost anything to get close to their heroes; this proximity enhances the opportunity to copy them. Thus, they read everything they can find about them (which is why magazines like *OK!* and *Hello!* sell so well), they want to have their signature (which proves they have got up close and personal), they want to wear the same clothes, look the same, and they are even prepared to go through their rubbish bins to get a piece of them. (Again, fans may not be aware of the evolutionary motive behind their behaviour; evolution has done the thinking for them, and fans are conscious only of the compulsion to emulate.)

Politicians are aware of this. When they give a speech, they want as large an audience as possible for their oration. They know that large crowds will attract more followers. Novelists and book publishers also know that many people will buy a book just because it features in the bestseller list. A bookworm's line of reasoning goes something like this: this book is a bestseller because loads of people have bought it, and loads of people can't be wrong. There must be something in it, so let's take it to the till.

Sometimes, though, this 'follow the majority' rule backfires; we end up following individuals who have no redeeming qualities (or certainly none that one would aspire to). Their only qualification for prominence is media ubiquity, which gives us the false impression that the person is worth following. This, we argue, has brought us to this curious point in human history, where people are famous for being famous.

Big Brother is a reality show in which ordinary people are watched night and day for weeks as they complete amusing, pointless or humiliating tasks for the benefit of viewers. The programme's producers are flooded with applicants each year; these hopefuls know that it is a route to instant fame because they receive intense media exposure. This media bombardment hits our psychological weak spot. Our Stone Age brains are tricked into believing that when an individual earns a lot of attention, he must boast a particular skill or quality and thus deserves following; it is only on closer inspection that we realise that those who bask in the limelight don't really justify their time out of the shadows. It is a perfect example of a mismatch (a concept we explore more fully in Chapter 6). We have recently designed an experiment where we show various leaders on a computer screen surrounded either by a few or many other individuals. Furthermore, we have manipulated the gaze of the surrounding individuals so that they are either looking at the leader or away from him. Then we ask participants in this experiment to rate the leadership qualities of the leader. Results are not yet available, but we expect participants to attribute more leadership qualities to a person surrounded by many individuals, especially if those individuals are looking at him.

A comic illustration of this propensity to 'follow the leader, any leader' was devised by the British comedian Danny Wallace. In 2002, he created an international cult of followers through his 'Join me' campaign (http://www.join-me.co.uk/). He toured the world asking people to follow him as the leader of a 'collective' while being deliberately obtuse about what the purpose of the 'Join me' movement was. This did not prevent thousands of people from all over the world signing up. With minimal effort, Wallace did indeed become a leader.[28]

Of course, we need to note that all followers are not the same: they have their own preferences, values and personalities. Christians come in many forms, from the devout to the lapsed. Followership comes in many flavours – reluctant, enthusiastic, unquestioning, critical, slavish, obsessive. Again, there has been little investigation of these different styles, because of the focus on leadership. But we suggest that the questions that have been traditionally asked about leadership – what the styles are, how those styles come about, how effective they are in different contexts – should be posed about followership.

Some theorists have attempted to answer the questions: they distinguish, for example, between dependent and independent followers. The first simply follow the leader's orders, while the latter take a more critical and questioning approach.

A distinction can also be made between active and passive followers. Active followers take initiatives (in this respect, they are a little bit like leaders) but passive ones don't. They wait and see.

Some psychologists, such as Ira Chaleff, believe the distinguishing feature of followership lies in how much a follower is prepared to challenge the figure at the helm. Certainly, a follower who is prepared to question an incompetent or dangerous leader – the courageous follower, as Chaleff termed him – is worth studying. We need to understand the courageous followers who dare to stand up to immoral leadership, such as the people who tried to rescue Jews in Nazi Europe or the whistleblowers who brought down Enron.[29]

From an evolutionary viewpoint, though, the most important distinction is that between good and bad followers. We don't mean this in the moral sense; rather, we mean that a good follower is one who is geared to achieving the outcome desired by the leader. Good followers are those able to coordinate smoothly and efficiently with the leader in a bid for success – for instance, reaching the preferred waterhole without compromising group unity. Bad followers are the difficult ones – they go their own way, speak out of turn, and don't care much for the path their leader has carved out for them. In moral terms, whether followership is morally good or bad depends on the aims of the leader. Thus the Nazis who followed the orders of Hitler blindly were good followers but morally corrupt. The Nazi officers who plotted against Hitler were bad followers but their motives were morally sound. In the main, a good follower of a morally bad leader amplifies the misery created by the leader, whereas a good follower of a morally good leader amplifies the happiness created by the leader.

Not all followers are equally committed to a leader's goals, as demonstrated by Barbara Kellerman. In her book *Followership*, she grades them on the basis of commitment to the leader's objectives (although she does not distinguish between the two very different breeds of follower who act either in consort with, or against, their leader).

Kellerman's taxonomy of followership commitment contains five categories. First, isolates. They are at the apathetic end of the spectrum, and comprise, for example, people who can't be bothered to vote. A leader dismisses them at his peril, because apathy among followers raises questions about a leader's legitimacy. There may be no legal or constitutional difference between a president who wins 51 per cent of his country's vote and one who wins 80 per cent, but instinct tells us that candidates who achieve the latter enjoys a greater mandate to act.[30]

Loitering in the second category are the bystanders: they show little or no commitment to any particular leader. Where an isolate practises apathy, a bystander specialises in ambivalence, taking a neutral position.

The third group, practising middling commitment, are called participants. Examples include reasonably satisfied employees who are willing to put in extra hours when the job requires it.

Then comes category four: the activists. These activists are more highly engaged than participants, and will consistently work hard to either support their leaders or to oust them.

But no category is more committed than the diehards, who are ready to lay down their lives for their leaders or the cause. Diehards show a dedication and devotion that are all-consuming; this defines everything they are and every action they take. Terrorists, whose lives are totally shaped according to an ideological agenda, occupy this end of the spectrum. Suicide bombers are, of course, the ultimate diehards.

If you are a leader, it pays to know how to shift followers farther up the commitment spectrum. What you want is a psychological sales technique, capable of turning bystanders into participants, and activists into diehards. The most important of these, according to Robert Cialdini, an appropriately influential psychologist in the study of influence, is the foot-in-the-door technique, in which the leader starts off making small requests and then follows up with more exacting demands. In this favoured modus operandi of terrorist organisations and religious cults,the commitment dial gets cranked up relatively gradually; minor activities such as distributing leaflets slowly escalate into more extreme actions, such as renouncing friends and family. The follower acquiesces more out of consistency with previous actions than any deep desire to make the requested sacrifice.[31]

Even corporations can begin to behave like cults. The most startling revelation in *The Devil's Casino*, an account of the 2008 downfall of Lehman Brothers, was the cult-like loyalty demanded of the bank's senior executives and their wives. Spouses were expected to dress in a certain way, support the same charities, join company vacations and keep quiet about marital troubles. The culture was never questioned, even when one wife was pressured into leaving her sick child's bedside to go on a company outing. The financial services behemoth subsequently became one of the largest bankruptcies in American history.[32]

Another way to shift commitment levels is by obtaining a follower's agreement to a specific task – such as attendance at a political meeting – and then changing the terms of the arrangement (e.g. 'If you want to attend this political meeting you must become a party member'). A third way is through temptation: for example, telling followers they will be paid for distributing leaflets at a political rally. Once they have committed – well, wouldn't you just know it? There's simply not enough money to pay everyone so would you mind volunteering? Finally, flattery is surprisingly effective: a smart leader will describe his followers in glowing terms – 'you are all fantastic, understanding employees' – and then, after deploying this labelling technique, ask them to take a pay cut. And why do most of us fall for this trick? Because nobody wants to look like a bad employee.

There are, however, gaps in these analyses of followership. They point out that followers show different levels of commitment to a cause – but neglect the fact that the nature of what is being followed varies. What is it that followers are trying to achieve? What are their motives? What differentiates first followers from those that come on to the scene later? Are they trying to be good group members (to foster cohesion)? Are they following in the hope of one day jockeying for power (to become a leader)? Or are they following because, in the absence of the capacity to lead, they are left with no option but to follow?

As we saw earlier in this chapter, evolutionary leadership theory gives three reasons for followership: group cohesion, uncertainty (not knowing which is the poisonous mushroom) and the possibility of emulation. These provide adaptive justifications for followership (in other words, followership in these situations makes the person more likely to have offspring). And so the mode of followership depends not just on commitment level, but also on the nature of the adaptive problem that leads to the followership behaviour.

We propose a new taxonomy of followership based on evolutionary leadership theory. It contains five categories of follower: apprentice, disciple, loyalist, supporter and subordinate.

If a follower wants to be a leader one day, he is an apprentice (one of the most successful television programmes of recent years has been *The Apprentice*, a reality show in which about fifteen young, thrusting types compete for a lucrative job under a famously rich, demanding tycoon. In the UK, the tycoon is computer entrepreneur Sir Alan Sugar; in the USA, it is Donald Trump). This kind of follower is carrying out the evolutionary imperative to emulate.

If a follower seeks moral wisdom or guidance about how to live, he is a disciple (like the disciples of Jesus Christ), and is enacting the evolutionary imperative to combat uncertainty. If you eagerly devour books by business 'gurus' such as Tom Peters, Peter Drucker and Michael Porter, you can count yourself as a disciple.

If a person follows a leader because he values group cohesion, upon which evolution has also placed a high value, he is a loyalist (like senators or MPs who put aside personal objections to vote with their parties; or football fans; or employees headed for their long-service awards). If a follower's devotion stems from personal attraction to the leader, he is a supporter (think David Beckham or Brad Pitt); this is where charisma comes in, and this quality helps to rally fans behind a single figure.

Finally, if someone is a follower simply because someone farther up the hierarchy wants him to be, he is a subordinate (like most employees). A subordinate is following the evolutionary motivation to stick with the herd, perhaps because the prospect of leadership is just not on his radar, because of a lack of aspiration and ability.

The distinction between apprentices, disciples, loyalists, supporters and subordinates is useful because understanding a follower's motives – in addition to comprehending their commitment, à la Kellerman – can help leaders and their groups recruit, retain and reconnect with those beneath them. For example, a charismatic CEO who champions his employees and is generous with his wisdom, while delivering profits that are shared among employees, is going to appeal to followers across the board. He will be a teacher to his apprentices, a source of inspiration to his disciples, a defender to his loyalists, a figurehead to his supporters and a provider to his subordinates. It's a tall order – and, as we'll see in the next chapter, it takes a Big Man to keep all followers happy.

4

Status-seeking on the savannah: the democratic ape

People may choose to ignore their animal heritage by interpreting their behaviour as divinely inspired, socially purposeful, or even self-serving, all of which they attribute to being human; but they masticate, defecate, masturbate, fornicate and procreate much as chimps and other apes do, so they should have little cause to get upset if they learn they act like other primates when they politically agitate, debate, abdicate, placate and administrate, too.

Arnold Ludwig, *King of the Mountain*

In most organisations we can usually guess who's in charge. In the business world it's the person who occupies the largest office, wears the most expensive suits, and drives the biggest company car (or has the chauffeur). In the military, the guy with the most metalware on his chest is a good bet. In the world of science and education it's the person with the longest string of titles attached to his name (professor, doctor, master of science, honorary fellow, etc.), and in politics it's the person who sits at the short end of the table during meetings.

Such status markers might be covert but we do take notice of them. And they make sense in large organisations because they subtly convey how a person is ranked; who he should defer to and, in turn, who should defer to him. In addition, the visible privileges associated with rank (such as a bigger office) motivate lowlier employees to aim high. These status markers also transmit information beyond company walls. If, for example, you walked into a business meeting with another company to discover that its CEO was that scruffy fellow who arrived in the clapped-out banger, you might surmise the company is not doing that well, and so decide against a commercial partnership. Therefore, perhaps counter-intuitively, many employees are quite content for their boss to earn more than them, and to drive a company car. The status symbols reflect well on the company and, by extension, reflect well on them.

In an age when rank is enshrined in job descriptions (assistant shop manager, team leader, deputy headteacher, chief executive), it is easy to forget that status was not always a conspicuous feature of human life. Status mattered, yes, but when there is little to go round in terms of worldly goods, there is a cap on how showy any one person in the tribe can be.

If we take today's nomadic hunter-gatherer societies as the model for how our ancestors lived for millions of years, the picture is much less stratified than we see in contemporary corporate life.[1] In this chapter, we'll travel back in time, in the company of missionaries and ethnographers who lived with and studied primitive tribes, to find out just how flat ancestral society may have been. We'll also accompany primatologists into rivalry-ridden chimpanzee colonies and gorilla groups, where dominance hierarchies make for a very different kind of primate society, and theorise about how evolution steered us away from the despotism of our primate cousins and towards a society of (relative) equals, under the protection of the wise, benevolent leaders predicted by evolutionary leadership theory. Along the way, we'll digest how the practice of food sharing may have seeded the beginnings of politics, by teaching both chimpanzees and humans how to forge alliances and coalitions; we'll discover how we balanced the need for leadership (putting power into the hands of the few) with the desire not to be dominated (by developing schemes for taking it away); and we'll see how our own species perfected the art of speaking truth to power, allowing our ancestors to keep aspiring despots in check using strategies that ranged from the salacious to the murderous.

Our first stop is Tierra del Fuego, at the southernmost tip of South America. Our brief companion is the missionary Esteban Lucas Bridges, himself the son of a missionary, who grew up among the Ona, a band of nomadic foragers. In 1948, Bridges would write an acclaimed account of his time with the Ona, the Yaghan (another indigenous tribe) and white settlers. Here, he marvels at the Ona's rather flexible approach to leadership:

The Ona had no hereditary or elected chiefs but men of outstanding ability almost always became the unacknowledged leaders of their groups. Yet one man might seem leader today and another man tomorrow, according to whoever was keen to embark upon some enterprise. A certain scientist visited our part of the world and, in answer to his inquiries on this matter I told him that the Ona had no chieftains, as we understand the word. Seeing that he did not believe me I summoned Kankoat, who by that time spoke some Spanish. When the visitor repeated his question, Kankoat, too polite to answer in the negative, said: 'Yes senor, we, the Ona, have many chiefs. The men are all captains and all the women are sailors.'[2]

Beyond status, the Ona did not even have a concept of personal property. When Ona hunting grounds were overrun by Westerners establishing sheep ranches, the clash of cultures proved disastrous. The Ona would routinely steal the animals. Ranchers employed hired gunmen, offering bounties for the heads of Ona thieves. The tribe is now extinct; its last member is thought to have died in the 1970s.

The overriding message from the study of primitive band societies such as the Ona, the !Kung San in the Kalahari desert, the Yanomamo of the Amazon river basin, the Inuit of the Arctic coasts and the Aborigines of northern Australia is that they do not have designated tribal leaders or formal hierarchies. If you were to meet a tribesman, and ask him to 'Take me to your leader', he would be bewildered by your request. From the ethnographic evidence, however, it is also clear that some individuals did have more influence than others based on their personality, temperament, intelligence or skill. Yet this influence was confined to narrowly prescribed areas of expertise; the best hunter, for example, had the final say in the choice of hunting territories, the most formidable warrior in combat decisions, and the tribe's leading herbalist in how to treat the sick. If these individuals attempted to claim authority beyond this, or tried to dominate the group, they would have been guilty of a serious violation of social etiquette.

Academics who have spent time with these societies believe this is how we lived for most of human evolutionary history (our own species, *Homo sapiens*, emerged about 200,000 years ago). As the anthropologist Bruce Knauft states in his analysis of band societies, 'Before twelve thousand years ago humans basically were egalitarian. They lived in what might be called societies of equals with minimal political centralization and no social classes. Everyone participated in group decisions and outside the family there were no dominators.'[3]

So, what changed? Historical evidence suggests that, in particular places in the world, band societies snowballed into larger tribal societies – perhaps to exchange information, goods and brides – comprising different clan groups that were nevertheless still fiercely egalitarian. Such social coalescence may have seeded the beginnings of a more hierarchical set-up, because larger societies create opportunities for trade. People who traded successfully – agriculture, as we'll see in the next chapter, provided the perfect opportunity for early salesmanship – would have accumulated more resources than others. This wealth would have afforded them more influence in the public sphere, because others would have looked up to these figures, called Big Men, endowed with economic prowess.

Big Men first emerged in places like Polynesia and Papua New Guinea, the North Pacific and parts of sub-Saharan Africa; in some regions, the Big Man still exists. According to anthropologist Marshall Sahlins, whose studies of ethnographic accounts of tribes in such places as Papua New Guinea did much to develop the idea of the Big Man, this character is 'reminiscent of the free-enterprising rugged individual of our own heritage. He combines with an ostensible interest in the general welfare a more profound measure of self-interested cunning and economic calculation.'[4] Thanks largely to Sahlins, the term Big Man entered anthropology; he observed that it was a loose translation for 'leader' in many local languages. It is worth noting that the term is still used elastically, with some scholars ascribing the title only to heads of individual tribes rather than clusters of tribes. We shall be magnanimous in our definition, and employ it to describe a man of benevolence who exerts influence over one tribe or a small group of tribes (we'll see in the next chapter that tribes grew in size as foraging gave way to agriculture).

The tribal societies governed by Big Men were largely flat and their influence was very limited. For instance, a difference in wealth acquisition was tolerated only if the whole community benefited. A Big Man was expected to redistribute his wealth through giving gifts and lavishing favours on his extended family. Some primitive societies even introduced gambling in order to spread the riches more evenly; the Big Men would play until they were cleaned out. The anthropologist William Mitchell wrote of the Wape, a tribal society that dwell in the West Sepik region of Papua New Guinea: 'A man will not tolerate a situation where a neighbour has more than he has. A man should not possess either goods or power to the disadvantage of others.' Mitchell would later write a paper entitled 'The defeat of hierarchy: gambling as exchange in a Sepik society', about the Wape's unusual means of ironing out financial differences.[5]

In native cultures in the Pacific North-West, such as

those of the Haida and Tlingit, wealth redistribution used to take the form of a ceremony called the potlatch, in which a Big Man of one tribal village would simply give away valuable gifts and goods such as canoes to neighbouring villagers.[6] By showcasing such wealth and generosity, usually to mark special occasions such as a birth or a daughter's first period, he could strengthen his political position in the tribe and form alliances with other Big Men. Sometimes Big Men would simply burn valuable goods such as canoes or blankets to signal their riches. Potlatches were outlawed by the Canadian government in 1885 for their wastefulness; the ban, criticised for its cultural insensitivity, was repealed in the mid-twentieth century.

In a recent study we created a potlatch in the lab.[7] Individuals received a monetary endowment which they could put either in a private fund or a public fund. We then set up two different scenarios: in one, the donors remained anonymous, and in the other, they were named. We then created a situation such that the public fund was already filled with contributions from the other players. Essentially, any donation would thus be wasted. Yet we found that when people were publicly identifiable they wasted their money on making a needless public-good donation. Importantly, those who did so received status from the other players, just like the Big Man burning his goods to show off his wealth. We interpreted this conspicuous behaviour as a costly signal which individuals use to attract collaboration partners and sexual mates ('look at how wealthy I am, I can afford to spend money on useless things such as a diamond ring or an exotic holiday'). This happens for real: some charities which assist after high-profile disasters, such as the Haiti earthquake, report that donations continue to flood in even after appeals for the money stop. We can assume that donors do it for reputational reasons, as well as philanthropic ones.

On the surface, the potlatch seemed the epitome of egalitarian behaviour, but it was actually a show of status.

And we know that status is a powerful motivator for human behaviour, because it comes with its own repertoire of emotions. This explains why we feel elated and proud when we or a close relative gets a promotion or a first-class degree; and our feelings of disappointment and humiliation in the face of defeat or demotion. The potlatch is a performance of competitive altruism, an overt form of generosity that is, deep down, motivated by the desire for status (a stepping stone on the way to get sex, evolution's main incentive to encourage reproduction). In this way, with the potlatch serving as a benign status symbol, Big Men could maintain the illusion of egalitarianism while still showing off their elevated position within their communities. Our research shows that competitive altruism is a very powerful drive that probably accounts for much charitable and philanthropic behaviour (why else do donors want theatres, schools and hospitals named after them?). This explains the ubiquity of 'Top Philanthropists' or 'Giving' lists, such as those compiled by *Business Week*, *Slate* and the *Sunday Times*; if we are interested in how much money people are making, we seem even more captivated by how much they are giving away. And, to judge by our laboratory experiments, showing your generous side is a guaranteed way to raise your status among peers.

In our experiments, players were randomly assigned to teams of three, and identified only by number. Each player got £1, any portion of which they could invest in a private fund or a group fund. At the end of each round, the amount in the group fund would be doubled and shared equally among team members. Clearly, a contribution to the group fund was a charitable act because the players were less certain of the pay-off.

When people played anonymously, group funds didn't attract many donations. But when a player's number and his contribution were made public, the coffers of the group fund swelled. Clearly, people were contributing to enhance their reputation. Indeed, when we solicited opinion, players said they respected generous benefactors the most, and wanted to elect them group leaders. In another study we found that randomly assigning people to the position of group leader increased their public generosity and improved their mood.

This experiment shows that, even today, people like to be seen behaving benevolently and fairly, like Big Men, and do not like to be viewed as graspers motivated purely by self-interest. Modern philanthropy is a direct successor to the potlatch: it has emerged as a way of acquiring status through benevolence. But where does this benevolent streak come from?

We can try to date it by looking at the primates that are genetically closest to us. We share a common ancestor with the gorilla – our lineages parted about eight million years ago – and the gorilla leader is a despot. Indeed, most ape and monkey species have a clear dominance hierarchy in which the alpha male is a dictator and political inequality is the norm. For instance, among gorillas the silverback male heads the group and he holds all the political power. He hogs the resources in the group and exercises a mating monopoly with receptive females. If your boss were a gorilla, he would arrive unannounced at your house, help himself to your food, kill your children and then go to bed with your wife. Lower-ranked male gorillas can only watch helplessly; they often leave the group to mature and return to overthrow the silverback when age has weakened him.

Since (we earnestly hope) humans don't behave like gorillas, we need to scale a few branches on the family tree and look at our closer relatives. Chimpanzees, which share a more recent common ancestor with us, are also at the despotic end of the political spectrum. Chimpanzees, however, possess one characteristic that gorillas lack, which may have been crucial in the evolution of egalitarian behaviour: the ability to form coalitions. Humans also do this very effectively (without it, politics would look even messier than it does today). This coalition-building skill may have evolved separately in both species, but it seems more likely that this capacity was already present to a rudimentary degree in the common ancestor of humans and chimps, which lived between four and seven million years ago.[8]

The ability to cooperate with others means dominance hierarchies can be kept in check. Why? Because two (or more) subordinate individuals can team up against a domineering aggressor. Thanks to the pioneering work of Dutch primatologist Frans de Waal at Arnhem Zoo in the Netherlands, we know that chimpanzees are astute politicians, constantly sniffing out opportunities to form coalitions to help them scale (and subvert) the hierarchy. In fact, de Waal, who is now at Emory University at Atlanta, even called one of his books *Chimpanzee Politics*; Newt Gingrich, a former Speaker of the US House of Representatives, included the book on his 1994 reading list for incoming politicians.[9]

In one notorious episode observed by de Waal, three male chimps in the Arnhem colony – Yeroen, Nikkie and Luit – were competing to become group leader. Initially, Yeroen was the alpha and ruled the colony with the support of the female chimpanzees (without female back-up a putative alpha is powerless). Luit lurked on the periphery of the colony, having been forced out by Yeroen. When Nikkie had sufficiently matured he formed an alliance with Luit and together they started to beat up the females, not for the sake of it but to expose Yeroen's inability to defend them. After about four months the females switched allegiance to Luit, almost certainly to avoid further beatings. Luit was now the leader.

He then adopted a very smart policy. In front of the females, Luit acted as the peacekeeper in the group; this strengthened female support for his status. When it came to the males, however, he would intervene in fights to support the loser. Thus, even though his rise to leadership had been secured with the help of Nikkie, who was by now the second-most powerful male in the colony, Luit routinely sided with Nikkie's opponents.

This made tactical sense. If Nikkie had won, he might have felt emboldened to steal Luit's crown. It also meant that Nikkie's opponent would feel indebted to Luit and therefore support him in further conflicts.

The power of this story lies in its uncanny resemblance to human politics, strengthening our case that leadership is an evolved behaviour. Modern politics is all about taking sides, building coalitions, forging alliances and undermining rivals. When Barack Obama appointed Hillary Clinton, who ran against him in a bid to become the Democrat's presidential candidate, as Secretary of State, it was a deliberate ploy to widen his coalition base and make an ally out of someone who very probably would have become a powerful critic. It seemed like a gracious appointment but it was also a self-serving one. The British election of May 2010 resulted, at the time of writing, in a coalition between the Conservatives and the Liberal Democrats. The unlikely alliance came about because, although the Conservatives won more seats than any other party, they did not secure enough to govern alone. That parties with such different ideological outlooks were able to come together testifies to our evolved artfulness at maintaining group unity (especially in the face of a common enemy, Labour). It is also fascinating that both David Cameron and Nick Clegg, his Lib Dem opposite, declared publicly they were compromising for the sake of the country. Both men, whether knowingly or not, wished to be seen as servant leaders.

These instances, again, illustrate how human politics mirrors chimp politics, and that evolutionary leadership theory can shed light on both. Leaders in both species strive to keep the peace and avoid party divisions (which can be exploited by enemies); they also deal harshly with potential rivals, striking up allegiances and pacts that can be called on to put upstarts in their place. As for the role of women, courting the female vote is seen as a shrewd strategy, in both human and ape politics. These similarities point very strongly to a common origin of the capacity for alliance-building in humans and chimps, which suggests it may have been driven by an important need. And what, in the battle for survival, could be more important than filling your belly?

Evolutionary scientists believe that the ability to form alliances originally evolved in humans and chimpanzees for the purpose of sharing food. If you are lucky enough to have gathered more food than you need for the day, then it pays to share your surplus with a less fortunate individual (without a fridge there is not much point hanging on to the extra grub). Your kindness means you might get a share on days when your own basket is empty. This is called reciprocal altruism, and it is one of the cornerstones of human and primate sociality.[10]

It is not limited to primates. Vampire bats share blood meals with their neighbour in the cave. This works because (a) vampire bats always return to the same spot in the cave and therefore have the same neighbour and (b) not all vampire bats are lucky enough to get blood every night. These two conditions led to the evolution of reciprocal altruism in the species.

Over time this propensity to share food may have developed into more complex trading behaviour in brainier species, in which one currency was exchanged for another. Chimpanzees, for instance, are known to trade meat for sex; a male who's been hunting will share some of his kill with a female in order to mate with her. Chimpanzees and baboons also form long-lasting grooming relationships where the time they spend beautifying each other (in reality picking off fleas and offering soothing, friendship-reinforcing massage) is reciprocated. Similarly, the ability to take sides in fights with the dominant male may have emerged from this reciprocity principle – 'I'll watch your back if you watch mine.'

Reciprocity is linked to fairness, and most of us have a highly attuned sense of workplace justice. If you have a colleague who consistently steals your ideas, or a manager who claims credit for your hard slog, it arouses intensely antagonistic instincts which usually sour the chance of any fruitful alliance. You're not being oversensitive: that churning feeling in your gut has been honed over millions of years, and is shared by capuchin monkeys who feel similarly hard done by.

This was demonstrated in a wonderful experiment designed by Sarah Brosnan and Frans de Waal, who got pairs of monkeys to do tasks.[11] The animals were rewarded with either a grape or a slice of cucumber. Being sweet-toothed primates like us, monkeys regard a grape as a greater prize than cucumber. First, the researchers ensured each monkey got the same reward for doing the same task (returning a token to an experimenter). Then things changed – after performing the same task, one monkey would consistently get the cucumber and the other the grape. The monkey given the cucumber – who observed his counterpart getting a better reward time after time – became reluctant to continue performing, and, if the inequity continued, it would simply mutiny, either by not carrying out the task or by refusing the cucumber. Refusal of food is highly unusual in an animal; it never happened when both monkeys were getting cucumber, only when the rewards differed. Capuchin monkeys knew when they were being short-changed and wanted out. This shows that monkeys demonstrate 'inequity aversion', just as humans do. Brosnan and de Waal concluded that these animals understand the concept of fairness, again suggesting that this capacity is not unique to humans and probably pre-dates our own lineage.

In the behaviour of the grape-seeking monkey, we can glimpse the shrouded origins of the human drive towards egalitarianism and a fair society. To recap, we don't care for individuals who are motivated entirely by self-interest; neither, we think, should they ride on the coat-tails of others. We do not feel comfortable with huge power differences – and will form coalitions to keep dominators in check – but we do seem naturally inclined to accord greater status to those who have demonstrated that they place the welfare of their group above self-interest (as shown by the keenness to bestow leadership status on players who gave the most to group funds). These instincts – for reciprocity, fairness and a hierarchy built on generosity – are lodged in our psyches: when we give a birthday present to a friend we expect to be similarly rewarded on our own birthday. When we accompany colleagues to the pub, we expect everyone to buy a round; if they don't, we 'forget' to invite them again. When we help a political candidate into office by, for example, donating to his war chest, we expect privileges in return: the larger the donation the greater the privilege. Reciprocity is so strongly ingrained in the human psyche that we have evolved a whole set of emotions to regulate it: anger if someone fails to return a favour and guilt if you have failed to reciprocate. Anger and guilt thus serve the function of keeping reciprocal relationships going, and they are nothing to be ashamed of. In fact, you wouldn't want to get too close to a person who does not experience either guilt or shame after a transgression – psychologists term these people psychopaths. It has even been suggested that instead of *Homo economicus*, the coldly rational person who takes economic decisions based purely on self-interest, it would be more accurate to call ourselves *Homo reciprocans*, reflecting the premium we have evolved to place on reciprocity (particularly the way we will punish those who don't reciprocate, even at cost to ourselves).[12]

Let's return to coalitions: individuals shared food on a roughly equal basis, so both parties had full stomachs and neither party felt short-changed. But we also developed the ability to build more sophisticated alliances and coalitions. While it is common for two weaker individuals to decide to team up against the alpha male, why, we might ask, doesn't a weakling side with the dominant or go it alone? Coalition game theory can help us to understand this. Suppose there are three players, A, B and C, who each differ in strength. A's got a strength of 4, B of 3 and C of 2. For the sake of the argument let's suppose these are political parties and their

strength equates to the number of votes. The party or coalition of parties with the highest number of votes gets to form
the government. Let's also stipulate that none of the three
parties can form a government on their own, so they need
each other.

Party A would prefer to team up with C – just as Luit wanted
to team up with Nikkie – because A will then be the strongest
party in the coalition and hold more power relative to C (the
power differential with B would not be so favourable). Yet for
precisely this reason C does not want to team up with A, and
prefers to go with B (this reflects the allegiance between the two
weaker males, Nikkie and Yeroen). Because B also prefers C, a
coalition between B and C is the most likely outcome. B and C
form what is called a 'minimum resource' coalition – they have
the minimum number of votes to form a coalition. Paradoxically, the most powerful party, A (Luit, the alpha), gets excluded
from the coalition, and this is called the power inversion
paradox. Coalitions, therefore, are a surprisingly effective way
of diluting power.[13] Incidentally, after the inconclusive May
2010 election result, the Liberal Democrats (C) came under fire
for even negotiating with Labour (B). The Lib Dems, had they
formed a Lib–Lab coalition, would have been accused of prop-
ping up a party that the public had voted out of office. That is
why the Lib Dems joined forces with the Conservatives (A).

When people play out this scenario in the laboratory
they often form such minimum resource coalitions. Studies of
national elections across Europe also bear this out (although
in many countries the biggest party gets the first shot at
forming a coalition to avoid ending up with a weak government). Grand coalitions – when A, B and C team up together
– are relatively rare and really emerge only when there is an
external threat. The Great Depression of 1929 triggered a
grand coalition in Britain; the country also mounted a united
front, in the form of a National Government, in response
to both world wars. Interestingly, in our lab, we tested out
coalitional game theory and found that grand coalitions

were formed under only two circumstances: first, when the players in one group were told that a rival group was in the lab (the mere presence of another group was enough to elicit a defensive reaction) and, second, when women and physically weaker men (with strength assessed by hand grip) were participating.[14] Interestingly, a recent study showed that both physically formidable men and attractive women are tougher negotiators in business transactions: Presumably because they represent high mate value, they feel entitled to a bigger share of the pie – so forming coalition relationships with these individuals may come at a cost.

Coalitions can curtail the power of any particular individual very effectively, certainly more successfully than any one wimp going it alone. This has been a major force in the evolution of egalitarian and democratic societies in humans. Fast-forwarding to the modern world, we still see that governments and political leaders will, reluctantly, make concessions towards power-sharing and democracy when their regime is under threat. Think of the power struggle between King Charles I and the English parliament headed by Oliver Cromwell, which severely weakened the stranglehold of the monarchy. In Nepal, the recent struggle between the monarchy and the Maoist rebel government has led to the monarchy relinquishing considerable power in order to survive.

After coalition-building, a second key condition in the evolution of egalitarianism and democracy is the threat of subordinates leaving. When faced with this prospect, dominants are often prepared to throw in the towel. Chimpanzees (at least the males) can form coalitions but they cannot leave their troop, and this makes them dependent on the alpha. Our human ancestors, however, were nomadic hunter-gatherers who lived on the savannah in areas with low population densities. They always had the option of breaking away with other aggrieved individuals, and leaving the bully behind. We'll see shortly that the prospect of desertion by the group was a potent strategy for keeping overbearing leaders in check.

Since a king without a kingdom is not much of a ruler, the prospect of being deserted – especially by an influential follower whose actions trigger an exodus – should have tempered any domineering tendencies. An aspiring leader would need to keep subordinates happy and offer them protection to induce them to stay. Egalitarianism and democracy, we suggest, would have been the result. We can see this line of thinking in action, in the sequence of events leading up to the collapse of the communist regime in eastern Europe. When one communist country, Hungary, opened its border with Austria on 19 August 1989 – for the three-hour symbolic Pan-European Picnic, organised by Hungarian dissenters to give their countrymen a taste of a borderless Europe – the opening in the Iron Curtain attracted more than the expected handful of holidaymakers. Between 700 and 1,000 East Germans whose desire to exit had been thwarted by the presence of the Wall saw an opportunity to flee.[15] The chink became a gaping hole, the human trickle became a flood, and quickly Hungary decided to open its border for good. Trainloads full of East Germans flocked to Hungary and crossed the border to Austria, en route to West Germany. On one day in 1989 no fewer than 14,000 people made the journey from East to West. Ultimately, this event contributed to the collapse of communism and the spread of democracy in eastern Europe. In the parlance of psychology experiments, the gap in the Iron Curtain represented an 'exit option'; we'll soon see how the availability of exit options tempers dictatorial tendencies in leaders.

So, the move from despotism to democracy in our early human ancestors probably resulted from the interplay of two forces: the ability to form alliances and the emergence of exit opportunities. The laboratory, we have found, provides an ideal testbed for this 'origins of democracy' hypothesis. Individuals come to the lab and play a game in pairs in which they can earn money by dividing up, say, £10. One of them is assigned the role of leader and the other the role of follower.

In one version known as the ultimatum game, the leader proposes how to divide the £10 and the follower can either accept or reject the offer. Rejection means neither leader nor follower gets anything. This, essentially, reflects a democratic set-up. In an alternative version, called the dictator game, the leader simply dictates how much of the £10 he wants to give and the follower must accept.

Suppose you are the leader. In which scenario would you give more to the follower? We bet you would show more generosity in the democracy scenario (because you don't want to risk rejection and slink away with zilch). Research shows that leaders do offer substantially more to followers – roughly eight times more – when they are a democratic leader. On average they give away almost 40 per cent of the booty, while a dictator parts with an average of 5 per cent. In the democratic version, the threat of being rejected and walking away penniless provides a compelling reason for leaders to behave decently.[16]

We recently conducted a slightly more democratic version of the ultimatum game in which followers could consider offers from many leaders and reject the ones they disliked. In other words, followers were given exit options. With this refinement, most leaders opted to give away a fair share (50 per cent). Some gave almost all of their money to the follower, which, in this case, is the rational option (since you want to give your follower as little reason as possible to reject your offer, to avoid ending up with nothing).

The potency of an exit option in fostering democracy was further demonstrated by a group experiment in our lab. We invited groups of six players each to participate in a group investment task in which they could plough their start-up money of £3 into a public fund. A bonus of £5 was on offer for each player – but only if four out of six players invested their start-up money. The bonus would be paid to all members in the group, whether or not the group member was one of those making the investment. The group members did not have face-to-face contact, instead communicating with each other via computer.[17]

We assigned a leader – in reality, a computer programmed to issue standard messages – to each group, to coordinate between players. And we varied the leadership style between groups: dictatorial, democratic or laissez-faire.

The message from the dictator read: 'Hi: I will be your group leader during the tasks. In order to ensure that you win the group bonus I will automatically remove the start-up money from four of you. I will not consult anyone about my decision so you will not have a say in whether you make an investment or not. Each time I will simply remove the start-up money from four members I choose to make sure your group gets the bonus.'

In contrast, the democratic leader introduced 'himself' like this: 'Hi: I will be your group leader during the tasks. In order to ensure that you win the group bonus please let me know whether you are willing to contribute or not. I will then remove contributions from four of those who have volunteered. If not enough people volunteer, however, I will have to remove the start-up money from someone who has not volunteered, just to make sure that four people invest their money.'

Finally, the laissez-faire leader sent out this: 'Hi: I will be your group leader during the tasks. For each task let me know whether you are willing to contribute, and I will remove the start-up money from those of you who have volunteered. Hopefully, at least four people will make a contribution in each task.'

In the initial three rounds of the game, the players in each group were told that their group had been successful in stumping up enough money to win the bonus. Each of the players could then indicate whether they wanted to continue playing the game in their existing group, or to join another group that had no leader. Almost 40 per cent of players under the dictator wanted to leave, despite their group being successful in pocketing the bonus. In comparison, only 11 per cent of players under the democrat wanted to leave. The exodus led to many groups in the dictator condition collapsing, because they no longer had the required number of players (at least four) to continue.

Perhaps most intriguingly, only 3.4 per cent of players wanted to desert the group with the laissez-faire leader. It suggests that most people do not want to be led unless it is strictly necessary (our dislike of power or status hierarchies again). This experiment – in which subordinates exercised their right to abandon ship, in spite of the prospect of missing out on a bonus – is another powerful demonstration of why dictatorships do not work. There is a lesson for dictatorial bosses here: your best employees will have exit options (other teams or companies to jump ship to) and they are more likely to exercise those options if they feel they are being dominated. Managers do seem to be aware of this: evidence shows they treat subordinates who have no exit opportunities worse than subordinates who do (this is called the selective exploitation effect).

Most of our primate cousins are despots, while humans appear to possess a more democratic disposition (in the shape of the food-sharing, inequity-averse tribesman). Given the despotism still found among chimps (despite their ingrained sense of fairness), this transformation is most likely to have happened after our ancestral line veered away from the chimpanzee line, between four and seven million years ago. It is plausible that the psychological divergence between the species was set in train 2 million years ago, when our ancestors came down from the trees to colonise the savannah, eventually adopting a nomadic hunter-gatherer lifestyle in small bands. In these small, mobile bands, we can speculate, food-sharing became essential for the survival of the tribe.

An aside: some scientists recently suggested that the death knell of despotism in our species may have been sounded by the evolution of stone-throwing. This practice could have been effective in attenuating the dominance hierarchy in a group because it allows weaklings to attack a more physically formidable opponent while avoiding hand-to-hand combat. The problem with ascribing human democracy to stone-throwing is that chimps indulge in it too.[18] In one zoo, a male chimp was seen not only throwing stones but also stashing them away before the zoo opened. He systematically stockpiled caches of stones and hurled them when visitors arrived. Crucially, the chimp never displayed this behaviour when the zoo was closed in the off season, suggesting an astonishing level of cognitive forethought and planning once thought to be unique to our species.

Whenever it originated, this long egalitarian epoch probably persisted until the spread of agriculture some 13,000 years ago, when differences in wealth and status started to emerge and band societies were integrated into Big Man tribal societies and later chiefdoms with designated leaders, as we will see in Chapter 5. Obviously democracy returned at various times in recent history and most readers of this book will be fortunate enough to live in a democratic society (the majority of the world's population do not share this privilege). It is therefore mistaken to ascribe the origins of our modern democracy to Athens or Rome around the fifth century BC (despite the etymology of 'democracy', made up of the Greek words *demos* = people and *kratos* = rule; thus 'government by the people'). These were merely manifestations of ancestral tendencies towards egalitarianism and democracy that had perhaps been with us for at least 2 million years (when we left the trees for the savannah).

Before we congratulate ourselves on our long, equitable ancestral past, we shouldn't forget that humans still harbour a tendency, shared with other primates, to dominate and exploit weaker individuals (in fact, there is still some scientific debate about whether our 'true' nature is egalitarian or despotic). Five minutes in a children's playground confirms the continuing existence of bullies, who physically dominate other children and steal their toys. Egalitarianism could have been achieved only through a reversal of the dominance hierarchy, in which the many were able to control the few by sticking together and mounting a united front against their superiors (it's the power of coalitions again). As the anthropologist Harold Schneider famously stated: 'All men seek to rule but if they cannot they prefer to be equal.' The idea of a reverse dominance hierarchy, in which the rank and file rise up to collectively quash their self-appointed superiors – much as trade unions mobilise the masses to give them negotiating power with their bosses – was explored by Christopher Boehm in his book *Hierarchy in the Forest*, a comprehensive study of stratification (or its absence) in human societies the world over. Boehm repackages the sentiment expressed by Schneider – that if domination fails, equality will suffice – like this: 'The disposition in question is not one that orients us specifically to equality, but one that makes us resentful of being unduly subordinated ...'[19]

This disposition leads us to mistrust those who overtly seek power, prompting us to think them greedy, grasping and self-interested (something recognised by Machiavelli, who wrote in his political treatise *The Prince* that the power-hungry should keep their appetites well hidden). Indeed, the ethnographic evidence suggests that hunter-gatherer groups apply a rich variety of strategies for keeping the greedy graspers locked down. We could call these sanctions, which differ in severity and ingenuity, Strategies To Overcome the Powerful (STOP).

The first line of defence in a primitive society against an overbearing individual is, believe it or not, gossip. Spreading negative rumours about a leader – about his meanness or sex life – can damage his standing in the group and, as a result, chip away at his ability to do the job. Whispers about Bill Clinton's affair with the White House intern Monica Lewinsky unquestionably damaged his presidency; the fact they were true, as so many rumours turn out to be, confirmed in

Clinton a lack of judgement. Public preoccupation with the affair detracted from genuine political issues.

It has been persuasively argued by Robin Dunbar, an evolutionary scientist at Oxford University, that human language evolved for the purpose of spreading gossip, and we can envisage how it was employed to maintain egalitarianism.[20] Spreading rumours doesn't take much effort and can be highly effective; when a person becomes wealthy and/or powerful, gossip inevitably follows. Gossip is a way of raising a question mark about the character of a person – vital if ancestral groups were to root out the free-riders taking more than their fair share of collective resources. Today there is a media industry devoted to spreading tittle-tattle about leaders and other stellar individuals, such as film stars or sporting celebrities. Effectively, gossip columns act as a restraint on power, including corporate power, as there are so many avidly read newspaper columns devoted to the movers and shakers in the business world; and however much we complain about the paparazzi pandering to a downmarket obsession with trivia, they play an important role in protecting our democracy. Randy Cohen, the *New York Times* ethicist, is a great defender of gossip; his opinion is that the only difference between gossip and news is the intention of the messenger, rather than the veracity of the information (gossip often turns out to be true). His distinction is that gossip, unlike news, is motivated by the wish to do harm (and here, followers would use it to damage the reputation of those in power).

After gossip, public discussions are our second STOP. Most bands and tribes have public meetings where adult males gather to make decisions that affect the group as a whole, such as decisions about whether to invade a neighbouring territory. This is the arena in which criticisms are aired. There is a script that leaders must follow closely; they should not be perceived as domineering. For example, the late Australian anthropologist Mervyn Meggitt described the complex social choreography displayed by the Mae Enga, a tribal society in Papua New Guinea, when deciding whether to initiate hostilities:

The men who initiated the conference or their spokesperson briefly indicate their view of the clan's position and the action they favour. They may argue that now is the time to launch a full-scale attack on the neighbouring clan with the aim of occupying a specific section of its territory. The major Big Man [leader] then solicits Responses from the audience. Ideally, everyone present has a voice and being among his own clansmen can speak with complete freedom. The task of the Big Man at this stage is to ensure that all have a chance to offer their opinions and facts in full and to make no attempt to cut off any but obviously irrelevant speeches.

Only in this way it is believed can each clansman truly ascertain the thoughts of his fellows and the evidence behind them. So instructed, he can cleave or modify his own ideas and his reactions in turn affect those of others. Naturally the Big Men and fight leaders have their own opinions of an appropriate outcome of the discussion; but none of them, especially in the early sessions, reveals much of his hand or tries patently to push for the acceptance of his suggestions.[21]

Parliamentary or Senate sessions are the modern versions of this STOP, as are annual general meetings and shareholder meetings in the business sphere.

When an influential person steps out of line there is also evidence that hunter-gatherer groups engage in a third STOP: satire, which is direct criticism leavened with humour. The Canadian anthropologist Richard Lee learned this the hard way, during his time living with a band of the !Kung San tribe.[22] He gave the band a fattened cow – a gift that was rejected and ridiculed because, to the tribe, it signified arrogance and an ulterior motive. As Lee recounted it, the refusal was justified like this: 'When a young man kills much meat, he comes to think of himself as a chief or a Big Man. And he thinks of the rest of us as his servants or inferiors. We can't accept this. We refuse someone who boasts for someday his pride will make him kill somebody. So we always speak of his meat as worthless. In this way we cool his heart and make him gentle.' Not that Lee should have felt particularly bad; the practice of 'insulting the meat' is a common one among the !Kung, with (usually) good-natured teasing routinely dished out to those who make the biggest kills. Such ribbing tempers the tendency to boastfulness, which is regarded as detrimental to the group's egalitarian ethos.

This technique – using humour as a weapon of criticism – is surprisingly ubiquitous. Our own research suggests that humour and its product, laughter, are great ways to relieve tensions within groups and can smooth relationships between superiors and subordinates. Court jesters were often used to express the thoughts of the people; no offence could be taken if truths were embroidered with song, dance and juggling. In *Fools Are Everywhere*, a study of court jesters throughout history, Beatrice K. Otto writes: 'The court jester is a universal phenomenon. He crops up in every court worth its salt in medieval and Renaissance Europe, in China, India, Japan, Russia, America and Africa. A cavalcade of jesters tumble across centuries and continents, and one could circle the globe tracing their footsteps.'[23] Today's equivalent of the court jester is media satire, such as the British panel show *Have I Got News for You*, which lampoons politicians, and its American cousin, *The Daily Show with Jon Stewart*, not forgetting satirical blogs and magazines.

When gossip, public discussions and satire fall on deaf ears, a fourth STOP is disobedience. A range of actions come under the disobedience umbrella, from simply ignoring a leader's instructions to killing him. In ancestral societies, bossiness – even if it came from individuals who enjoyed a position of authority through, say, peacekeeping duties – was not tolerated. For example, among the Iban, a tribal people in the Philippines, no one listens to a leader who issues a command as opposed to making a suggestion. Hunter-gatherer groups are proudly autonomous, and the notion of obedience outside the family domain does not exist. Schneider once noted that East African tribal leaders 'cannot order people to do anything'.

A darker shade of disobedience is the act of deposing errant leaders. Denuded of their status, these disgraced individuals are then returned to the rank and file of the hunter-gatherer group, or ostracised. For instance, among the Bantu, a chief can be dethroned by his own kinsmen; among the Panamanian Kuna, a chief is removed if he fails to consult the people before making a decision, or if he shows violent anger, or indulges in immoral behaviour. A modern manifestation of this strategy is 'bossnapping' – holding management hostage in protest at job cuts. In early 2009, companies including Sony France, 3M and Caterpillar experienced the ire of French employees through bossnapping episodes. Interestingly, French polls suggested widespread support for such desperate measures. *Newsweek* reported: 'Almost two thirds [of those polled] said these methods shouldn't be punished because "they are often the only means employees have of being heard".' In other words, the public will often approve of subordinates taking matters into their own hands, even if such action is unlawful.[24]

Desertion also comes under the disobedience umbrella, and it happens in nomadic tribes such as the Bedouin in Saharan Africa. The leader loses the protection of the group and can be killed at will by other tribes. As demonstrated in our investment experiment, desertion is quite a common tactic among disaffected followers. In sedentary communities, however, upping sticks is not an option: ostracism is more effective. In fact, recent experiments have shown that when people are ostracised in a laboratory setting, the 'pain' centre in the brain is activated. Being ignored really can feel like a kick in the teeth.[25]

The fifth and most drastic STOP is assassination. Leader

assassinations have been documented by anthropologists in many primitive societies – it is not a contemporary phenomenon. For instance, in Papua New Guinea a leader who seriously oversteps his prerogatives can face a death sentence from his own community – with his kin encouraged to carry it out (to avoid tit-for-tat killings between different families). With the spread of weaponry such as spears and knives, and later guns, it became easy for disgruntled followers to finish off a chief (as various American presidents have found, to their cost). Paradoxically, the spread of weapons among band members may have fuelled the spread of democracy because it is a cheap and effective way to keep dictators out of power.

All these STOPs are extreme: most band societies practise dispersed leadership, in which individuals lead only in spheres they know about. Thus, the most competent hunter is entrusted with finding food, and the best warrior leads the battle; outside these realms, individuals remain in the rank and file. This expertise-based leadership is very common in both hunter-gatherer groups and modern societies. For example, people with a talent for numbers will often become CEOs of major accountancy firms. Many restaurant owners cut their teeth as chefs (you'll recognise from Chapter 3 that these are the well-trodden paths of our 'apprentice' class of followers, who reach leadership positions by learning the trade).

This is leadership based on prestige rather than dominance, with status conferred through ability rather than size.[26] It sounds meritocratic but prestige-based leadership isn't as straightforward as you might think. There are still avenues for what we might call 'leadership creep': routes through which leadership can spread from one domain to others, opening the door to aspiring dominators.

First, modern leadership often requires more than expertise in one area; a leader also has to keep his group together. So, an army general must not only know his machine guns from his missile launchers, but he also has to keep the spirits of his platoon up.

Second, in the absence of remuneration packages, it is possible that ancestral leaders agreed to dispense their hard-won wisdom on condition they were accorded greater influence over other matters. This form of leadership creep happens today: Joanna Lumley used her prestige as an actress to mount a campaign on behalf of Gurkha soldiers (the British government eventually acceded to her request that Nepalese soldiers who fight for Britain earn the right to settle here). Sir Bob Geldof used his fame as a musician to create Live Aid, thus becoming an important face in the fight against global poverty. Leadership creep is the phenomenon behind every celebrity-endorsed clothing line. Famous people, such as David Beckham, Tiger Woods and Madonna, turn themselves into brands, because their excellence in one sphere fools our prehistoric minds into believing that their opinion counts in other spheres too.

A third reason for leadership creep is that some of the attributes that make people better warriors or more natural diplomats are generic traits that transcend specific domains – and therefore propel these people to lead in a range of realms (so, a head girl becomes a CEO, and then a governor). Examples of generic traits could be intelligence, personality and drive. A person with an abundance of these three qualities is likely to accumulate power across many different domains, and so earn a major role in public affairs. This may also give him or her an opening to dominate.

Prestige-based leadership also presents another challenge: how does a group know who is good at what? If there is an Einstein in a project management team but the other members fail to recognise the genius in their midst, then it is highly unlikely that the Einstein will emerge as leader. This is a hurdle that many groups face – how to recognise each other's unique expertise. How do people identify who is the best colleague to lead their new advertisement campaign, or which is the most suitable politician to lead the country into war? In other words, how do we identify the best person to follow? This is exactly the sort of dilemma we confront when we elect politicians and appoint executives, particularly those with little experience or back story. That will form the basis of Chapter 6. But first, in the next chapter, we'll conclude our journey through human evolutionary history. We'll discover that, after a long period of living in egalitarian communities, a historic shift in the way we fed ourselves rekindled our primatological propensity to dominate. This propensity was perfected by a colourful cast of tyrants, despots, kleptocrats and dictators, bent on staying in power and reaping the immense reproductive benefits.

5

The birth of corruption

Do not imagine, comrades, that leadership is a pleasure. On the contrary, it is a deep and heavy responsibility. No one believes more firmly than Comrade Napoleon that all animals are equal. He would be only too happy to let you make your decisions for yourselves. But sometimes you might make the wrong decisions, comrades, and then where should we be?

George Orwell, *Animal Farm*

One of the most noteworthy achievements of Mobutu Sese Seko, who ruled Zaire (now the Democratic Republic of Congo) from 1965 to 1997, was to build an airport in his home village of Gbadolite with a runway long enough to accommodate Concorde. This allowed him to charter the aircraft on a whim, to transport him from the jungle to deliver speeches at the United Nations, and to whisk his family shopping in Paris. As the Mobutu clan drank pink champagne and filled their bags with designer booty, the nation's infrastructure rotted away, public workers went unpaid, and the Congolese starved.[1]

The name Mobutu has come to symbolise a form of government known as a kleptocracy, which essentially means government by thieving. During his reign he creamed off an estimated $5 billion of state income (accrued from Congo's vast reserves of natural resources such as cobalt, copper and diamonds), which were funnelled into foreign bank accounts belonging to both him and members of his extended family. Mobutu, protected by bodyguards drawn from his own Bangala tribe, boasted holiday homes in Paris and on the French Riviera, as well as grand residences in Spain, Portugal, Morocco and Senegal. Corruption was so endemic that Mobutu was often taken advantage of himself. A family member revealed: 'Mobutu would ask one of us to go to the bank and take out a million. We'd go to an intermediary and tell him to get five million. He would go to the bank with Mobutu's authority and take out ten. Mobutu got one and we took the other nine.'

President Mobutu ruled his country through a combination of terror and clever political manipulation. In the early years, he had political rivals executed in open-air spectacles witnessed by thousands of people. He once lured a political rival out of exile with the promise of amnesty, and then tortured him to death, gouging out his eyes, removing his genitals and amputating limbs. Mobutu later resorted to bribing his political rivals and creating a personality cult around him. He changed his name to Mobutu Sese Seko Nkuku Ngbendu wa Za Banga, which means 'The all-powerful warrior who because of his endurance and inflexible will to win goes from conquest to conquest leaving fire in his wake.' He gave himself such titles as Father of the Nation, Saviour of the People and Supreme Combatant. His portrait hung in all public places. Each evening, the television news opened with an image of him descending through clouds from the heavens. In presidential elections, voters were once offered two ballot choices: green for Mobutu and Hope, and red for Chaos. Mobutu won with a vote of 10,131,699 to 157.

Surprisingly for a dictator, Mobutu died a natural death in 1997 while still in office (77 per cent of dictators in the twentieth century have had assassination attempts made against them). Yet in some ways Mobutu is still with us today. He fathered seventeen children, suggesting that even today despotism still pays out in terms of reproductive success.[2]

Why do despotic rulers such as Mobutu crop up time and again in our apparently egalitarian species? We are not, after all, a species in which males engage in life-and-death battles to seize power and much else besides (well, women and food). Most of human evolution took place in small band societies with minimal power differences between individuals, in which leaders could wield influence only in narrow realms. If this period has moulded our leadership and followership psychology, then how do we account for the emergence of dictators, despots and tyrants in recent human history? From which corner of the evolutionary room do these aggressive and manipulative people, who exploit and dominate subordinates, crawl out? Are these despotic rulers historical accidents or are they the flesh incarnations of an innate dominance drive that is part of our primate origins? Evolutionary leadership theory favours the latter explanation – that our primal tendency to dominate and exploit others, shared with chimpanzees and gorillas, was unleashed by the agricultural revolution about 13,000 years ago. Food no longer needed to be shared; it was plentiful (to those in power) and could be stockpiled. This simple fact would create a very different social architecture and dynamic: sedentary societies, the birth of professions (because people no longer needed to forage) and, as we shall see, corruption.[3]

Before agriculture, followers were a powerful force: through collective action using STOPs (Strategies To Overcome the Powerful) they could keep overbearing leaders in check. After agriculture, this dynamic shifted in favour of leaders, who could stockpile resources and use them as leverage to preserve power. This constantly shifting balance of power makes followers feel fundamentally ambivalent towards leaders and vice versa. Followers want to be led but not dominated, and it is easier for leaders to dominate than to persuade. We can call this the ambivalence hypothesis of leadership.

Nomadic hunter-gatherer societies go to great lengths to preserve equality among group members because these societies live at marginal subsistence levels. In order to survive, members must stick together and share their resources with each other. If someone is lucky enough to get a kill, the band makes sure that the meat is distributed fairly. Even if the hunter resists, the band simply takes it – a lot of meat-sharing is in fact a form of tolerated theft. This sharing ethos is practical because (a) foraging bands cannot store any surplus meat for long, and (b) an individual who lands a kill one day might not be as lucky tomorrow and therefore depends for his future survival on the gratitude of others. Anthropologists suggest that food-sharing is a form of risk reduction (it is also sometimes called risk reduction reciprocity). The evolutionary legacy of meat-sharing remains with us today: in many cultures dining is governed by a strict etiquette, with guests usually offered the finest cuts.

The agricultural revolution that rippled around the globe around 13,000 years ago changed this egalitarian practice because it created vast inequalities in wealth and power between individuals. The domestication of wild plants, such as corn and wheat, and animals, such as cows and chickens, turned hunter-gatherers into farmers and bred a completely new social structure. In rich arable lands such as the Fertile Crescent in contemporary Iraq and the Rio Balsas drainage of Mexico (where maize is thought to have been domesticated[4]), farming was very productive and for the first time in human history there were food surpluses. It is hard to grasp just how significant this milestone was – and the vast social, cultural and political changes that would flower with this new, agrarian life of plenty.[5]

To till the land, people stayed close to their farms, leading to the blossoming of settlements and a decline in the nomadic way of life. Communities became sedentary (although in pastoral societies people still moved around seasonally with their cattle) and food became plentiful. This nutritional bounty is thought to have caused the population to expand. The reliability of the food supply freed people from the necessity of foraging, allowing them to develop other skills – and led to new professions such as toolmaking, pottery and weaving. It is also speculated that since women no longer needed to carry their young on foraging expeditions, children could be more closely spaced and left in the care of non-relatives.

In this way, the advent of agriculture, sometimes called the Neolithic Revolution, would, we think, have had considerable consequences for leadership and followership. There is even evidence that agriculture left a biological imprint on the human genome. The ability to digest dairy milk in some adult populations, especially in Europe and North Africa, is a direct consequence of cattle farming. At least twice in human history (once in Europe and once in Africa), this cultural practice selected for a gene allele that made adults lactose-tolerant (lactose is the main sugar found in milk). In cultures that did not develop dairy farming, the genome shows no sign of having adapted to the availability of milk, and dairy products can be tolerated only in babyhood (when an infant is receiving his mother's milk). This explains why half the world's adults suffer from cramps and diarrhoea after consuming dairy products.[6]

It is difficult to say whether the agricultural revolution produced a corresponding genetic shift in our innate leadership psychology, but farming certainly produced a cultural shift as it gave rulers the opportunity to accumulate more power. This was due to two factors: first, farming and trading allowed inequalities in wealth and status to emerge between families, creating an upper class, the elite, and a lower class, the commoners; second, as populations swelled and people began spending more time in settlements, there was an impetus to regulate interactions between them. Unlike nomadic hunter-gatherers, who simply moved on when they came into social conflict, settled inhabitants needed to find a more permanent way of resolving disputes. On top of this, cooperation between villages became essential to fend off threats from enemies intent on plunder and pillage.

Back to farming: the practice led to tribal societies spring-ing up around the world. Each tribe was made up of several interrelated clans and they could number several hundreds of people. Each tribe had its Big Man – and now, in this larger social grouping, they had to jostle with other Big Men for influence.

As farming settlements ballooned, and societies became more unequal, Big Men were no longer big enough for the job. An expanded settlement meant that life was no longer spent exclusively in the company of close genetic relatives, each beholden to the others. The consequence was that the familial needed to become more formal, in order to regulate the coming together of different families. From this accretion of unrelated tribes and bands – no longer bound by blood – came the impetus to appoint leaders, invent rules and write laws, to better regulate social interactions.

In tandem with this internal pressure to stick together, societies also needed to shield themselves from external threats from marauding neighbours, intent on seizing food and wealth. Settlements became not just sedentary but forti-fied, protected by walls and armies. In the blink of an evo-lutionary eye, human society changed: thanks to farming, a simple tribal structure propped up by Big Men was usurped by chiefdoms kept together by a stiffer leadership structure. We can speculate that, around this time, Big Men keen to assume more power pushed themselves to the forefront in an attempt to lead these chiefdoms.

The first chiefdoms emerged around 7,500 years ago in the Fertile Crescent and around 3,000 years ago on the American continent, in the regions of Mexico and the Andes, and on the islands of Hawaii and Polynesia.[7] Chiefdoms were much more populous than tribes, ranging from several thou-sand to several tens of thousands of people, and these newly enlarged settlements faced fresh social perils. For the first time in human history, people had to rub along with others who were not blood relatives. The potential for violence was ever-present and could only be contained by appointing one individual, the chief (think of him as a Big Man who has won promotion), and giving him the monopoly on the use of force.

These chiefs were immediately recognisable through their uniforms, often colourful and extravagant, which served as symbols of their prestigious position. They occupied the biggest house in the village and transmitted power through the bloodline; this is the first appearance in human history of hereditary power, with the baton of influence usually passing from father to firstborn son. With power came responsibility: chiefs bore the responsibility of maintaining peace and distributing public goods, such as food (to have failed in this most basic of tasks would surely have invoked one of our STOPs, such as disobedience or desertion). Their remit included creating and maintaining public works, and protecting the chiefdom.

One chiefly task was to receive wheat at harvest time from every farmer and then throw a public feast (or store the crop to hand it out again in the period between harvests). Some of this food was not redistributed at all but purloined by the chief, his family and the bureaucrats looking after the system. This amounted to a rudimentary form of taxation. As well as physical goods like wheat, chiefs demanded labour from the commoners. This was mostly to build civic structures for the public good, such as irrigation systems for watering farmland. But corruption crept in: some works, such as opulent homes and lavish tombs, seemed to serve no benefit except to massage the egos of the chief and his lucky kin (remember Mobutu's luxury pads?).

Finally, chiefs had the authority to rally groups of armed men to defend their own territory and snatch others (sometimes making slaves of those in vanquished settlements). These warriors played an important role in protecting and expanding the chiefdoms. Again, chiefs could put their warriors to nefarious use, employing them to settle personal disputes and suppress public rebellion. Mobutu was always guarded by soldiers from his own tribe; they amounted to his personal army.

So, the emergence of chiefdoms created a tense situation between leaders and followers; this new social order, rendered necessary by large settlements with surpluses to protect, provided the perfect opportunity for despots to make their big-hatted, flamboyantly attired appearance. Not that everyone was on the make: sometimes chiefs were agreeable rulers who provided valuable services that raised the standard of living for everyone. But, more than occasionally, they were power-crazed kleptocrats, exploiting and tyrannising commoners by stealing their labour and wealth to enrich themselves and their family.[8]

Despots wouldn't have minded the unpopularity, because the pay-off was so huge. Specifically, Darwinian theory predicts that any behaviour that maximises offspring will spread. And the fact is, the bad guys out-reproduce the good guys. If you take a cross-cultural sample of 104 traditional societies (from the Aztec in the Americas to the !Kung Bushmen), rank them in terms of power inequality (using questions such as 'are conflicts resolved with bias such that one individual is immune to sanctions?') and then rank the societies again in terms of how many women are kept in the leaders' harems, you get a substantial positive correlation between despotism and reproductive success.[9] It comes back to our three S's of salary, status and sex: chiefs could cream off food or other resources, increasing their power (a proxy for status) and thus expanding their sexual opportunities. As for women, they pursue high-status men because they know their children will be cared for. That is why so many tycoons of unremarkable appearance find it easy to attract beautiful women.

Nowhere was this dark connection between despotism, power and sex clearer than in Dahomey, a pre-colonial kingdom in West Africa founded in the seventeenth century and conquered by the French in 1894 (it is now Benin). The

kingdom gained notoriety for its penchant for human sacrifice and the Dahomean Amazons, its female warriors. Any
woman, married or unmarried, could be taken away and
added to the harem of the king. As one writer stated, 'Fantastic accounts of the numbers of wives married to the potentate
have been handed down; speaking in round numbers, the
Dahomean informant ordinarily mentions several thousand.'

The King of Ashanti – the Ashanti empire is now a con-
stitutionally protected mini-state within Ghana – was said
to have as many as 3,333 wives. In terms of the number of
offspring, the record seems to be held by Moulay Ismail the
Bloodthirsty, the emperor of Morocco at the turn of the seventeenth century. His harem of 500 women supposedly produced 888 children. A woman who reached the age of thirty
was banished from the emperor's harem and replaced by a
younger bride. The trend for African statesmen to work prodigiously on their genetic lineage was continued in modern
times by leaders such as Idi Amin, the dictatorial former
president of Uganda. He is reported to have had six wives
and fathered at least thirty children. Jacob Zuma, the current
polygamist president of South Africa, has sired twenty children, one of them very recently from an affair, to the dismay
of many South Africans who believe their leader should show
some restraint. This public outcry is exactly what evolutionary leadership theory would predict.

This is not a purely African phenomenon. On the Samoan
islands chiefs could marry up to 50 times, and the cabin of
the Natchez chiefs in North America could contain 4,000
beds. In the contemporary incarnation, wealthy men enjoy
more sexual liaisons and, as their income rises, the age of the
women they liaise with drops (thus increasing their chances
of conceiving). It is not uncommon to find a trail of marriages
behind rich businessmen: Rupert Murdoch and Jack Welch are
on their third marriages, while Larry Ellison is on his fourth.

The anthropologist Napoleon Chagnon, who spent much
of his professional life among the Yanamano, was quite clear

about the relationship between power and sex: 'If we consider polygyny [a form of polygamy in which a man takes more than one wife] to be a prerequisite of leaders and a mark of measure of inequality then in the world's so-called egalitarian societies not all men are in fact equal ...' Despotism is an easy route to riches – and, through the three S's, a highly effective way of spreading one's genes. Since despotism paid out genetically, it continues to this day in our species.

As agriculture intensified, more people could be fed and settlements expanded. Chiefdoms evolved into kingdoms, which were early prototypes of the nation-states we are familiar with today. These fledgling states arose in Mesopotamia around 7,500 years ago and around 1,000 years ago in West Africa. They shared many features with chiefdoms; they had kings as hereditary leaders, who monopolised decision-making and the use of force. States were, in effect, chiefdoms writ extremely large. Most modern countries have more than a million citizens and China now exceeds one billion citizens. Furthermore, states are subdivided into cities and regions, one of which will be the seat of power (where the ruler and his elite live, usually the capital).

The king in his kingdom was far mightier than the chief in his chiefdom: a king's authority and his power to redistribute wealth were much more extensive. A bigger population also meant a greater division of labour and more specialisation. The ruler's administration was greatly expanded, and different branches of government emerged to oversee disparate aspects of public affairs such as taxes, water management, police and foreign relations. Internal peacekeeping became increasingly formalised, encompassing laws, a judiciary and a police force. The laws were often written down by the literate elite (interestingly, writing is thought to have been invented independently at the same time in Mesopotamia and Mesoamerica, suggesting that the practice, dating back to about 3500 BCE, may have emerged as a means of coordinating and unifying large groups of people).[10]

Early states were also held together through organised religion and temples of worship. Many early kings considered themselves answerable only to God, providing citizens with the reassurance they were answerable to someone, and this idea was used to justify royal absolutism (the right of the monarch to govern as he pleased, otherwise known as 'the divine right of kings'). Early kings were themselves heads of state religions or else had separate high priests.

As states expanded, by seizing territory, warfare became inevitable. This led to the rise of the military, making warlords of kings. An example is Charlemagne, the eighth-century leader whose military sprees across western Europe led to the founding of Germany and France. Warlords were tough, aggressive men who built coalitions of followers around the common purpose of extracting resources by force, with followers rewarded for their loyalty with riches, power and privilege. State expansion is likely to have seeded the beginnings of the social class structure, with the ruler and his devotees comprising the upper class, and the vanquished filling the ranks of the servant underclass.

Warlord societies were the norm in early pre-industrialised states such as medieval France. A substantial portion of modern humanity, including people living in parts of Asia and much of Africa, the Middle East and South America, is still governed in this oppressive way. Whenever centralised state governments break down, such as in Afghanistan and Somalia, tyrants or warlords tend to emerge. Their power-seeking agendas often conflict with our innate and fundamentally democratic leadership psychology.[11]

So, after a long evolutionary history as first a dominant primate, then a democratic human and, finally, thanks to agriculture, a despotic one, we arrive at the final period that shaped the leadership landscape. It corresponds roughly to the beginning of the Industrial Revolution 250 years ago. Modern nation-states emerged that contain a diversity of people from different cultures and who spoke different languages. Division of labour was taken to an extreme, with specialists selected on the basis of ability and skill, rather than on kinship or tribal loyalty (as had been the case in chiefdoms and early states). Unlike their enslaved predecessors, citizens of modern nation-states – and workers – were freed from overbearing leaders because they had the option of defecting elsewhere. This liberty shifted the balance of power away from leaders, striking a blow for democracy. Leaders could no longer rule without regard to their followers. Those who did quickly lost valuable trades: the French city of Lyons lost most of its silk weavers when they fled to Britain in the late seventeenth century. The Huguenots, as the fleeing French Protestants were called, crossed the Channel to escape persecution by the Catholics. Lyons' loss was London's gain: the weavers, armed with a newly invented technique for giving silk a lustrous sheen, developed a flourishing trade that is commemorated in the street names of London's East End, such as Silk Street and Loom Court. A contemporary analogy would be the brain drain that hit America after George W. Bush clamped down on stem cell research. Many top biologists went abroad, including to the UK. Now that Barack Obama has lifted the restrictions on such research imposed by his predecessor – and earmarked millions of dollars in research money – British institutions fear that talented young scientists will defect across the Atlantic.[12]

To keep culturally diverse states and companies running smoothly, leaders were no longer appointed on the basis of blood ties. Countries such as France, Germany and the USA abandoned the principle of hereditary governance carried over from chiefdoms. Some compromised by creating a constitutional monarch as symbolic head (Queen Elizabeth II in Britain or Queen Beatrix in the Netherlands), with a bloodline of succession, and, separately, a prime minister in charge of a democratically elected government who, in reality, runs the country like a manager. These hybrid structures might actually foster political stability because power is not concentrated in the hands of one individual. In difficult times, a state with both monarchy and government at the helm might fare better: the prime minister can afford to take unpopular measures because the country is held together by the monarch as the symbolic head of state.

To recap, over human history there has been a steady increase in the size and social complexity of political units, from bands and tribes to chiefdoms, early states and modern nation-states and businesses. The agricultural revolution played a key role in the transition from a relaxed Big Man governance to a more formal leadership structure in which chiefs and kings accrued astonishing levels of power over their subordinates. In return for providing public services they received taxes or kickbacks that enabled them and their kin to live in style. This provided a window for corruption to flourish. Devious, manipulative chiefs, kings and warlords saw opportunities to abuse their power to enrich themselves and their family. Many consolidated their inflated rank by taking multiple wives and siring lots of children, thus ensuring that their own descendants would come to power and retain the family wealth. Only in the last 250 years have we witnessed a move away from despotic leadership in which governments of multi-ethnic and multilingual nation-states and businesses have relinquished powers and privileges to attract citizens and employees with a wide range of abilities and skills. (See Appendix B for a table displaying the four phases of the natural history of leadership.)

Now we come to the sordid relationship between leadership and corruption. Leadership is power and, as Lord Acton, one of William Gladstone's contemporaries, famously insisted, 'power tends to corrupt and absolute power corrupts absolutely'. Is this true? We can return to the zoo for a reunion with our closest primate cousins, the chimps, to get a glimpse at the distorting influence of power. When a male chimp attains the status of alpha male, his elevated status does indeed distort his behaviour – and even his appearance. His body grows, and he adopts a stern facial expression. Even testosterone levels reflect pecking order, rising when he comes to power and falling when he is dethroned. Richard Wrangham and Dale Peterson described the psychology of primate power in *Demonic Males: Apes and the Origins of Human Violence*:

A male chimpanzee in his prime organizes his whole life around issues of rank. His attempts to achieve and then maintain alpha status are cunning, persistent, energetic, and time-consuming. They affect whom he travels with, whom he grooms, where he glances, how often he scratches, where he goes, and what time he gets up in the morning. And all of these behaviours come not from a drive to be violent for its own sake but from a set of emotions that, when people show them, are labelled pride, or more negatively, 'arrogance'.[13]

There is evidence to suggest that people who ascend to power are similarly transformed by their new-found status. People who acquire power, for example, walk faster and are less emotionally expressive. Those in lower ranks laugh and cry more often and, notably, tend to laugh at jokes made by their superiors, suggesting that the laughter is a form of ingratiation. And, in general, people dislike moving down the hierarchy: in one experiment, we told participants that we would assign them to the role of either leader or follower in a group task. We then told some of the 'leaders' that we had misassigned them, and they were, in fact, to be followers. This demotion had a surprisingly strong effect on their mood, causing them to feel sad, depressed, anxious and pessimistic. People who were initially told they were followers, who were subsequently promoted to be leaders, reported an increase in positive mood. The emotional gain for followers-turned-leaders didn't compensate, however, for the emotional loss for the leaders-turned-followers.[14]

It is surprisingly easy to demonstrate how power distorts human behaviour. Psychologists simply prime people with a simple instruction such as 'think of a time when you felt that you had power over others', and then ask them to carry out a task. The performances of these primed subjects are strikingly different from those of people who are instead asked to recall situations in which they felt powerless.

Such experiments show that the main effect of power is to induce action. For instance, powerful people are more likely than the powerless to make a first offer in a negotiation task and they are also more likely to hit (take a card from the dealer) in a blackjack card game. In both cases, the result tends to come out in their favour. People of high rank are also more likely to help in emergencies, presumably because power is allied to a sense of responsibility. Psychologically, power can change someone's mood and render them more optimistic about the future (an unsurprising result, if we remember that power comes with perks). But there is a downside: they take more risks and have an unrealistically optimistic view of their own abilities.

Powerful people also find it more difficult to empathise with others. In a highly original experiment, people primed to recall moments of power were asked to write the letter 'E' on their forehead so that others could read it. The powerful were three times more likely to write the E from their own perspective (meaning it would look like a reflected E to others).[15] One possible explanation is that power decreases the ability to take on the perspective of others, or to show empathy for their situation. This inability to walk a mile in someone else's shoes is a handy trait for a dictator such as Mobutu, who lived a life of luxury while his subjects starved, or for a highly paid CEO charged with sacking people.

People in power are also inclined to abuse it. In one experiment in the 1970s, people were asked to supervise groups of students working on a task.[16] In one condition leaders were given the power to praise a good performance and punish a bad one. In the other condition, leaders were permitted only to praise. The group performance was standardised so that in both conditions the groups did equally well. Yet when the leader got the power to punish he used it surprisingly often, despite the group performing respectably. With power comes the potential for abuse, a truism that is stamped all over human history.

Encouragingly, research shows that the misuse of power is not a human universal. When people playing a money game are given power, some of them become more generous and others corrupt. It turns out that whether a person acts selfishly or generously depends upon his personality. People with a prosocial personality become benefactors, whereas those with a pro-self personality become hoarders. What drives this personality difference is largely a mystery, but one suggestion is that prosocial types tend to come from larger families (with the number of sisters being particularly influential).[17]

If personality is the key to the mystery of corruption, can we home in on a particular personality type associated with corrosive behaviour? Well, we can conjecture that power is very attractive to those with a pro-self personality, because it provides an opportunity for personal gain. With that personal enrichment come greater opportunities for mating (which is why rich men have no trouble finding girlfriends). And so, in keeping with evolutionary leadership theory, a person who relentlessly seeks out power is likely to succeed in spreading his genes.

This might account for the emergence of the 'Dark Triad', a constellation of personality traits that is widely seen as undesirable but is often found at the top of the power pyramid. People with the Dark Triad score highly on three particular dimensions of personality: narcissism, Machiavellianism (Mach) and psychopathy. This triumvirate makes them self-centred, emotionally cold and aggressive. Part of their 'talent' lies in image management: they are adept at cloaking their sinister motives, and may appear outwardly normal, charming even. These cunning people think mostly of themselves and cannot empathise with others. Were such a means of identification allowed, they'd be distinguished by foreheads stamped with a backwards E. They are, we can assume, rife in commerce and politics today, or wherever there is power to be gained.[18]

Let's not beat about the bush – these guys are bastards. Worst of all, there is plenty of evidence that, in evolutionary terms, it sometime pays to be a bastard. Study after study has found that these nasty pieces of work out-reproduce the good guys in certain situations, such as if there is a lot of movement between groups and tracking the reputations of individuals becomes burdensome (this is why employers should be wary of a candidate who changes jobs frequently). Women seem to especially like the bad guys when they are in the fertile stage of their reproductive cycle, though they prefer the nicer guys to care for the offspring. This explains why as many as 10 per cent of children are reared by men who are not their biological fathers. When societies break down, say during a war, these selfish types also seize their moment, often to grab control. If personality is partly heritable (as most scientists think), their ability to smooth-talk and manipulate women into bed results in a fresh generation of corrupt individuals, and explains why this sinister personality type is still with us today.

Let's home in on the three dimensions that lurk behind the Dark Triad. First, narcissism. Narcissists long to be admired; their lives are a quest for status and glory. In moderation, narcissism can be a healthy trait, because the narcissistic desire to look good is kept under control by a capacity for self-reflection, an openness to new information and the willingness to take sound business decisions. Healthy narcissists can be creative strategists who grasp the bigger picture and navigate risky challenges to leave a positive legacy.

Unhealthy narcissists, on the other hand, often wind up as executives in very competitive, high-risk (and high-gain) businesses. They will do anything to earn a fat bonus, to the extent of making dodgy short-term decisions (the kind that might conceivably precipitate an international banking crisis). Their *raison d'être* is success and glory, and they don't really do empathy. They pursue their goals aggressively and single-mindedly, and blame others when they fail.

In turbulent times, such ruthless leaders seem seductive because they can often pull off radical changes. That's because they don't lose sleep over making staff unemployed, for example. We shouldn't, therefore, be surprised that leaders commonly have narcissistic personalities.

The second element in the Dark Triad is Machiavellianism. The term is a nod to the political writer Niccolò Machiavelli, who wrote *The Prince*, a sixteenth-century manual for seizing and holding political power through cunning and manipulation.[19] Unlike narcissists, High Machs do not suffer from feelings of self-grandiosity. They remain realistic about themselves and their goal is not to impress. But they display a strong selfishness and will stop at nothing to achieve their objectives. For a Machiavellian, the ends justify the means – period. On the one hand, Machiavellian traits such as charm, cunning and confidence seem desirable in a leader. On the other hand, High Machs tend to be coldly calculating and arrogant, often behaving in ways that inspire mistrust and sabotage cooperation. They might seem aloof and uninterested in social interactions, and they don't care to forge deep emotional connections. Like narcissists, High Machs regard other people as objects to manipulate. They often gain short-term success but the truth eventually comes out: the merciless pursuit of self-interest allied to a lack of empathy works against their leadership.

The third trait is psychopathy. Psychopaths have an antisocial personality characterised by deceit, a disregard for others and a general lack of empathy and remorse. Like narcissists and High Machs they are utterly self-interested but, unlike them, psychopaths are not troubled by anxiety. They are fearless and immune to stress, allowing them to keep their heads when all about them are losing theirs (they even have trouble spotting when another person is fearful or sad). They remain unflinching in the face of punishment, which makes them almost impossible to sanction. This is why psychopaths are over-represented in prison. The one string to their bow is their ability to face down an extreme threat; their supreme decisiveness and fearlessness can prove pivotal on the battle-field or in the boardroom. Some evolutionary theorists have argued that this is why we tolerate these monsters in our midst.

And we have little option but to tolerate them, because they are exceptionally good at breeding. In a survey span-ning 35,000 people in 57 countries, David Schmitt of Bradley University in Illinois uncovered a link between the Dark Triad and reproductive success in men.[20] 'It is universal across cul-tures for high Dark Triad scorers to be more active in short-term mating,' Schmitt told New Scientist. 'They are more likely to try and poach other people's partners for a brief affair.' You certainly wouldn't want this kind of guy turning up as your new neighbour or boss.

This chapter is entitled 'The birth of corruption', and from what we've seen, there appears to be a horribly circular nature to the association between personality, power and cor-ruption. People who relish glory and rewards are more likely to strive for power, and once there, the rewards they accrue allow them to have more children. This produces a fresh gen-eration of selfish, power-hungry individuals, ready to start the cycle anew. The rest of us appear to accept this state of affairs grudgingly: we recognise the need for leaders who can coordinate our activities and provide us with valuable goods and services that could not otherwise be provided, and we are keen to reward them for taking on these responsibilities. On the other hand, we resent being dominated and exploited. This leads us to apply the STOPs we discussed in Chapter 4 (including gossip, criticism, disobedience and, in extremis, assassination).

Being hypocrites, however, it is in our nature (at least for some of us) to commit exactly the same abuses when we seize power (or are given it). This brings us to the counter-strategies that leaders can apply to enhance their power base. We can call them STEPs (Strategies To Enhance Power). What follows is – with tongues firmly in cheeks – the seven-STEP programme to seizing power and hanging on to it.

The first STEP is to expand one's power base through nepotism and corruption. This is not just a tactic adopted in Third World countries; the British scandal over MPs' expenses, in which politicians made claims ranging from the embarrassingly trivial (a bathplug for under a pound) to the ridiculous (a duck island for a castle moat), demonstrates that the powerful will always find ways to abuse privilege.[21] Be warned, though: you will eventually be rumbled, so corruption tends to work only in the short term.

The second STEP is to curry favour by providing public goods efficiently and generously. Benevolent dictatorship was practised by Lee Kuan Yew, prime minister of Singapore for 31 years. Lee believed that ordinary people could not be entrusted with power because it would corrupt them, and that economics was the major stabilising force in society. To this end, he effectively eliminated all opposition by using his constitutional powers to detain suspects without trial for two years without the right of appeal. To implement his economic policies Lee allowed only one political party, one newspaper, one trade union movement, and one language. He encouraged people to uphold the family system, discipline their children, be more courteous, and avoid pornography. As well as setting up a government dating service for single graduates, he urged people to take better aim in public toilets and handed out hefty fines for littering. Singaporeans tolerated these restrictions on their freedom because they valued their economic security more. On this point, Lee did not disappoint, turning Singapore into one of the world's wealthiest countries (per capita). If a despot can spin wealth and stability people are more inclined to forget their liberty. In fact, one of our experiments shows that a Lee-style form of leadership, in which one person is vested with the power to punish free-riders and cheats, is very effective at maintaining cooperation in groups.[22]

STEP three is to instigate a monopoly on the use of force to curb public violence and maintain peace. Dictators cannot survive for long without disarming the people and buttering up the military. Former dictators such as Pervez Musharraf of Pakistan, Mobutu of the Congo and Idi Amin of Uganda were high-ranked army officers who co-opted the military in order to overthrow democracies in favour of dictatorships. Yet democracies are not always more popular than dictatorships. In reality, people prefer dictatorships if the alternative is chaos. This explains the nostalgia for rulers like Stalin and Mao, who were mass murderers but who provided social order. One retired middle-ranking official in Beijing told the *Asia Times* last year: 'I earned less than 100 yuan a month in Mao's time. I could barely save each month but I never worried about anything. My work unit would take care of everything for me: housing, medical care, and my children's education, though there were no luxuries ... Now I receive 3,000 yuan as a [monthly] pension, but I have to count every penny – everything is so expensive and no one will take care of me now if I fall ill.'

When given the choice in the laboratory, participants will desert an unstructured group (analogous to an anything-goes society) and seek the order of a 'punishing regime', which has the authority to identify and reprimand cheats.[23] This lawlessness can be seen in hunter-gatherer tribes (egalitarianism is no guarantee of peacefulness). When anthropologists visited a New Guinea tribe they found that a third of males suffered a violent death. When women were asked to describe their domestic life a typical answer ran like this: 'My first husband was killed by Elopi raiders. My second husband was killed by a man who wanted me and who became my third husband. That brother was killed by the brother of my second husband, seeking to avenge his murder.'[24] Any aspiring dictator who restores order, even through coercion, is likely to earn the gratitude of his subjects.

The fourth STEP is to exterminate your political enemies – or, more cleverly, embrace them in the hope that the bear hug will neutralise them. This is exactly what David Cameron has done, by teaming up with Nick Clegg in a British coalition government. Mobutu abandoned the unpopular practice of murdering political rivals and instead bribed them, with political office, for their support. Idi Amin, who came to power in Uganda after a military coup, stuck with the murderous route: during his eight years at the top, he is estimated to have killed between 80,000 and 300,000 people. His victims included cabinet ministers, judicial figures, bankers, intellectuals, journalists and a former prime minister. At the lower end of the scale, that's a hit rate of 27 executions a day.

STEP five: nothing is as effective at strengthening a leader's position as defeating a common enemy. By facing down Nazi Germany, Churchill, de Gaulle, Roosevelt and Stalin sealed their reputations as great leaders. Legendary warlords such as Alexander the Great, Genghis Khan and Napoleon were military geniuses who expanded their countries' territories through invading their neighbours. Dictatorships feed on wars and other external threats because these justify their existence – swift military action requires a central command-and-control structure. More than half of twentieth-century rulers engaged in battles at some point during their reign, either as aggressors or defenders. Among dictators the proportion rises to 88 per cent. Democratic rulers find this tactic more difficult to adopt because most wars are unpopular with voters.

To attract support, the ruler must be perceived as a defender, not a warmonger. The former British prime minister Margaret Thatcher received a lucky boost to her popularity after Argentina, a military dwarf, invaded the British-owned Falkland Islands; she triumphed over her Argentine enemies. Another former British PM, Tony Blair, was not so lucky.

Although the 9/11 attacks did much to strengthen his government, his decision to attack Iraq (ostensibly to defend Britain
from a long-range missile attack) sullied his legacy.

There is some experimental evidence that when democratic leaders feel threatened, they are more likely to wage
war than in secure times. Replicating an earlier study, we
had two groups of participants play a game where they could
either cooperate or compete with each other. Each group
had a leader. The leader of one group was told his appointment would last the duration of the experiment. The other
leader was informed that his performance would be evalu-
ated halfway through, after which his group members could
decide whether to replace him. The leaders in the latter group,
who thought their position might come under threat, were
more likely to attack the other group. The lesson here is that
leaders can consolidate and extend their power over followers
by creating a common enemy and, ideally, defeating it; or by
playing the tough defender.[25]

The sixth STEP for leaders is to accumulate power by
manipulating the hearts and minds of followers. One of the
first actions of any aspiring dictator should be to control the
free flow of information, because it plugs a potential channel
of criticism. Mobutu and Amin eliminated the free press
in their countries and turned the media into propaganda
machines for their regimes. Other leaders, such as Burma's
ruling junta, shut down media outlets completely (the charity
Committee to Protect Journalists identifies Burma as the worst
country to blog from). Democratically elected leaders are
somewhat more restrained, but if they have enough powers
they can rig an election (like Mugabe in Zimbabwe), do away
with meddlesome journalists (like Putin's Russia) or, if money
is no object, build their own media empire. The Italian prime
minister Silvio Berlusconi owns nearly half the Italian media,
encompassing national television channels, radio stations,
newspapers and magazines. Unsurprisingly, these outlets
carefully manage Berlusconi's public image and shield him

from criticism. Aspiring dictators should note, however, that muzzling the media is most effective in an ordered society: a 2007 poll of more than 11,000 people in fourteen countries, on behalf of the BBC, found that 40 per cent of respondents across countries from India to Finland thought social harmony more important than press freedom.[26]

Finally, leaders have a seventh STEP at their disposal: the creation of an ideology to justify their exalted position. Throughout history leaders have used or, in some cases, invented a religion to legitimise their power. In the original chiefdoms like Hawaii the chiefs were both political leaders and priests, who claimed to be communicating with the gods in order to bring about a generous harvest. Conveniently, this ideology often passed as an explanation of why the chief should occupy the role for life, and why the post should pass to the chief's descendants. Accordingly, these chiefdoms spent much time and effort building temples and other religious institutions, to give a formal structure to the chief's power.

In later kingdoms, followers became wise to the ruse, and politics and religion were officially separated, although the king still headed both. When priests became pesky, however, some monarchs simply started another religion. Henry VIII of England pulled this trick when the Pope refused to annul his marriage to Catherine of Aragon. He created the Church of England, appointed himself Supreme Head and granted his own annulment.

Other ideologies include personality cults such as Mobutism or Maoism; some serve to unite a nation divided by ethnicity, religion or language. For example, Mustafa Kemal Atatürk, the founder of modern, independent, secular Turkey, attempted to soothe the ethnic and religious tensions threatening the country by propagating a belief system his countrymen could buy into. According to sun-language theory, the first utterances of mankind were based on sun worship and this proto-language most resembled Turkish (because Sumerians, one of the first civilisations to devise writing, came from central Asia). Atatürk, in an act of expedient presumption, thus claimed that Turkish was the original language of mankind. The lesson here is that you need to somehow convince your followers that you are 'The Special One' (as José Mourinho, Chelsea's ex-coach, famously said when asked by the media why he landed the job), and no justification is strange enough.

Thus, for any leader out there with dictatorial aspirations, we have identified the seven-STEP path to power: (1) be corrupt and nepotistic, (2) provide public goods generously, (3) maintain order, (4) turn political rivals into allies, (5) find an external threat, (6) control the media and (7) invent an ideology that legitimises your power.

All of these strategies have been used, to varying degrees of success, by dictators in the past. That rulers are capable of both extreme benevolence and extreme malice is down to the fact that human nature is complicated. The primate inside us craves power and dominance because that is how we spread our genes. Yet our evolutionary history as foragers in simple societies has taught us the benefits of cooperation and equipped us with an egalitarian ethos. Evolutionary leadership theory is the only conceptual framework that comfortably explains this apparent contradiction: these competing psychologies are continually vying for supremacy. In hard times, we show generosity and fairness because an act of kindness might one day lead to a reciprocal act that saves our own skins; when starvation is a distant prospect, as with the move to agriculture, the prevailing ethos, at least among leaders, is that greed is good.

In the next chapter we'll haul our Stone Age brains into the 21st century, and find that there is evidence of a psychological mismatch. Our evolutionary preference for being members of small, egalitarian tribes sometimes jars with the reality of modern life, comprising corporations numbering thousands and cities numbering millions, both governed by a remote bureaucracy. Picture, for a moment, our savannah-dwelling ancestors swapping their shelters for high-rise living, their tribal roles for white-collar management, and their limited, trusted social networks for the sprawling cyber-tentacles of Facebook. The term 'fish out of water' doesn't even begin to describe it.

6

The Mismatch Hypothesis

It is [fear] that makes people so willing to follow brash, strong-looking demagogues with tight jaws and loud voices; those who focus their measured words and their sharpened eyes in the intensity of hate, and so seem most capable of cleansing the world of the vague, the weak, the uncertain, the evil. Ah, to give oneself over to their direction – what calm, what relief.

Ernest Becker, *The Birth and Death of Meaning*, 1971

If you enjoy studying incompetence, the average office would make a fitting laboratory. It is estimated that around 60–75 per cent of managers fall well short of the leadership ideal, with flaws ranging from tyrannising subordinates to failing to call tough decisions.[1] In fact, there is a well-trodden path that leads from managerial incompetence to bankruptcy. The banking industry is a textbook model of how not to do leadership. Executives lent money they did not have, giving themselves huge bonuses in return, even as governments bailed them out with billions from irate taxpayers. In America, two-thirds of employees name their boss as their biggest headache, and there is no reason to think this dismal statistic differs wildly in other economies. Common reasons for disgruntlement among employees are the feeling they are being micromanaged; rude or abrasive managers; workplace indecision; and perceived favouritism. As for political leaders, it is a rare leader who lives up to the promises he makes on the campaign trail.

What lies at the heart of failed leadership? According to evolutionary leadership theory, the answer lies back on the savannah. Just look at the current complex social environments in which our leaders currently operate, and compare them to the relatively simple ancestral environment in which human leadership first emerged. Could it be that there is a mismatch between the way we live today and the way we lived for much of our evolutionary history? We think so, and, in this chapter, we'll see how evolutionary leadership theory explains the misguided decisions people make – without even knowing they are making them – which propel certain candidates into power. We call this element of ELT the Mismatch Hypothesis.

One consequence of a mindset wired for ancestral life is that we often select leaders on the basis of physical and psychological traits that once would have served those small, ancestral, egalitarian hunter-gatherer groups well, but which are of less importance in today's large-scale, fast-paced environments.

In this chapter, we will first explain what we mean by 'mismatch', and set out, using creepy-crawlies and top-shelf gentlemen's reading material, why we believe our brains still house a set of ancient emotional triggers and templates. These vintage templates are elicited whenever we are confronted with situations that echo those faced by our ancestors. We'll show that, while these templates were the ideal psychological equipment for the savannah, they are somewhat outmoded for the 21st century.

We'll discover a host of mismatches in leadership psychology which, to our lack of surprise, have been linked to leadership failure. So, for example, the top-down way we recruit managers and assign wide-ranging responsibility to executives clashes with the bottom-up, specialised style of leadership that our species practised for thousands of years. Our enthusiasm for people who look like us (as if they could belong to our tribe), and our paucity of enthusiasm for women leaders, is a throwback to the Stone Age; we'll see how this parochial mindset is plaguing us in today's global village. We'll also discover that when we select our leaders, we consistently favour tall, fit-looking males. We call this the Savannah Hypothesis, and it contends that we still choose our leaders as if we are appointing Big Men to protect us from aggressors and predators on the savannah. This is the idea reflected in the quote at the beginning of this chapter. Sometimes we want our leaders to look warm, sometimes steely. All those traits that we pay close attention to – height, age, perceived masculinity, gender and reputation – can be thought of as 'savannah traits' of leaders. We have folded the Savannah Hypothesis into the Mismatch Hypothesis chapter because focusing on savannah traits can blind us to better candidates with proven competence, and ranks as an obvious example of a mismatch.

Lurking at the end of the chapter, like a mysterious character lingering in the wings, is our old friend, charisma. We have included it as a particularly intriguing savannah trait. We'll examine theories of why charismatic individuals have always held such allure for us, from ancestral times right through to today. Something in their mesmerising personalities allows them to bypass our rational thought processes and hot-wire their way into our emotional hubs. This ability to forge an intensely personal, emotional connection seems to lie at the heart of charismatic leadership and followership, which explains their endurance throughout evolutionary history. We should, though, be aware that charisma is not always a force for good, and that through today's mass media, charismatic leaders enjoy a greatly magnified sphere of influence. Hundreds of thousands of years ago, charismatic leaders influenced perhaps 150 people; today they can inspire – even lead astray – followers in their millions.

Mismatch is a concept from evolutionary science. All organisms, including people, possess traits (biological and behavioural) that have been passed down through generations through natural selection. That you are here at all, reading this book, is because your ancestors had inherited qualities that made them winners in the game of life, better able than their competitors to survive and have children. They have, through your family lineage, bequeathed those winning genes to you (although exactly which genes you get from each parent is a lottery). Yet we suspect that the evolutionary environment that shaped your and your ancestors' traits was quite unlike your current surroundings. From at least two million years ago until 13,000 years ago, everyone lived in tight-knit foraging communities of about fifty to 150 people, rarely encountering outsiders.[2] Food was hunted or gathered, and the lifestyle was active. Today, half the world's population lives in cities, many in so-called mega-cities, numbering more than ten million people.

So traits that were adaptive, or useful, in ancestral times are no longer necessarily adaptive in these new, different surroundings. As the experimental psychologist Steven Pinker writes: '... our ordeals come from a mismatch between the sources of our passions in evolutionary history and the goals we set for ourselves today'.[3] Witness, for example, the rising rate of obesity in the West, where energy-dense foods are widely and cheaply available. Our ancestors did not live in a time when food was so plentiful; when they came across such bounty, they made the most of it. Unfortunately, we still carry the ancestral propensity to tuck into fatty, sugary foods whenever we can. Couple that with a more sedentary way of life today, and it is no wonder that our waistlines are expanding.

Remember, traits evolved because they produced reproductive and survival benefits in the past. Our genomes change extremely slowly – it is estimated that each of us carries between 100 and 200 random genetic mutations, which represent less than 0.000013 of our genomes.[4] Measurable evolution happens when a useful random mutation spreads through an entire species; humans separated by hundreds, even thousands, of generations are, genomically speaking, indistinguishable (although, on occasion, such as with the dairy-digesting gene mentioned earlier, a really advantageous mutation can spread in a matter of ten thousand years). This means we must retain many ancestral traits, many of which may not be useful to us, or adaptive, today. After all, our physical and social environments have changed dramatically in the past 13,000 years, since the agricultural revolution; environmental and social change has mostly outpaced the rate at which our genomes can keep up.[5]

Convincing evidence for this Mismatch Hypothesis can be found not only in the obesity epidemic but in any cobwebbed attic. Many people have a fear, even a phobia, of creepy-crawlies such as snakes, spiders and scorpions. Yet when was the last time you heard of someone dying from a snake or spider bite?

Snakes and spiders were common foes for humans in ancestral environments (and they still are for hunter-gatherer groups in remote parts of the world). Today, in America, they kill fewer than twenty people a year. Most victims are the animals' owners. In contrast, car accidents kill about 40,000–50,000 people a year in America alone. Yet experimental research has shown that a fear of snakes and spiders is more easily learned and less easy to shake off than a fear of more lethal, recent dangers such as cars or electrical appliances.[6]

In these experiments participants looked at pictures of snakes, spiders, cars and various household appliances. On several consecutive occasions, these pictures were followed by a mild electrical shock, so that people learned to associate the objects with an unpleasant sensation. In the second part of the experiment, the same pictures were shown several times but without the accompanying electric shock. On being shown these pictures again without the shock, the participant showed physiological signs of fear (for example, a rise in skin conductance) – as if he or she had actually received a shock – but, in the case of the modern threats (cars, electrical appliances) this response gradually disappeared over time.

When it came to spiders and snakes, however, the fear

response remained. It was activated every time the picture was flashed up. So, although we know that, by and large, spiders won't harm us, many of us have an instinctive fear of them.

Another mismatch is the trust we place in complete strangers (provided they look 'in-group', or as if they could belong to the same tribe as us). When someone knocks on our door we open it. When we purchase goods on eBay we transfer money to people we are unlikely ever to meet and still expect that they'll send the booty. Experiments with economic games further show that about 40–60 per cent of participants are prepared to send money to a stranger, even if the donation brings no obvious payback.

This makes little sense, unless we take ourselves back to the savannah. Everyone we knew was a trusted member of our tribe, usually a blood relative. Encounters with strangers were extremely rare. It is plausible that our brains are not geared up to deal with one-off interactions; we are inexorably conditioned to believe that we are likely to meet that stranger again. Our instinct, therefore, is to give him the benefit of the doubt.

Research indeed shows that people are more likely to trust and help strangers if they trigger 'in-group' cues (belonging to the same family or tribe). One experiment involving secret cameras showed that participants, who had previously been asked about their sporting allegiances, were much more likely to stop and help an injured individual if he was wearing a shirt from the team that the participants supported. On four out of five occasions, Manchester United fans stopped to help an actor wearing their team's shirt; if, however, the actor wore a Liverpool shirt, the fans tended to walk by. We are currently looking at the role of local dialects as in-group markers because they are very difficult to fake by outsiders. In general, we are more trusting towards, and more helpful to, people who look like us, speak like us, share the same values, and even people who mimic our behaviours.[7]

Good salespeople know how to exploit these evolutionary weak points. They are adept at pulling off the 'chameleon effect': mirroring your behaviour, using your language, seeking out the things you might have in common (how many salesmen ask you where you're from, and then claim to have been there?).

The whole of the pornography industry is predicated on a mismatch. Men become sexually aroused at pictures of nude women even though their sexual excitement does not lead to reproduction. Somewhere deep in the brain, a picture of a naked woman is interpreted as a real naked woman; this photographic invitation to reproduce elicits the usual male physiological response. Going to a sperm bank would be a more successful strategy for men to increase their reproductive success (without the commitment) but very few men find the prospect stimulating. Sperm banks were not around on the savannah, so men have not evolved to appreciate the reproductive benefits.

So, there are many behaviours that were adaptive in ancestral environments – in the sense that they boosted reproductive success – but now risk cutting our childbearing prospects.

Spider phobias, pornography and obesity show that many modern fallibilities have Stone Age origins. What, we need to ask, are the implications for leadership? Our leadership psychology evolved over 2 million years during which time we mostly lived in small egalitarian bands of brothers and sisters, and leadership was informal, consensual and situational. The best hunter decided when the tribe would go hunting; the best warrior decided when a showdown with neighbouring tribes was necessary. That was to change dramatically just 13,000 years ago, when the birth of agriculture fuelled a steady increase in the size and complexity of societies. Happy family clusters were rapidly replaced by complex social structures of chiefdoms, states, nations and empires in which thousands or even millions of people were encouraged to live and work peacefully together.[8]

This change in social circumstances is brand new on an evolutionary timescale. To illustrate how new, imagine that the existence of humans from 2 million years ago to today can be mapped on to a 24-hour period starting at 00:00. The last 13,000 years don't even start until the clock has ticked past 23:59. Our evolved leadership psychology is out of synch with the new times. But before we can convince you of a mismatch, we should first revisit the reasons why we believe that our leadership psychology is largely a consequence of evolution, rather than, say, upbringing or social conditioning.

As we have seen, humans evolved for at least several hundreds of thousands of years in small-scale societies without any formal leadership structure. There were near-equal power relations between adult male group members. If evolutionary leadership theory holds, this social structure should be reflected in the way modern humans evaluate leadership. In particular, we would expect there to be universal agreement on what followers regard as positive leadership qualities, and these qualities should closely match the prototype of the Big Man, the ancestral leader type.

Data confirm this. The GLOBE research programme – the Global Leadership and Organisational Behaviour Effectiveness research programme, based at Wharton Business School at the University of Pennsylvania – studies perceptions of desirable and undesirable leadership attributes all over the world. In a study of 62 cultures, its academics uncovered a remarkable consistency in the way leaders were described.[9] Examples of universally positive attributes are integrity – good leaders can be trusted; generosity – good leaders are helpful; fairness – good leaders are just and equitable; diplomatic – good leaders handle conflict well; decisiveness – good leaders make sound, timely judgements; intelligence and competence – good leaders contribute to the group's performance; and vision – good leaders can describe a desirable future. These leader prototypes closely match the perception of respected Big Men in traditional band societies. Big Men were able to exercise influence through their personal qualities rather than through a divine or inherited right to rule. In order to lead they needed to prove they were an asset, not a drag, to group living, helping it to survive and prosper (in terms of providing a safe, well-resourced environment in which to raise families).

Generosity (for example, helping younger men in the tribe to make a traditional payment to the bride's family), fairness (sorting out arguments) and competence (the ability to grow food) are important Big Men traits and these qualities remain sought after today. It is amazing how closely these virtues match those of universally admired figures such as Nelson Mandela, Kofi Annan and the Dalai Lama; it is as if there really is a universal psychological template of what a good leader should be like, just as ELT predicts. In the business world, Bill Gates has also regularly topped 'most admired' lists, owing to his commercial acumen as well as his philanthropic activities. As we have shown with the potlatch example, it matters less what the benefits of this philanthrophic act are to the recipients. What counts in terms of status is the amount of money a person gives, because that is an honest signal of someone's wealth.

An important aspect of Big Men leadership is that they exercise influence through persuasion rather than coercion. Big Men would be foolish to throw their weight around: members of hunter-gatherer societies don't like being bossed around and, as we saw in Chapter 4, it is not unknown for them to ignore, disobey or even kill a person who assumes too much power and authority (murder is thousands of times more common in these tribes than in modern society). In an echo of our ancestral past, we still dislike bossy, self-centred and corrupt leaders today. The GLOBE project data are useful here. Dominance, despotism and selfishness are universally loathed, as are leaders regarded as arrogant, vindictive, untrustworthy, emotional, compulsive, over-controlling, insensitive, abrasive, aloof, too ambitious, or unable to delegate or make decisions.

The challenge, then, for any evolutionary framework, is to explain why leaders with these attributes still make it to the top. One possibility is that they appear benign when angling for power but show their true dictatorial colours once in office. This is where, we suggest, the Dark Triad comes into play: men who score highly on all three traits – narcissism, Machiavellianism and psychopathy – often rise to leadership positions because their cunning allows them to present a likable face to the world. Only once enthroned do they unveil their manipulative, selfish and power-hungry personalities.

In the absence of a personality test result, we do not know for sure whether Robert Mugabe, who started life as a freedom fighter in Zimbabwe against British colonialists, is a member of the Dark Triad fraternity, but we can be certain he is no longer seen as a noble liberator of his people. In 2009, while Zimbabwe starved, Mugabe ordered tonnes of lobster, champagne and chocolates to be flown into the country for his 85th birthday celebrations. Today, despotic leaders such as Mugabe can stay in power with the help of the army (because armies benefit from being 'in' with the ruler) and maintain the monopoly on violence. In traditional societies, such behaviour would not be tolerated for long.

How does this apply to leadership and followership? We can list a litany of phenomena that point to our evolved leadership psychology being at odds with the modern world: the recruitment process for managers; the forcing of multiple responsibilities on people who have proved competence, or prestige, in only one field; a bias for people who look like us; the lack of women in top posts; the fact that military men often become political leaders; and our fondness for tall, fit and often masculine leaders (this is the Savannah Hypothesis: more on this later). It is no coincidence, we believe, that all of these mismatch phenomena, which we examine in turn, have been implicated in leadership failure.

Recruitment

Unlike in traditional Big Men societies, leaders in modern collectives, such as corporations and public sector organisations, are not chosen from the bottom up (i.e. by subordinates) but installed by people higher up the hierarchy, in a top-down way. This may produce leaders with qualities that superiors like to see – for example, the ability to execute orders from on high. But just carrying out orders from the guys upstairs isn't classed by most people as leadership, and won't necessarily raise your reputation among those underneath you. And so, very often, we'll find leaders and managers who don't possess what their subordinates would regard as prime leadership qualities.

Prestige-based leadership

In hunter-gatherer societies, a leader earns his position through his competence in a particular field. Big Men wield influence only within their realms of expertise, and they lead by example. This is known as prestige-based leadership. Prestige is given to individuals with specific skills who can help the group achieve its aims.[10]

Since a variety of people held leadership positions in the tribe in different, complementary areas, there was no evolutionary motivation for one tribal figure to be a Jack-of-all-trades. But there is pressure for leaders to be good at everything today, to be what we might call 'rainbow leaders'. This is because people who show skill in one area are often promoted into corporate positions where they have to take on other kinds of responsibility. So, rainbow leaders are expected to be good at inspiring, coaching, accounting, planning and delegating. If, however, someone has risen through the ranks because she's great at inspiring her colleagues, but it turns out she is lousy at filling in a balance sheet, it can be a recipe for failure. Not all skills transfer easily.

The sports pages also provide ample evidence of how prestige-based leadership can go awry. In competitive team sports such as football (soccer) the best players earn a lot of prestige – and money – while playing, giving them an edge in the competition for management jobs when they retire from the pitch. Yet there is absolutely no evidence to suggest that great players make great managers. If anything, league tables point the other way. Some of the most successful managers in English football – Sir Alex Ferguson at Manchester United, Arsène Wenger at Arsenal and José Mourinho, formerly at Chelsea – were mediocre footballers, and began their management careers at an early age. It helps here to think of a football player as a follower, and the manager – who picks the team, decides on their formation and their playing strategy – as the leader. When a football club puts its best player in a suit with the expectation that the team will reach the top of the table, it is making the classic error of assuming that a great follower will always make a great leader. Some clubs replace managers as often as a catwalk model changes her dress, but our analysis of the English Premier League suggests that a management change in football is nearly always detrimental to the club's performance record.

We like people like us

When two groups are competing against one another – say, on the football pitch, on the battlefield or in the tendering process for corporate contracts – our research has found that followers prefer a leader who is not only aggressive but also regarded as 'in-group'. That means he endorses group norms and shares group values. This preference persists even if the in-group candidate is demonstrably less competent than an out-group rival. We conducted an experiment that demonstrated exactly this apparently irrational behaviour.[11]

We took four students, sat them in neighbouring private booths, and gave them £5 each. The students were told the following: they could walk away with the money or they could pool some or all of it in a group fund. If the fund reached £12, the researcher told each student, the fund total would be doubled and divided equally among the group members, without anyone needing to know who had contributed.

The students were then allowed to communicate with each other by email, ostensibly to work out how much each would donate to the effort.

If a student – let's call him Adolf – was really scheming, he could lie to the others about his own contribution and hope the other three would pool theirs to make the £12 tally. That way, he would keep his initial fiver plus any share of a pooled kitty.

Now let's say that Adolf's group failed to make the £12 tally (there was a lot of fibbing going on in those booths). The group was then given the option of someone else joining the group as a leader, to coordinate the email exchanges within the group. Two candidates, Ben and Cameron, were offered up, both of whom had participated in the experiment previously. Ben's team had managed to reach the £12 target; Cameron's team had not.

Which did Adolf's group choose? Cameron, who was known to have already failed at the very task for which he was being taken on. Why? Because Cameron came from the same university as Adolf's team; Ben, a better choice on paper because he outperformed Adolf on a leadership competence scale, came from a different university. In other words, our personal liking for a potential leader often matters more than competence, which seems irrational. Our preference to be led by people like us probably comes down to a matter of trust: someone from our own tribe is less likely to betray us.

Women

This innate favouritism for 'people like us' can work against success, as it did in Adolf's group. Sometimes, the most competent leader is a different colour, a different gender or a different social class from us; and yet our evolved psychology prevents us from fully embracing this fact. For example, there are very few women directors on the boards of companies (and even fewer CEOs). A study of the 500 top US companies in 2006, however, as listed by *Fortune* magazine, showed that those with women directors are more profitable than those with no women on the board. The women-friendly companies are especially strong on corporate governance. A study from Leeds University Business School has found the same phenomenon: the data suggest that a 50:50 ratio of men and women on a board makes for a healthy balance sheet. All-male boards are not good: adding just one female director cuts the risk of bankruptcy by 20 per cent.[12] The Savannah Hypothesis will show how our gender bias is very probably a consequence of the time our species spent on the savannah.

Military leaders

Our penchant for war-savvy leaders also has the hallmarks of a mismatch. In traditional societies leaders had to manage relationships with neighbouring tribes and fend off mutual enemies. Raiding and warfare were common threats on the savannah; such threats could, and indeed did, wipe out tribes (such as the Incas). For this reason, Big Men were often warriors; only they could display the decisiveness, bravery and even aggression needed to fend off attacks and perhaps quell internal unrest. In fact, the social science literature abounds with examples of human tribalism, in which in-group members are treated well and outgroup members harshly. We think that intergroup conflict has shaped the social psychology of men, an idea we call the male warrior hypothesis.[13]

This instinctive link between military might and leadership extends to contemporary times: senior figures in the military are often found in politically prominent roles. Dwight Eisenhower became US president in 1953 on the back of his pivotal role in commanding Allied troops in the Second World War. But today, when politicians have to do far more than their Big Men predecessors, there is scope for a mismatch.

They have to run countries and build coalitions, as well as make war. Talented soldiers often wilt under the pressure of having to widen their circle of competence.

In addition, the scale of warfare has changed dramatically from our days on the savannah. Although it may have been wise for small ancestral societies to endorse a more aggressive leader when conflict loomed, is it wise today? The costs of modern warfare are much greater – even for the winning side. Hawkish leaders can increase the probability of war without increasing the probability of reaping any benefits.

Also, ancestral leadership was essentially situational, and once the threat had gone the nominated war chief would see his influence diminish. Today, however, leaders tend to serve a fixed term of office, say four years. Once the threat has evaporated, countries can be stuck with an authoritarian head of state for longer than they would wish, as Pakistan was with Pervez Musharraf.

Leaders, aware that military accomplishment confers political legitimacy, have been known to strengthen their power base by starting a conflict with another group, something we witnessed in our lab too. 'When the tyrant has disposed of foreign enemies by conquest or treaty and there is nothing to fear from them, then he is always stirring up some war or other, in order that the people may require a leader,' wrote Plato. The resulting 'siege mentality' deflects attention from a leader's deficits, and funnels it into maintaining group unity. This is, incidentally, a well-practised technique in football management: when a team is performing badly, a management will often redirect criticism to match officials, the opposition or the media.

Tall, fit, male leaders (or the Savannah Hypothesis)

The Savannah Hypothesis is the conceptual cocktail you get when you blend evolutionary leadership theory with the

Mismatch Hypothesis. And we can give you an inkling of what we mean by asking you to consider the word 'statesmanlike'. What does it mean? You could answer: it means looking or acting like a statesman. We have certain expectations of a 'statesman': he should be male, authoritative, wise, benevolent. But to earn this epithet a leader must also have a special demeanour or even physique about him. It is hard for a nervy beanpole who stutters to look statesmanlike; a short, tubby fellow with a high-pitched voice would be similarly challenged. Where do we get this mental image of what a statesman should be like?

The truth is, voters approve of candidates who look, sound and behave in a certain way. Height, physique and attractiveness matter.[14] Political scientists have consistently noted that taller presidential candidates are more likely to be voted in; rotund hopefuls are extremely unlikely to become wedged behind the desk in the Oval Office (the last overweight candidate to roll into the White House was William Howard Taft, in 1909). Voters also generally favour mature leaders over young ones. Barack Obama bucked the maturity trend, partly because some voters thought that, at 72, John McCain was a little too mature to start ruling. Not that Obama coveted the gift of youth: there were rumours that the dynamic lawyer dyed his hair grey in order to heighten his air of authority.

Traditional leadership theories have some difficulty explaining the seemingly irrelevant correlations with age, height, weight, health and gender, and tend to see them as spurious (and the preference for male leaders as an example of social conditioning). After all, ruling is more of a cerebral activity than a physical one. But view these same correlations through the lens of evolutionary leadership theory, and these preferences begin to make sense. In ancestral environments, choosing a poor leader was potentially so costly that any notable personal trait would be folded into the selection process. After all, hunter-gatherer tribes didn't do interview boards, leaving physical appearance and personality as the only viable metrics for competence. For leadership activities requiring physical strength and stamina, such as group hunting or warfare, our ancestors would have wanted the physically fittest man for the job (in retrospect, a wise judgement, because you are testament to their success). Height, weight and health would have pointed to fitness. Evolutionary leadership theory explains it like this: evolution has burned into our brains a set of templates for selecting those who lead us, and these templates are activated whenever we encounter a specific problem requiring coordination (such as in times of war or recession). The Savannah Hypothesis spells out what those criteria, or savannah traits, are.

Our Savannah Hypothesis contains four broad ingredients. First, it proposes that individuals with a particular set of physical features and psychological traits were more likely to emerge as leaders in ancestral societies. To the extent that these traits were reliable predictors of effective leadership, followers started to pay closer attention to these cues. Over time, using these cues, followers built up cognitive profiles or prototypes of good leadership, and individuals who slotted most closely into these moulds were more likely to be accorded leadership status.

Second, the Savannah Hypothesis maintains that these cognitive ancestral leader prototypes (let's call them CALPs for short) varied according to the task in hand. For instance, the CALP of a peacetime leader would look very different from the CALP of a war leader, because different leadership traits are required for fighting wars and maintaining peace.[15]

A third plank of the hypothesis is that, over time, these CALPs became hard-wired in our brains. This is how it works: if a particular action (say, following Thor to go hunting) is consistently associated with a particular, positive outcome (say, filling one's belly), the mental association between action and outcome becomes reinforced over time. So, whenever Thor dons his hunting boots, he attracts followers. This cognitive association can then be generalised to other situations in which Thor wants to take the lead – such as going into battle with another group – as well as to situations in which people who look or behave like Thor want to take the reins. Over many generations, this reinforced association becomes a cognitive template. So, people lacking in experience might still become leaders simply because they fit the CALP template.

A fourth and final implication is that we still spontaneously evaluate aspiring leaders based on these CALPs, even though the templates are no longer relevant (because most of us don't need to hunt for food). Think of the automatic fear response towards snakes and spiders. Although they hardly threaten modern humans, these creatures – and even pictures of them – consistently elicit a powerful fear response. We don't respond in anything like the same way to cars, which are much more threatening to human survival in terms of the number of genetic lines they bring to a premature end. So, our brains seem to be primed to instantly respond to dangers that were lethal in ancestral times, rather than to modern killers; and we are similarly psychologically primed to this day to seek out leaders who would have surpassed themselves on the savannah. Astonishingly, young children who are shown photographs of election candidates are extremely accurate at forecasting the winner, even though they base their judgements on looks alone. In the rest of this chapter, we'll size up the savannah traits that appear to influence the perception of leadership potential, and delve into why they have become such strong psychological triggers. We'll look in turn at the following savannah traits: overall health, height, age, a masculine appearance, gender, reputation and, finally, charisma.

Overall health

In ancestral times, the only real selection process for aspiring leaders was through appearance and demeanour. Physical features would have indicated leadership potential via the following logic: attractiveness has been found to correlate with facial and bodily symmetry (the higher the degree of symmetry, the higher the beauty rating), which in turn is an indicator of genetic fitness. A pleasing face signals that its owner is in good physical health and is therefore worth following (he won't drop from exhaustion before the hunt has concluded). Every time you see an attractive person, that skipped heartbeat is evolution's shorthand for saying they've got great genes and therefore any offspring you have with them stand a decent chance of survival.

The first of four televised debates between presidential candidates John F. Kennedy and Richard Nixon in 1960 proved, semi-scientifically, the importance of appearance: Nixon looked pale and ill (in fact, he had just come out of hospital, and decided against using make-up) while Kennedy looked healthy and attractive. While television viewers rated Kennedy the winner, radio listeners came away with a much more favourable view of Nixon. These were the first televised presidential debates in America, and they taught a lesson to aspiring politicians that has become even more pertinent in today's media-soaked political world: it is not only what you say that matters, but how you look when you say it. This explains the deep public fascination for televised debates between political candidates. Britain held its first such debates prior to the May 2010 election: David Cameron, soon to be the new prime minister, appeared dynamic and fresh compared to the older man he deposed, Gordon Brown.

Current and aspiring political leaders continue the fashion for showing off their physical health. During his presidency Bill Clinton was regularly filmed jogging. Nicolas Sarkozy, president of France, has embarked on a well-publicised fitness and diet regime (although this may also have had something to do with having a supermodel wife thirteen years his junior). Fascinatingly, he also told his ministers to lose weight and get fit. Both Barack Obama and his wife Michelle make a daily trip to the gym; the president also plays basketball and football when he can. Vladimir Putin, the Russian president, regularly demonstrates his pectorals to the press, which has photographed him fishing bare-chested in Siberia, horse-riding and playing judo.

It drove one female political commentator to write: 'In what other non-sporting line of work are there similar expectations of physical prowess? No one expects a senior economist – Mervyn King [the governor of the Bank of England], for instance – to jog ... or do judo ... But retired politicians point out that it would now be unthinkable for a man with a build along the lines of, say, Aneurin Bevan [the stocky health minister who created Britain's National Health Service] to find work at the top of politics. Even for superior physical specimens, the price of political success is now per-petual exercise.'[16]

Furthermore, there is a keen public appetite for news about the health (or otherwise) of leaders; a keenness that is not shared by those in possession of the facts. For instance, in the last US presidential election John McCain and Joe Biden – both older than Obama – refused to disclose medical information.

In business, too, customers and investors seem to link a healthy CEO to a healthy balance sheet. When rumours began circulating about the health of Steve Jobs, the CEO of Apple, share prices plummeted. A poorly leader, our ancestral brains reason, bodes ill for the group he heads. The news that Jobs had had a successful liver transplant in 2009 was 'leaked' on a Friday evening, when the news would do least financial damage to the company. Dr Alexa Perryman, a management academic at the Neeley Business School, at Texas Christian University, who has examined the impact of CEO sickness on the fortunes of companies such as McDonald's and EarthLink, has argued that the Securities and Exchange Commission should classify a CEO's ill-health as a material fact requiring disclosure.[17]

Height

Leaders with towering ambitions need to be, well, towering. Consistent with our Savannah Hypothesis, which argues that we choose leaders on the basis of how they look, voters elect taller leaders (although the evidence for heightism is restricted to competitions between male candidates only). For instance, a look at the US presidential elections shows that the loftier candidate usually wins (one notable modern exception is George W. Bush defeating the taller John Kerry). Nicolas Sarkozy (who defeated a female opponent to win the French presidency in 2007) and Silvio Berlusconi appear sensitive about their modest stature; both have stepped on to platforms when meeting taller international counterparts and both wear shoes designed to give them a few extra inches. In Sarkozy's case, his diminutive physique – allied to his consciousness of it – is a constant source of amusement to cartoonists and sketch writers. When the French president visited a company recently, newspapers reported that short employees were bussed in specially to meet Sarkozy, because they would not make him look small.

This perception that tall politicians are taken more seriously was taken to heart by a female Australian politician, who had her legs broken and stretched by three inches. 'I want people to take me seriously and to be known for the work I do as a politician in my local community,' Hajnal Ban, a councillor in Queensland, told *The Times* in 2009, without spelling out why she felt that her contributions to community life would be ignored if she were shorter.[18]

We can offer an explanation: in ancestral times height was an indicator of genetic quality and good physical growth (and therefore all-round health). Furthermore, a taller person would have been a more formidable warrior in hand-to-hand combat, and a better peacekeeper (it is easier to prise two fighters apart if you can enter the fray from above). It has been suggested that potential aggressors might have backed off from taller opponents, making tallness a valued trait among those entrusted with defending the group. Given that tall men would be expected to be healthy, height would have been a reliable signal of fitness in the Darwinian sense, i.e. indicating likely number of offspring. Tall men would thus find it easier to attract mates than short men.

This ancestral rule of thumb still holds true today: Robin Dunbar, an evolutionary psychologist at Oxford University, scanned the medical records of thousands of adult men in Poland and found that taller men are more likely to get married and to have children.[19] Childless men were, on average, an inch shorter than fathers. Dunbar carried out the study after noticing that men advertised their height in personal ads only if they were tall.

More generally, there is a well-documented correlation between height and success in the workplace: one July 2004 study of more than eight thousand British and American workers calculated that a six-footer earns, on average, nearly $166,000 more during a 30-year career than someone who is 5 feet 5 inches – even when controlling for gender, age and weight.[20] The researchers found that salesmen reaped the biggest rewards from extra inches, implying that height affected customer perceptions (we come back, again, to the three S's: tall men earn more, have a higher status and find it easier to attract women). Tall people are in the enviable position of being looked up to, rather than down upon; the resulting boost in self-esteem and confidence contributes to a positive image overall. This might explain why tallness is a common attribute of successful businessmen: Malcolm Gladwell noted in 2005 that 30 per cent of Fortune 500 CEOs were 6 feet 2 inches or over, compared to 4 per cent of the general population. Jack Welch, however, stands out – if that is the right term – as an exception. Some observers attribute his success to the fact that the 5-foot-7-inch tycoon rose within the ranks of GE rather than being appointed from outside, and so was judged more on what he accomplished than how he looked.

Just as with height, researchers also find consistent correlations between leadership and weight. Leaders tend to be heavier than average; the extra weight would once have signalled that a person was healthy and resourceful. A bigger leader has, literally, more gravitas than a skinny one. A heavy man is also likely to be a formidable warrior in hand-to-hand combat. In fact, the title Big Man – used to describe archetypal leaders – could well have come about through the unwritten leadership rule devised by our ancestors that 'heavier and taller is better', although, as we saw earlier, voters are quick to distinguish between weighty and fat.

Age

Another facial cue that is perceived to be linked to leadership potential is age. Like gender, it is one of the most obvious physical characteristics of a face, and this characteristic encodes important leadership information. When juries appoint a spokesperson, for example, they will often look to an older male to represent them; there appears to be a subconscious assumption that a mature male is wise and authoritative. A mature face speaks of expertise and wisdom; professions that require specialised knowledge, such as academia or the clergy, tend to have older leaders. These jobs require experience and training, and age is therefore viewed as a positive. Wrinkles can, though, also hint at physical frailty and perhaps conservatism, disadvantaging the older candidate in situations that call for energy, dynamism and innovation. For example, in the army, the platoon commander – a physically demanding post – is usually of comparable age to the soldiers he directs. In the higher echelons of the military, where physical combat is not important, age rises with rank.

In a recent study in our lab we morphed the faces of individual leader candidates – males and females – to make them look older or younger. We then asked participants to rate the suitability of these individuals to become president of beloved Taminia, the fictional country dreamt up by a member of the research team, Brian Spisak.[21] In one scenario the country was in a period of transition:

Your country of Taminia is experiencing a time of change. The foundation of your economy is switching from steel and coal to 'hi-tech' commerce. Overall, people are open to the experience and see it as an opportunity for growth. Presently, your country needs to attract new investors, encourage long-term development and retrain its workforce. This requires everyone to be motivated and energetic. Likewise, for this shift to work, Taminians must stay inspired and focused. The near future will be unfamiliar territory filled with challenges. Currently, your country is in the middle of a presidential election. Vote for a face in each pairing you think looks 'most' like the leader in a transitional period.

In the alternative scenario, the country needed some stability:

Your country of Taminia has recently experienced the worst natural disaster in its history. Tens of thousands of people have unfortunately perished as the result of large scale flooding. The rebuilding of the physical infrastructure has started without problem, but psychologically the citizens have a strong sense of loss and uncertainty. This collective insecurity is taking a toll on the country's well being. People in general lack focus and are quite anxious. Presently, Taminia is holding presidential elections. Vote for a face in each pairing you think looks 'most' like the leader to provide reassurance, understanding and closure.

When confronted with the first scenario, with Taminia undergoing change, participants plumped for younger-looking leaders. In the second scenario, they preferred the older-looking candidate. Since the candidates up for election were essentially the same face aged by computer trickery, we can safely assume that participants were making their decisions based on age. Manipulating the context in which leaders are selected, we can deduce, changes the desirability of particular leader faces.

These studies provide a possible insight into Barack Obama's resounding victory; his youthfulness played well with voters seeking change. Obama deliberately and cleverly presented himself as the candidate for change (the word 'change' appeared on all his election posters), taking advantage of his relative dynamism and presenting his lack of experience as a positive sign that he was different from other politicians. This might also explain the success of David Cameron and Nick Clegg, the two tall, attractive leaders who now govern Britain. Both sought to present themselves as a change from the past, ready to face the country's economic problems with freshness and vigour.

A masculine appearance

How did the shorter Bush trump the taller Kerry in the 2004 presidential election? Age is unlikely to have been a factor: fewer than three years separate their births. According to our Savannah Hypothesis, voters tailor the CALP they are seeking to the problem in hand. That means that desirable attributes of leadership are context-dependent. In the case of Bush and Kerry, the other salient physical difference between them, apart from height, is facial. Could Bush's victory have been down to his jawline?

Anthony C. Little at Stirling University recently conducted a fascinating study to find out.[22] The facial features of Bush and Kerry were blended and superimposed on a neutral male face in such a way that people did not recognise either candidate in the composite. The face was then tweaked to make it look more Bush-like or Kerry-like (without it being obvious). Participants were then asked who they would vote for if their country was at war, and who they would vote for in peacetime. They went for the enhanced Bush face in the war scenario but the enhanced Kerry face in the peace scenario. At the time of the real election, the country was engaged in wars in Afghanistan and Iraq.

Since the voters were making their decision on appearance alone, it seemed to be the relative masculinity of the Bush face which won him the election (in real life, as well as in the experiment). A typical masculine face has a strong jawline with pronounced eyebrows and narrow eyes, small lips and a lot of facial hair (which obviously might be removed through shaving). A feminine face, in contrast, is delineated by a soft jawline, large eyes and full lips. A very masculine face is a sign of relatively high testosterone levels (to digress, one theory suggests that, since only men with very good immune systems can cope with high testosterone levels, women find strong-jawed men attractive because their masculine looks are a sign of a top-notch immune system, a heritable trait that increases the likelihood of children surviving).

To test the idea that voters were responding to facial cues in their voting choices, our lab replicated the Scottish study using the faces of Obama and McCain as templates. Obama's face is more feminine whereas McCain's is more masculine. As expected, the softer faces (in which Obama's features were enhanced) were preferred in peacetime; the McCain-like faces were chosen in a war scenario. A war-weary American electorate would therefore have two reasons, according to the Savannah Hypothesis, to vote for Obama in the 2009 presidential elections: his softer features and his height. Additionally, researchers at the Kellogg School of Management have suggested that Obama's softer features contributed to his historic election because they were a 'disarming mechanism' that signalled to white voters that this black candidate was non-threatening. The psychologists also studied black CEOs and had whites rate them for 'babyfaceness' – yes, that really is the technical term – and found that the more babyfaced the black CEO, the higher his company was placed in the Fortune 500 ranking.[23]

Fascinatingly, babyfaceness hinders, not helps,

prospective white CEOs because it is associated with weakness, the Kellogg academics found. This is backed up by a separate, older study, which discovered that the CEOs of higher-ranked companies in the Fortune 1000 tend to have 'stronger' faces – as rated by neutral observers – than CEOs of lower-ranked companies.

Back to our facial cues study: to guard against the possibility that our lab voters had recognised Obama's and McCain's features, we tried another version of the experiment. We took various neutral-looking faces, male and female, and, again, tweaked them to look more masculine and more feminine. For each pair of faces, we asked participants which they would vote in as president of the imaginary country of Taminia. To prime them, we presented them with fictional scenarios. In one, Taminia was at war; in the other, the election was for a peacetime figure.

Our results echoed those found with the Obama and McCain faces: masculine-looking candidates were favoured during war, and more feminine-looking candidates were preferred in peacetime.[24] The masculine faces were considered more dominant and aggressive (the kind of qualities we expect in war chiefs). The feminine faces were rated as being more gentle and agreeable. It is interesting to note that the last three people in the role of US Secretary of State, America's most senior foreign peacekeeping position, have been female: Madeleine Albright, Condoleezza Rice and now Hillary Clinton. We can speculate that countries lacking women in positions of authority might be more prone to warfare (although, conversely, it might be the case that war situations reduce the chances of women being elected).

Gender

We took the masculine/feminine experiment to its logical conclusion – by actually offering our players the option of choosing a male or female leader. We invited four people at a time to our laboratory to play an investment game. Half the groups were told that the aim of the game was 'to earn more money with your team than the other teams in the game' (we call this the war scenario, because teams are pitted against one another). The other half were told that the aim of the game was 'to earn more money than the other players in your team' (the peace scenario).

Each group was then asked to choose a leader from two candidates, described like this: 'Sarah, a 21-year-old university student in law. Her hobbies are exercise, travelling, and going out with friends' and 'Peter, a 20-year-old university student in English literature. His hobbies are reading, music, and attending parties.' In other words, the only salient difference between the two leaders was gender. Predictably, most players (78 per cent) voted for Peter in the war scenario, and there was an overwhelming preference for Sarah (93 per cent) as leader in the peace scenario. Furthermore, these leaders were also more effective in the situations that members thought them most suited to; Peter raised more contributions in the war scenario and Sarah in the peace scenario.

Interestingly, there was also a version of the game which combined elements of both war and peace. The players were told that the goal was 'to earn more money than other teams and to earn more than the other players in your team'. In these hybrid cases the players preferred Sarah to lead (75 per cent). There is some evidence from other research that women have a more flexible leadership style, making them exceptionally capable of dealing with situations involving high degrees of complexity, such as when there are simultaneous opportunities for conflict and collaboration (and those women diplomats come to mind again).

Our relative reluctance to choose women leaders explains their absence in the top echelons of politics and business; only a third of the FTSE100 companies boast women directors, and most of those are non-executive. Just 3 per cent of executive directors are female. Female presidents and prime ministers are few and far between, and tend to be daughters or widows of previous leaders (Benazir Bhutto and Corazon Aquino, for example). Where does this reluctance come from? In hunter-gatherer societies, leadership often includes a physical component. Duties include spearheading group hunts, organising raids and breaking up group fights. Because men are usually bigger and stronger than women, they are more likely to rise to prominence.

We must also remember that the perks of leadership – salary, status and sex – militate against women. Men hunger for high-status positions because it makes them more desirable to women (Darwinian logic explains the sexual allure of rich men: women know their babies will be well provided for). Women don't benefit evolutionarily from acquiring personal status and riches in quite the same way: they can best serve evolution's end (which is the propagation of the species) by nurturing their children rather than chasing a promotion or salary increase (in fact, there is some indication that career women have fertility problems because of job-related stress). These evolved differences in the way men and women view status – men care about it much more than women do – might be responsible for strengthening the already robust bias towards male leaders.

Some women do make it the top but they seem to be penalised for excelling at stereotypically masculine tasks. Carly Fiorina, the former CEO of Hewlett Packard, has often remarked on how sexist the coverage of her tenure was. It is true: we don't ask male CEOs what it's like to be a man at the top.

Society tends to assume it is the natural order of things; a woman wielding great power is still somehow seen as unnatural, especially if she is of childbearing age. We find it hard to shake the feeling that she should be at home looking after her brood. Post-menopausal women, however, appear to be taken more seriously in politics and business. Angela Merkel, the

Chancellor of Germany, Hillary Clinton and Kraft CEO Irene Rosenfeld are all highly respected. In *Fortune*'s 2009 ranking of America's leading businesswomen, only two were under 40.

Personal reputation

The public takes a compulsive interest in the domestic minutiae of leaders' lives, and the lives of those closest to them – and there is a media industry devoted to sating it. We want to hear about how Malia and Sasha are doing at school (see, we don't even have to give you their surname) and check out how the First Family decorate their home. We soaked up details of Euan Blair's drunkenness and listened disapprovingly to Senator John Edwards's confession that he had cheated on his cancer-stricken wife. When Gordon Brown appeared on television discussing the death of his baby daughter, it was viewed as a career-saving attempt to humanise him. Why are we interested in our leaders' lives beyond the office, and why do politicians so often opt for a public confessional prior to elections?

The Savannah Hypothesis predicts that we should be interested in personal information about putative leaders because this is how our ancestors judged those around them. In small tribes, everyone knew everyone else's business. This information, alongside evaluations of competency at the task in hand (e.g. foraging), would have been used to assess leadership potential. The logic is summed up in this conviction by Truett Cathy, the CEO of fast-food chain Chick-Fil-A: 'If a person can't conduct their personal life, you can't expect them to be a high performer in their business.'

It is interesting that we place a high value on 'authenticity' when we watch these confessional interviews. We really care about how sincere a candidate is when he vouchsafes information about himself, as if his authenticity is key to our judgement of his suitability as leader.

Our ancestors, we speculate, would also have made

character judgements of those most closely allied to a prospective leader, such as his spouse or children. These are the people most likely to influence his judgement and decisions, and a leader's relationship with them can give some insight into character. During his tenure as US president, for example, Ronald Reagan permitted his wife Nancy to consult an astrologer; it was reported that the president timed meetings, conferences and even the announcement of a re-election bid in accordance with this astrological advice. It is fascinating to note that this revelation was made only after Reagan had left office; it would have diminished his political reputation considerably.

So, why does this category of personal reputation belong in the mismatch chapter? The leader–follower relationship was much more intimate in hunter-gatherer groups than it is in today's large, formally tiered societies and corporations. Yet even in these bureaucratic collectives, we still crave a personal relationship with those at the helm. Given that a CEO of a ten-thousand-strong company is not likely to be able to share a drink with every employee, and a presidential candidate is not going to be able to meet every voter (even on the most painstakingly planned campaign trail), the information vacuum needs to be filled. This is where newspapers, magazines and strategically timed personal interviews with trusted TV hosts come in. Of course, it is possible that a prospective leader who thinks that his personal life is off limits is more likely than a voter to perceive prurient interest as a mismatch: the fact is, however, that public figures who refuse to broach personal topics look evasive.

Charisma

Finally, we come to the issue of charisma, which so often crops up in academic and popular discussions about leadership. We feel that evolutionary leadership theory can finally offer a scientific explanation of why charisma is seen as an essential quality in many kinds of leader, from political to corporate to religious. We believe that our desire to be led today by men blessed with charm and a gift for oratory harks back to our time on the savannah, when these leaders were able to rouse emotions that united a crowd, fostering group cohesion. That is why we have included charisma as a savannah trait.

These figures, we suggest, were great at creating an emotional connection with their followers, and sending out emotional tentacles throughout the group in order to bind followers together. But our preference for these leaders can, today, be highly problematic. And that is why we regard it as an example of a mismatch.

First, how do we define charisma? The German sociologist Max Weber offered the most widely used definition of charismatic authority (for which we can read leadership). It rests 'on devotion to the exceptional sanctity, heroism or exemplary character of an individual person, and of the normative patterns or order revealed or ordained by him'.[26] Weber may have been on to something but it must be more complex than this; the adulterous Bill Clinton did not have a flawless moral character yet this did not undermine his charismatic powers.

Charisma is indeed an odd beast: difficult to define but you know it when you see it. John F. Kennedy and Martin Luther King had it. It is thought to have evaded George W. Bush, but his successor Barack Obama has it in spades. Former British PM Gordon Brown seems to lack it; in comparison, his successor David Cameron looks blessed with it. Since Weber, psychologists have attempted to pin the quality down more precisely: a person with charisma seems to harbour an extraordinary gift for leadership, can cope in a crisis, thinks up radical ideas and can rise above the fray. He also attracts a loyal fan base.

Fascinatingly, psychologists have discovered that

charismatic leaders are able to press a psychological button buried deep in the human mind. They discovered this by using a clever experimental technique called mortality salience manipulation, which involves asking participants to imagine their dying moments. Its purpose is to make people feel anxious, to churn up the kind of mortal dread you don't get merely by sitting an exam (which people are also asked to imagine, by way of an experimental control). When, after describing their imagined death, they are subsequently asked to vote for one of three leaders – a doer, a peacemaker or a visionary – then the visionary fares surprisingly well.[27] We think this is because a fear of death creates an instinctive need for protection, and, on the savannah, we would have sought out a trusted person who would have known us intimately to give us that protection and comfort. A visionary – a charismatic leader – excels at putting himself in our inner circle, by giving us something of his personality in his oratory.

Research on traditional societies suggests that Big Men are often extremely charismatic; one famous example is Ongka, a Big Man in the Kawelka tribe of New Guinea, who starred in his own film.[28] Being intimate, inspiring, persuasive and visionary would have been important attributes of aspiring leaders in small face-to-face groups. That, we suggest, is why we judge putative leaders so strongly on personality. We can safely assume that the tribal leaders on the savannah were not shut away from their followers in an air-conditioned office, were not shielded by a snooty personal assistant (a wife, maybe) and didn't get to and from work in a chauffeur-driven Lexus. Our ancestors were not segregated from those who led them; there was little distinction between public and private personas. And so followers rated their leaders on what they saw: their personality, their communication skills, their family values. In the absence of qualifications, psychometric tests and CVs, it was the only information our ancestors had.

Of course, a crucial weapon in the charismatic leader's toolbox is language. These leaders use twice as many metaphors in their speeches as other types, and scholars dating back to Plutarch have associated leadership skills with a mastery of language and rhetoric. Modern research bears out the historical and anecdotal evidence: leaders score notably highly on verbal IQ, and the babble effect, discussed in previous chapters, shows that talkative people are perceived by others as leaders.

Patrick McNamara and David Trumbull suggest the crucial discriminator between speakers, as gauged by listeners, is 'relevance': in our evolutionary history, those individuals in the group who could collect and convey relevant, succinct, timely information would occupy a special status within the tribe.[29] This need to collect relevant information would drive memory capacity (ability to remember the information and where it had come from) and therefore intelligence. But a person would also need to have access to information from different sources, they suggest; this would imply the person was trusted and respected by many other group members of the tribe. Any of these traits is little use in isolation, as far as the group is concerned: it is no good being loquacious when one has little information and few opinions to disseminate, and it is next to useless if a person who may have gathered a range of views is too shy to pass the information on. On the other hand, one person harbouring all these skills – known and trusted widely, intelligent and verbally adept – would have an immediate leadership advantage. It could explain the correlation between leadership ability and extroversion and linguistic skills that we see today.

Of itself, though, language, which some researchers suggest possibly evolved in order to connect large groups of people, lacks the emotional bonding element necessary to arouse and synchronise emotions in crowds (it might help here to picture Bill Gates trying to deliver Martin Luther King's 'I Have a Dream' speech). We, and others, have recently argued that mechanisms like laughter, religion, dance and music – which are more or less uniquely human attributes – may have appeared in human evolutionary history to quickly release positive emotions through large groups of genetically unrelated people to help them bond.

We strongly suspect that charismatic leadership – which is language, body language and a certain *je ne sais quoi* – exerts similar psychological and physiological effects on followers as laughter, dance and religion. Great speeches stir people's emotions and unite listeners (think of Obama's inauguration speech, or the 'Give Me Liberty or Give Me Death' oration by Patrick Henry, one of the founding fathers of America). It is quite possible that rousing oratory stirs endorphins as well as emotions; this would make a fascinating subject for research. If this is the case, the earlier finding that people turn to charismatic leaders in times of need makes sense. Those leaders not only 'feel your pain', as Clinton once said, but can lessen it. When people are asked to make substantial sacrifices on behalf of their group, such as in war or recession, we can see that the ability to empathise with subordinates and feel their pain – reduce it, even – will be useful. We thus come to understand the allure of the charismatic leader.

Why do we believe that charisma deserves a slot in the Mismatch Hypothesis? Because personality and charisma do not always make up for competence, especially in today's world, which is so different from the savannah. Modern life has not yet rewired our brains to use newer techniques of assessing competence. Evolution has honed us to seek out information about the personality and oratorical ability of our leaders, because in ancestral times it was persuasion, personality and reputation – as well as physical factors such as height and age – which secured leadership positions in small tribes. But, today, we can and should compare applicants rationally, on the basis of relevant education and experience.

The fact remains, though, that, when choosing between two politicians, we often judge them not on what they say but on the conviction, sincerity and empathic resonance with which they utter it. Charismatic individuals – those who have the personal touch but not necessarily a mastery of the fine detail – have the edge here. Also, now that we no longer live in small bands but in cities, nations and geopolitical regions, charismatic individuals now have the potential to exert their magnetism over millions of people, rather than just 100. One bad apple risks rotting not just one basket but the entire orchard.

To recap, in this chapter we hope we've convinced you that the way we choose our leaders owes much to our time on the savannah, where our psychology evolved to help us operate in small hunter-gatherer tribes. But, because society today is much larger and socially more complex, we've become wedged in the gap between savannah and suburbia. However much we may employ our intellect, our brains have tunnel vision when it comes to leadership psychology. And we have been in that evolutionary tunnel for perhaps two million years since the emergence of the genus *Homo*: the 13,000 years since agriculture, which fuelled the growth of large settlements, don't even register on our evolutionary radar. And so we still hanker after certain leader prototypes: we like to be led by tall, strong, lantern-jawed men who know us personally. They must possess self-belief but not self-regard; they should be charismatic, but not charlatans. These revered figures should receive extra rewards and privileges, but not too many. Today, though, leadership is very rarely about foraging and fighting in 100-strong tribes of blood relatives; it's about ruling nations of millions (a billion, in the case of China), running multinational corporations with thousand of employees, and rubbing along in a global village where people don't look and behave the same way as you do. Is it any wonder that the leaders we choose today so often disappoint?

7

From savannah to boardroom: lessons in natural leadership

The truth is that maximizing personal compensation is not the only motivation that people have in their work. As we move up *Maslow's Hierarchy of Needs*, we discover that once our basic material needs are satisfied, money becomes less important to us. In my experience, deeper purpose, personal growth, self-actualization, and caring relationships provide very powerful motivations and are more important than financial compensation for creating both loyalty and a high performing organization.

John Mackey, blog, June 2009

We started our quest to understand leadership in the hot, dry African savannah of 2 million years ago, and we are about to conclude it in the 21st century. It is astonishing to think that this timeline is also a bloodline, connecting each and every one of us with our ancestors in the past. We have, to paraphrase Darwin, been modified in the descent. We have come down from the trees, acquired language, (largely) shaken off the dominance hierarchy of our primate cousins and built large cooperative societies in which people help and care for others. We are walking, talking organisms that come ready equipped with behaviours and instincts that enhance our reproductive success. And, just before the evolutionary clock struck midnight, those instincts and behaviours were well matched to our natural and social environments.

Today, though, in the urbanised, industrialised conglomerates in which most readers live, those instincts are catching us out. So, we gorge on the calorie-rich foods that would have been an occasional, welcome nutritional boost to our ancestors, and become fat. We run away from spiders and snakes, although they pose a negligible threat. Our ancestors lived and foraged in egalitarian tribes of fewer than 150 people; we are but tiny cogs in corporate and civic wheels, crushed under the weight of formal hierarchies. We are one employee among thousands, one citizen among millions.

What does this mean for leadership and followership? As evolutionary leadership theory explains, our psychology has been sculpted to thrive in small, flattened communities. So, we make the kind of instinctive judgements that our ancestors made. We follow people with charisma because we use it as a proxy for competence, but we often find out to our cost that a charismatic exterior can conceal a vacuous, even vindictive, nature. We vote for tall, fit men because those are the kind of people whom our ancestors sought out to provide tribal protection. We tend to exclude women (because they were confined to traditional roles in tribal life) and minorities (because we instinctively feel suspicious of people who are not like us). Today, there is no rational reason why height, age, weight, colour and gender should be used as sole qualifications for jobs or roles. Yet these savannah instincts continue to prevent us from picking the best person to fill a particular role, which we hypothesise contributes to the substantial failure rate of managers in corporate America.

Evolutionary leadership theory explains why: our minds are not wired to live and work as we do today. Sure, we get by – we are, after all, the most intelligent species on the planet, and can use technology and culture to adapt to our modern environments – but something about modern leadership just doesn't feel right. This might account for the rising popularity of terms such as 'authentic leadership', which aims to encapsulate a fundamental quality often missing in leaders.

If our ancestral past still affects the way modern humans think, feel and behave, then future leaders need to understand the phenomenon of Natural Leadership. Natural Leaders are those who pilot their organisations in a way that fits our ancestral psychology – and take pains to overcome the biases inherent in them. The obligation, we should note, is not one sided. Followers have the power to change the way they are led, and they need to learn how to assert themselves. As followers, we should ask how the organisations that govern our lives – governments, business, the Church, public sector bodies – could be redesigned to foster excellent leadership (by which we mean competent and moral) while minimising bad leadership (by which we mean excluding people who do not have our best interests at heart).

Evolutionary leadership theory gives us a valuable tool for improving the practice of leadership and followership in modern organisations. We set out the ten most important recommendations below, and relate them back to the chapters that explain the thinking behind them. Some recommendations are diagnostic, and can be used to investigate how well any particular organisational structure matches the ancestral environment; others are recommendations of courses of action that should improve the way people lead and follow 'naturally' given the constraints of our ancestral minds. An important note: we don't want modern workplaces to revert to the working practices of the Stone Age. Evolutionary leadership theory is about fostering an understanding of how group living, including leadership and followership, originated in our species. By gently tweaking our mindsets to properly accommodate the 21st century, we can make the dynamics of group living better for everyone.

1. Don't overrate the romance of leadership

In ancestral environments there were no formal leadership roles and there was little or no distinction between a leader's public and private life. In fact, personal information about an individual was crucial in determining whether he should occupy pole position.

Accordingly, we loathe our bosses when they make us work overtime and we love them when they give us a day off. Consciously we may be aware that our boss is simply following the orders of senior management. Yet our evolved psychology whispers to us that a boss who makes us work overtime is brutish, and the boss who gives us time off is a saint. This 'fundamental attribution error', also known as the 'leadership attribution error', is a product of our ancestral past in which office and home were the same place, and the only performance target that mattered was staying alive and having kids.[1]

That same error, or psychological short-circuit, leads us to romanticise leadership: we beatify leaders when a group is successful and blame them when things go pear shaped. British accounts of history portray Winston Churchill as defeating the Nazi regime virtually single-handedly. In contrast, George W. Bush's approval ratings were so low during his second term of office that it seemed as if he had personally orchestrated Hurricane Katrina, which devastated New Orleans in 2005.

This romantic view of leadership is epitomised by the Great Man theory we met in Chapter 1, and by the clamour for business biographies in which Jack Welch or some other business guru reveals his secrets. This romanticism may have been justified on the savannah, when good decisions spelt the difference between life and death, but is less justifiable today. Leaders today often operate as part of a coalition or follow orders from above, meaning the trail of responsibility is more opaque. The banal truth is that modern leaders deserve less credit and blame for their actions than their early predecessors.

Writing in *USA Today*, Alan M. Webber, a business commentator, revealed:

The best education I ever got on business leadership came from Jim Collins, author of the best seller Good to Great. I told Jim that I'd noticed that none of the companies that had made the leap from good to great were obvious choices. Even more to the point, none of those CEOs were famous or even recognizable. Was there a correlation between CEO anonymity and performance? I asked Jim. His answer: There comes a time in the history of most companies when the CEO has to make a choice: Do what is best for the company's future, or do what is best for the CEO's career.

So, which CEOs is Collins talking about who did what was best for their companies? Try taking this test: Can you name the CEO of Starbucks, one of the few US companies that has mastered the art of growing without losing quality? Can you name the CEO of Southwest Airlines, the only major airline to achieve profitability in the face of an industrywide economic disaster?[2]

The point Webber was making is that these unsung CEOs – who do not romanticise their contributions because they understand that great leadership today is about more than one figurehead – are actually among the most successful.

2. Find a niche and develop your prestige

In Robert Greene's entertaining book *The 48 Laws of Power*, the eleventh law states: 'learn to keep people dependent on you'. Greene writes: 'To maintain your independence you must always be needed and wanted. The more you are relied on, the more freedom you have. Make people depend on you for their happiness and prosperity and you have nothing to fear. Never teach them enough so that they can do without you.'[3] Ignore the Machiavellian overtones: the essential message is to find a niche for yourself. This will be good for you and good for the group. This is what Natural Leadership is about. In ancestral environments, we saw in Chapter 3, individuals gained a following because they possessed a skill that could benefit the group – such as flint knapping, hunting or navigating through unfamiliar territory – or some unique personal quality like tact, diplomacy or being able to communicate with the gods. These Natural Leaders attracted followers who were interested in learning the trade from them and those followers rewarded them with the three S's: salary (or, in the days before money, some extra privileges), status and, sometimes, sex.

Thus, over evolutionary time, there has been selection for traits that enable individuals to hone their abilities, especially those that are deemed 'useful' for the group they are in (where 'useful' is culturally determined). One manifestation of this is that people tend to love what they excel at. If you ask children why they like playing chess or football they often say it's because they are good at it. The talent-liking relationship makes sure that they continue practising until they reach an expert level. It has been estimated it takes 10,000 hours of training – twenty hours per week for ten years – to become an 'expert'.[4] Natural Leaders know their strengths and weaknesses and cultivate what they are good at.

Possessing specialised knowledge or a unique skill also makes someone seem irreplaceable. It helps to be involved in many aspects of how an organisation is run: you gain allies and appear indispensable. Henry Kissinger survived as a leading diplomat in successive American governments not because he was an exceptional negotiator or an agreeable person but because he anchored himself in so many political domains concerning security and foreign policy that it would have been destabilising to get rid of him. He advised on affairs with the then Soviet Union, China and Vietnam, Latin America and Africa; arguably, his presence ensured continuity in an otherwise turbulent world.

3. Keep it small and natural

The societies of our ancestors, which we toured in Chapter 4, were essentially extended, interdependent families in which everyone knew everyone else and their unique role. Groups were held together through informal, consensual and charismatic leadership. Ethnographic evidence suggests that these communities varied in size from around fifty (about the size of a chimpanzee group) to 150 members. This upper limit, called Dunbar's Number, is about the maximum number of people in a social network that can be held together informally and without external control. In a school of 150 pupils, the headteacher would know each child by name. Think of it as the total number of people on your Christmas-card list or the tally of people with whom you could resume a previous conversation if you bumped into them. It is no accident that 150 is the upper limit on sizes of such egalitarian religious communities as the Amish or the Hutterites. Once a Hutterite colony exceeds 130–150 people, a daughter colony is started.

Our brains are adapted to organisations of this size. Larger collectives are difficult to operate through informal means because members may not remember valuable information such as people's names or who said what in the past (the social networking site Facebook had to introduce 'defriending' so that users could prune back their networks to a manageable level). Creeping over the 150 limit leads to the need for formalised relationships and the writing down of policies and rules. Interestingly, the Dutch parliament has exactly 150 seats. The British parliament has 450 seats. Could this provide an explanation for the recent expenses scandal among British politicians, which might have been prevented had there been sufficient informal social control?

Effective organisations such as W. L. Gore and Associates, and Virgin, are designed and structured, whether wittingly or not, in a manner that resembles hunter-gatherer bands in certain respects. For instance, these companies delegate decision-making to managers far down the chain of command so that the size of functional units rarely exceeds a certain number (250 in the case of Gore). Decentralised forms of organising are associated with greater employee morale, involvement and commitment, which is in turn linked to greater productivity and better financial results and customer satisfaction. We'll come back to W. L. Gore and Associates later, to look at the other ways in which it is pioneering Natural Leadership.[5]

A Natural Leader must display the qualities associated with small-scale band leadership because this is the standard that we humans have applied for hundreds of thousands of years. International leadership studies from around the globe suggest that everywhere in the world, despite cultural differences, we value the same qualities in our leaders. These include trustworthiness, persistence, humility, competence, decisiveness and vision – the same qualities that propel individuals to Big Men status in pre-industrial societies. To be a Natural Leader means cultivating personal relations with subordinates. This means that even a CEO of a large business must develop and nurture relationships with subordinates at each level of the organisation (which is why it helps to decrease unit size). Although this sounds impossible, a bit of charisma and the use of modern communication technology can help foster an intimate relationship with many people at the same time (John Mackey's chatty email to his employees at Whole Foods Market, cited in the Prologue, is an example; Richard Branson, who heads the Virgin group of companies, also makes a virtue of informality).

4. Favour followers

Early humans, we saw towards the end of Chapter 4, realised the dangers of yielding too much power and influence to any one individual within their group because he (it was nearly always a man) could use it to dominate them and pursue his own selfish reproductive interests. We only have to look to our primate cousins, the gorilla or chimpanzee, to find out what life would be like in a dominance hierarchy ruled by a despotic alpha. As seventeenth-century philosopher Thomas Hobbes put it: 'No arts, no letters, no society; and, which is worst of all, continual fear, and danger of violent death: and the life of man, solitary, poor, nasty, brutish, and short.'

Dominance is part of our primate history and there is always the risk that people in leadership positions – the primates – will coerce and exploit their followers. This makes leader–follower relations fundamentally ambivalent. Throughout human evolutionary history there has been an ongoing arms race between leaders and followers to gain the upper hand in the battle for power. For large parts of history, when humans lived in egalitarian groups, subordinates were able to organise themselves effectively to curtail the power of leaders and keep them in check, using the Strategies To Overcome the Powerful (STOPs) mentioned in Chapter 4.

Anthropologists sometimes refer to this as a 'reverse dominance hierarchy', where the influence of a leader is derived from the legitimacy conferred by subordinates who are, therefore, the true holders of power. This power reversal made it possible for our ancestors to reap the benefits of cooperation and conquer the world. When leaders are kept in check, as has happened throughout most of human evolutionary history, and others are permitted to reproduce, then followers have a vested genetic interest in protecting the welfare of the group and stability results.

In a society ruled by a despot, subordinates have no interest in looking after the welfare of the group. They simply bide their time until they are strong enough to overthrow the dominant and take over. Since the agricultural revolution, we explained in Chapter 5, there have been periods when this reverse dominance hierarchy has been under threat, because leaders – kings, tyrants and warlords – could accumulate resources and build up powers which they sometimes used to exploit and coerce their citizens. These totalitarian arrangements are ultimately unsustainable, however, because there are simply not enough people who are willing to die on behalf of a despot. Regimes in which the common people have a shared interest – democracies – last longer because we will all defend societies in which we have a biological interest. It is interesting that much of the impetus to deal with climate change comes from a global desire to bequeath a better world to our children and grandchildren.

In short, although occasionally we see fascist and communist collectives emerge in special circumstances, these totalitarian regimes are at odds with our evolved psychology. We are not yet like other (ultra-)social animals such as ants and bees who have sacrified their own reproductive interests for the greater good of their society (think of how much misery the strictly enforced one-child policy has wrought in China). To paraphrase the great sociobiologist and ant aficionado Edward O. Wilson when he was asked about human communism: 'Great idea. Wrong species.'

Organisations would do well to consider the lessons from our ancestral past about leadership: it would be wise to take heed of the strategies that leaders traditionally use to accumulate power (the STEPs of Chapter 5), and perhaps more importantly, the ways in which subordinates can resist (STOPs). This is where followers must take responsibility for the way they are led.

One strategy is to accept leadership only from individuals – Natural Leaders – who have proven expertise. Most of the time employees and citizens can coordinate activities among themselves and do not wish to be micromanaged; a leader needs to show that he can achieve something above and beyond what can be achieved without him. It is worth making sure that checks and balances, along the lines of our STOPs, are in place to prevent the scales tipping too far in a leader's favour (although we are not including the most extreme STOP, assassination, on our list). Gossip should be tolerated (employers would be unwise to ban 'water cooler' gatherings, because the fear of loss of reputation is a powerful incentive for a manager to behave well). There should be regular public scrutiny through public hearings, shareholder referendums and elections. It is healthy to allow presidents only a fixed number of terms in office, and if they try to change this (as Hugo Chávez and Vladimir Putin recently did) they should go. Similarly, CEOs should be regularly appraised.

Organisations should also encourage recrimination-free whistle-blowing among employees. In extreme cases disobedience must be tolerated. The fact is, sometimes those in power make mistakes. Enron and Lehman Brothers might still be around had the organisations taken criticism from insiders more seriously; instead they have become synonyms for management failure. Natural Leaders, ideally, would have means in place – such as suggestion boxes and open channels of communication – that nip harmful practices in the bud. For example, the John Lewis Partnership, which owns a network of profitable department stores and supermarkets in the UK, holds regular meetings of its Partnership Council, at which any item may be discussed. Eighty per cent of council members are elected by employees (who are called 'partners') and any partner may attend any council meeting.

We also saw, in Chapter 5, the importance of exit options. Followers must be given exit options at all times. In ancestral times, individuals and (sometimes entire) groups could simply abandon an overbearing leader. When people are banned from leaving countries or discouraged from leaving workplaces (e.g. by the threat of a bad reference) they become slaves of those in power. It is an intolerable denial of our natural leadership and followership psychology and, as we've seen with the collapse of communism and fascism, ultimately unsustainable.

In a paradoxical way, then, the threat of criticism,

disobedience and even aggression when followers unite against leaders is a recipe for a healthy group dynamic. In the absence of these levelling mechanisms, societies and companies risk becoming more despotic as power differences between leaders and subordinates increase.

5. Practise distributed leadership

Leadership in the ancestral environment, we discovered in Chapter 4, was situational, fluid and distributed. The individual most qualified for the particular task had the greatest influence on collective action. Rarely would one individual coordinate all group activities or make all group decisions. With bureaucracy and formality reigning in the workplace today, however, the fate of an organisation often rests ultimately in one pair of hands.

The ability to perform multiple, even competing, leadership roles, or leadership versatility, is an important aspect of executive effectiveness. But few leaders (with the exception of such international leadership icons as Kofi Annan, the former United Nations secretary-general) are genuine rainbow leaders, i.e. have the range of skills needed to perform a wide array of duties. The demands we make on our leaders to pull off multiple roles partly accounts for the high failure rate of senior managers.

This explains the recent interest in the world of science and business in distributed leadership – the idea that leadership is a process that can be shared among individuals.

One of the most significant milestones in human evolution was the division of labour, something which only the social insects – some of which we met in Chapter 2 – have done better than our own species. In colonies of honey bees different groups perform different roles and together they make the beehive function more effectively. Worker bees do most of the foraging; scout bees influence the choice of foraging sites; the soldier bees look after the safety of the hive, and there is even an internal police force that ensures that only the queen is allowed to reproduce.

Natural Leaders recognise that expertise is widely distributed within his or her group, and that the organisation can prosper only if information flows freely and without recrimination. Natural Leaders also recognise the 'wisdom of crowds' in making decisions. The advantages of group decision-making are obvious; it allows organisations to pool information from many brains. The result is a global brain that has at its disposal more information than any single brain could possibly contain. Furthermore, group decision-making ensures that extreme opinions do not gain too much credence, thus preventing the well-known 'groupthink' phenomenon in which a leader or a small team, by failing to consult widely, makes a dreadful policy decision based on limited information.[6] Weak channels of communication between different arms of Toyota, allied to a culture of secrecy, are thought to have contributed to the company's belated recalls of cars with suspected faulty pedals. The recalls have shredded the company's reputation: it faces a multibillion-dollar bill for repairs, class-action lawsuits by families whose relatives have been killed or injured in accidents, and political censure. Whatever the much-vaunted managerial principle the Toyota Way was, the company lost it.

Don't be fooled by the psychological science literature on group decision-making, which too often concentrates on what is wrong with groups. Some literature claims, wrongly, that groups are poor decision-makers, that brainstorming doesn't work, and that groups make extreme decisions. These findings make headlines but the truth is more subtle. An understanding of human evolution suggests that group decision-making is natural. Groups are the optimum means for making complex decisions.[7]

Of course, some learned individuals will have a greater influence on the outcome but ultimately the decision is based on consensus and some form of democracy (although not necessarily the 'one person one vote' system, which is a recent human cultural invention). Consensual decision-making has been in place for millions of years and it explains the runaway success of humans and other ultra-social species such as ants.

One shining example of distributed leadership is the internationally acclaimed 'polder model' in Dutch politics. Much of the Netherlands lies below sea level and, to keep the sea from flooding polders (low-lying pieces of land), the Dutch have developed a network of interconnected dykes. Historically, these dykes and polders could be managed only through the collective efforts of the entire population; every citizen, from pauper to nobleman, took responsibility for maintaining the system. Today, various regional water boards oversee the system. Incidentally, the maintenance of dykes is an example of what game theorists consider a weak-link game, because the success of a group is determined by the weakest link in the chain, which is the lowest dyke that allows the waters in and thereby floods the country.

Because of this external threat, Dutch society is relatively egalitarian. There are strong norms militating against laziness and conspicuous wealth displays, as you would find in an ancestral hunter-gatherer band. In a distributed leadership model, everyone has the power to make a difference: and, as we saw in Chapter 5, assigning power to somebody usually results in action (although power can also be abused).

6. Mind the pay gap

Leadership in modern society often comes with perks and privileges. As we saw in the Prologue, before the credit crunch the salaries for CEOs in corporate America were, on average, 179 times higher than the salaries of the lowliest workers in their companies. In the UK, the multiple is around 100. Bankers and City traders walked away with bonuses worth millions. Before the economic crisis hit, nobody took any notice. Since then, there has been a global backlash. Belatedly, under public pressure, governments everywhere have promised to curb the culture of excessive pay and bonuses.

And so we should. For most of human evolution, we saw in Chapter 4, we lived in egalitarian societies with little or no wealth or status differences. Status is a scarce good with reproductive pay-offs, so there was always competition for status. Yet the power of a leader came ultimately from followers; leaders who overstepped the mark were dealt with by the group, sometimes even assassinated. The outrage at bankers' pay and perks – especially for those who ran failing institutions that required taxpayer bailouts – can be interpreted as a kind of ancestral bitterness directed at group members who did not pull their weight and who acquired reputations as freeloaders.

At heart, disproportionate executive pay is a mismatch, a concept we met in Chapter 6. Huge pay-offs unnerve us because they are at odds with our evolved psychology. On the savannah, semi-nomadic bands could not carry anything valuable around and, in the absence of a production economy, there was nothing to buy. Of course, just as today, there was a continuous jockeying for power between upstarts, but the benefits accruing from positions of power were relatively minor in terms of salary, status and sex.

Agriculture, Chapter 5 showed us, changed everything. Leaders could hoard enough resources to build harems; they protected their privileged positions through building armies and fortresses. The huge reproductive pay-off of these positions selected for the wrong kinds of leaders: warlords, tyrants, dictators and monarchs. These selfish, power-hungry individuals stole from their subordinates without giving anything in return, as if the the phrase *noblesse oblige* meant nothing.

Modern organisations must be aware that, as the relative benefits of taking on a leadership position rise, such positions become more appealing to individuals driven primarily by selfish interests rather than by the desire to serve the group well. Astronomical salaries and fabulous perks glint like diamonds in the dust – they are beacons to Dark Triad leaders, but off-putting to women and servant leaders. Furthermore, as the relative power of leaders increases, so does the likelihood that this power will be abused. Research shows that extreme power changes people: recipients empathise less with their subordinates and treat them less fairly.

From the perspective of the subordinates, paradoxically they might want their leaders to do well because this is a sign that a company is healthy. Would an employee who takes pride in his work really want to see their CEO drive around in a clapped-out banger? The trick is to get the power differential right. A Lexus might be acceptable, but a company Lexus plus company Ferrari plus company yacht might be pushing it. When power differences become too big, subordinates become alienated and disconnected, not only from those above them but also from social institutions. Fascinatingly, in March 2010 the UK-based Church Investors Group, which controls assets of more than £12 billion, commissioned a report on executive pay from leading theologians. The report recommended that the group sell off its shares in companies where the chief executive earns more than 75 times the average wage of the lowest-paid 10 per cent (this is, incidentally, the limit imposed by the John Lewis Partnership). The theologians said their advice was motivated by concern for the poor, a long-term outlook and, interestingly, a suspicion of the characters attracted by gargantuan remuneration packages.[8]

The psychoanalyst Hannah Arendt would undoubtedly approve of the CIG report's assertion that extreme economic inequality may well also have damaging social consequences: she argued that the alienation and indifference felt by citizens paved the way for the totalitarian regimes that swept into power in Germany, Russia and Italy in the early twentieth century.[9] This should serve as a warning sign for nations and businesses to take seriously the issue of power and income gaps between leaders and followers. When institutions favour leaders at the cost of followers, something has to give eventually. Sometimes that will be the forcible wresting of power by the common people, which explains political revolutions. Isn't it fascinating that the ideals of *egalité, liberté, fraternité*, forged in the French Revolution with its removal of the monarchy, epitomise the ideals of the typical hunter-gatherer society?

7. Look for leaders from within

In ancestral environments leaders emerged from the crowd because they had a particular skill or quality coveted by the group. For instance, a person who was knowledgeable about the natural world would earn his role, in his small tribe, as a shaman. We live in a complex world in which many organisations consist of multiple groups that are bound together through hierarchy. Consequently, in large organisations, leaders are often appointed by those above them in the hierarchy, such as senior managers. These leaders tend to be accountable to their seniors, rather than to subordinates. This top-down approach is unnatural. It undermines the Darwinian selection process of leadership whereby individuals with different traits compete for leadership positions (variation), those who show the best leadership qualities emerge from the group as winners (selection) and their leadership qualities are retained (retention).

Instead, we appear to have developed a form of artificial leadership selection. Senior managers appoint like-minded individuals who understand that climbing the ladder means pleasing their superiors. To these Artificial Leaders, the welfare of subordinates, even the welfare of their group, is a sideshow.

Artificial Leaders tend to perpetuate organisational failure (although senior managers may often appoint someone dynamic and innovative). Nevertheless, these externally appointed leaders often lack legitimacy, and struggle to gain the trust of subordinates. Our research suggests that followers work harder for leaders they have elected themselves than for externally appointed leaders.

Top-down leadership might also explain the disengagement and alienation felt by modern citizens and workers. This can be overcome by involving subordinates in the selection process. Research shows that hiring decisions for executive leaders are more likely to be successful if subordinates are given an active role in the hiring process. Jim Parker, the noted CEO of Southwest Airlines, pinpointed the importance of respectful manager–subordinate relationships when discussing the departure of a manager who had alienated his underlings. In *Do the Right Thing: How Dedicated Employees Create Loyal Customers and Large Profits*, Parker wrote: 'When this person finally left, I asked one of his former employees why she thought everybody disliked her former boss so much. She summed it up: "Because he was the kind of person who kissed up and spit down."' The title of Parker's book, ostensibly about distributed leadership, taps into the idea that we are equipped with an instinctive knowledge of the 'right' way to lead.[10]

W. L. Gore and Associates is a hugely successful company that makes, among other things, Gore-Tex, a fabric for extreme weather conditions. It is perhaps no coincidence that it has a particularly original way of choosing its CEO. It throws the post completely open, and invites employees to nominate candidates. Its current head, Terri Kelly, was shocked to be told she had got the job. She had been chosen by a confederacy of peers; the company philosophy is: if you attract followers, then you're a leader (which chimes with our definition of a Natural Leader, who must have qualities recognisable to followers). Interestingly, she doesn't have an MBA (around a third of CEOs have earned that coveted acronym).

Not that being a CEO is a big deal for Ms Kelly, because

nobody tells anyone what to do. The M-word – manager – is banned and employees are instead referred to as associates.

In another nod to evolutionary leadership theory, all company decisions, even on remuneration, are consensual and peer-reviewed. Kelly admits that this makes for slower decision-making but says that this is offset by the fact that all associates abide willingly by group decisions (she thinks this is preferable to reaching a quick decision which is then implemented grudgingly). The comparison to hunter-gatherer tribes doesn't end there: when groups get too big (more than 250 people), they split. The duplication in costs, Kelly reckons, is worth the benefits of intimacy. Furthermore, employee turnover is a very low 5 per cent, which suggests that this approach succeeds on the retention front.

8. Watch out for nepotism

Nepotism, we saw in Chapter 5, is in our blood – or, more precisely, in our genomes. We are descendants of individuals who looked after their families through the provision of love, parental care and other resources. Even today there is a higher infant mortality rate among children with an absent father, and, on the other side of the fence, kids who enjoy close contact with grandmothers fare better in life than their grandmotherless peers.[11] Human evolution has favoured individuals who lavished their resources on kin rather than on genetic strangers. One of the pillars of evolutionary theory is kin selection theory: it assumes that the stronger the genetic relatedness between individuals the more they help each other. This makes sense from an evolutionary perspective because, by assisting a close relative, you are helping to perpetuate a genetic legacy that looks a bit like yours, rather than the genes of a stranger.

It explains the success of family companies. Around 90 per cent of businesses in the USA are small family-owned concerns. These organisations seem to cope much better when the economic going gets tough.[12] Relatives cooperate more easily with each other and the levels of trust are high. The downside of this nepotistic arrangement is that preferential treatment is accorded to relatives irrespective of whether they are well suited to the job, and bloodlines make exceptionally fertile channels for corruption. It is doubtful whether every child of the late President Suharto of Indonesia was the best person to lead a large government department or a state-owned monopoly; nonetheless, the Suharto dynasty was reported to have helped itself to between $15 and $35 billion. Several relatives were subsequently convicted of corruption.

For businesses and organisations, keeping it in the family is a double-edged sword. If you are the boss of a small business then it helps having people around that you can fully trust, and who will willingly take on extra duties. In large organisations, however, where there is a stricter division of labour and more specialisation, Natural Leaders will recruit the people with the best job qualifications rather than relying on a narrow circle of relatives and friends.

9. Avoid the dark side

Dominance is part of our primate heritage. It is in our nature to settle disputes by referring to the rank we occupy in the pecking order: 'The boss says you have to do it.' In that sense, we are depressingly similar to our gorilla and chimpanzee cousins. Dominance is often the quickest way for leaders to get subordinates to obey. At times it is also the best way to maximise reproductive success, as indicated by the number of descendants that tyrants such as Genghis Khan or Mustafa the Bloodthirsty fathered. We met these prodigious sperm purveyors in Chapter 5.

Sometimes dominance is the last resort when reason fails (observe any parent who is trying, and failing, to reason with a child. Eventually, an exasperated parent will play her trump card: 'Because Mummy says so'). In a recent laboratory study we showed that after a number of trials cooperation broke down in groups that did not have leaders, whereas cooperation flourished in groups that had appointed leaders who had the power to punish free-riders. Thus, like parenting, some dominant leader behaviours are tolerated as long as it is clear that they are for the benefit of the group rather than the individual leader.

Yet we are very different from other primates in that we are able to exercise considerable self-control in conflict situations. As a result of our living for so long in highly interdependent, egalitarian groups, evolution has equipped humans with the ability to solve conflicts through consensus – anything to keep group unity – and this has shifted the balance in our power relations from dominance to leadership. Leadership is not about alpha male but *primus inter pares*, or the first among equals.

So Natural Leaders avoid, at all costs, this impulsive primate tendency to dominate. They seek consensus for their plans and build teams of dedicated but critical followers around them. Their Darwinian ambition – to achieve reproductive success through accumulating power – might still be there, but it is directed to ensuring the group succeeds. Reassuringly, research suggests that self-reported dominance does not predict leadership success in most modern organisations. This means that there is no scholarly basis for the commonly held idea that a person needs to dominate to get ahead. Occasionally, though, dominating and manipulating leaders do emerge. They usually harbour the sinister set of personality traits called the Dark Triad; the result is Artificial Leaders high in narcissism, Machiavellianism and psychopathy. Anyone scoring highly on any of these traits is capable of charming or forcing their way into positions of power. Charm offensives are hard to maintain, however, and Dark Triad leaders – whom we can think of as a shade of Artificial

Leader – are inevitably outed in the end as subordinates discover their true colours. Often, these leaders will move from place to place, to avoid being rumbled, or they are eventually dismissed. They thrive in today's global village, because they can move with ease from company to company, city to city, even country to country. Potential employers should be on their guard when confronted with an applicant who has moved job frequently, and should try to find out from a third-party source why.

Dark Triad leaders, however, come into their own if an organisation wants to dominate, exploit or outmanoeuvre outsiders. For example, Peter Mandelson, the British politician, is regarded as a cunning tactician and has even been labelled the Dark Prince (one British newspaper raised £739 by selling a copy of Machiavelli's *The Prince* that Mandelson had autographed). He is regarded with suspicion within British politics but excelled at his four-year posting as European Commissioner for Trade, deploying his artfulness on behalf of the UK in tough negotiations with other countries.

10. Don't judge a leader by his or her cover

Evolution has shaped our leadership psychology. Our argument, enshrined in evolutionary leadership theory, is that during the course of human evolution there has been selection for cognitive mechanisms that enabled our ancestors to make appropriate, fitness-enhancing decisions regarding who to follow and when. These psychological mechanisms, discussed in Chapter 6, consist of various if-then decision rules which trigger adaptive decisions about who to follow in critical situations. Each situation – say, hunger or attack – is associated with a certain kind of leader (a CALP, or cognitive ancestral leader prototype). Priming people with thoughts of war, for example, causes them to nominate a more masculine figure. In addition to warfare, we theorise that a number of other ancestral situations, such as peacekeeping, conflict management, exploring, teaching and sharing resources, selected for a certain kind of leader.

But here is the crucial point: these prototypes are part of our long, winding evolutionary heritage, and we should consider whether they are still applicable to our 21st-century lives, which are so dramatically different from the meagre existences eked out by our distant ancestors. There is little doubt that many prototypical personality traits associated with good leadership are still functional today; we still have universally valued traits such as trustworthiness, humility, moral integrity and competence. But we should question whether such factors as physique and gender are still functional (or useful) today. For instance, physical strength and robust health may have mattered in ancestral times, when food was scarce and battles were frequent, but should these characteristics still be critical to leadership success in today's well-fed, relatively peaceful societies? Today's leaders rarely lead from the front, in the physical way that our ancestors did, so we might expect psychological qualities to matter more.

Again, although male leadership is the norm in pre-industrial societies we should be wary of excluding women. In today's global village, business and politics bring people of different cultures together. Interpersonal skills and network-building are supremely valuable abilities. There is good evidence that women leaders, armed with superior empathic and verbal skills, cope better in these novel environments. While our 'think leader think male' bias might be difficult to overcome, we should be aware that it might prejudice our consideration of talented women candidates.

Status is a major factor in the gender debate: evolution has selected men to be more ambitious and status-obsessed than women because, for them, these behaviours translated into ancestral reproductive success. When men and women work together, men are quicker to assume the position of a leader even when a better-qualified woman is present. Illuminatingly, Charles A. O'Reilly III, a Stanford University business professor, concludes it is not gender per se which leads to the glass ceiling for women, but the overwhelming male desire to compete.[13] It is an interesting rewording of the evolutionary imperative we've already discussed (and he found it was the most masculine men who excelled).

So, the existence of these cognitive ancestral leader prototypes can bias the leadership selection process. How do we bypass these ancestral prejudices? By becoming aware of them in the first place, as some selection panels already are. In some countries, such as the USA, candidates omit their gender and age from application forms

It is also pertinent to rethink those astronomical pay packages; not only do sky-high salaries perpetuate gross inequality in companies and foster ill-will on the shop floor, they attract mainly men. Since rewards and privileges signal status, which increases a man's sexual allure, men are drawn to well-paid positions like bees to a honeypot. And many of these men, who regard the post as a way to further their own needs rather than those of the company or group, will be anything but a sweet deal for the company, especially if they turn out to be Dark Triad leaders.

Our suggestion is that reducing remuneration packages, and making it easier for women to combine professional with domestic responsibilities, would encourage more women to apply for and stay in top management positions. As we saw in Chapter 6, appointing women to senior management positions has proven benefits in terms of corporate governance. And you have to wonder whether the going rates for top executives are justified simply because they are the going rates for top executives. It is a circular argument that doesn't seem to have any genuine substance. Here is what Sir Stuart Rose, the newly crowned chief executive of Marks & Spencer, said, on gaining his dream job in 2004, which came with a £1.25 million 'golden hello' as well as a multimillion-pound salary:

'Much as I love the business, they would have thought I was soft in the head if I said I would come here for nothing. It was a very reasonable commercial rate for the job.'[14]

Our take on over-inflated CEO rewards? Someone has to blink first.

Envoi

For those of you who don't know Rick Rescorla, he was a warrior, a leader, and a friend.

Larry Gwin, at a reunion of Vietnam veterans after Rescorla's death, held to commemorate the 1965 Battle of Ia Drang, one of the first conflicts in the Vietnam War

Appendix A
Six Natural Leaders – a questionnaire

Evolutionary leadership theory suggests that Natural Leadership consists of a set of different leadership functions or roles, each with their own evolved psychology. As we have argued throughout the book, followers have specific ideas about what constitutes effective leadership in terms of achieving a variety of different adaptive goals, such as protecting the group, finding food and keeping the peace. We referred to these as CALPs – cognitive ancestral leadership prototypes. Based on the biological, anthropological and psychological literature, we speculate here on the existence of six different leader prototypes. You could think of them as six different types of Natural Leaders.

It is important to stress that research into this idea is at an early stage; our six types of Natural Leader remain a scholarly hunch. To explore this possibility, we have devised a questionnaire to test whether our classification is robust. If you are curious as to where your leadership talents might lie, we would suggest completing the test first and then reading on. Bear in mind that our intention is not to pigeonhole. It might turn out that people really can be split into six (or more, or fewer) leadership categories; or it might not. Only further research will tell; we will post updates on www.professormarkvanvugt.com.

Ancestral leadership prototypes questionnaire: what kind of leader are you?

In *Selected*, we propose a new way of measuring leadership that is based on evolutionary leadership theory. Our research, based on the most common leadership functions carried out in ancestral groups, suggests that there might be six leadership prototypes. We currently think that individual leaders differ in the emphasis they give to each of these roles.

Part 1

When you are in charge of a group, any group, to what extent are the following considerations important to your actions and beliefs? Rate yourself using the scale below, for each category, and then proceed to part 2.

1 = extremely unimportant
2 = moderately unimportant
3 = slightly unimportant
4 = neither important nor unimportant
5 = slightly important
6 = moderately important
7 = extremely important

Category A
Whether the group is doing better than other groups
Whether the group is strong and competitive
Whether the group is able to defend itself

Category B
Whether the group requires extra resources
Whether the group needs to expand
Whether the group should recruit new members

Category C

Whether the group has a positive reputation
Whether the group maintains friendly relations with other groups
Whether the group is being represented

Category D

Whether the group is cohesive
Whether group conflicts are being resolved
Whether group members are being too selfish

Category E

Whether the group accomplishes its tasks
Whether the group operates efficiently
Whether every group member gets a fair deal

Category F

Whether group members receive training
Whether the group traditions are being followed
Whether newcomers are being socialised into the group

Part 2

Please read the following statements and indicate your agreement or disagreement using this scale

1 = extremely unimportant
2 = moderately unimportant
3 = slightly unimportant
4 = neither important nor unimportant
5 = slightly important
6 = moderately important
7 = extremely important

Whenever I am in charge of a group …

Category A

I want the group to be ahead of other groups
I defend the group against criticism from outsiders
I am devastated when other groups do better

Category B

I am on the lookout for new members
I make sure that the group gets additional resources
I am concerned that the group is too small

Category C

I act as the spokesperson
I keep the group in good standing with authorities
I negotiate on the group's behalf with other groups

Category D

I intervene in arguments and conflicts
I make sure that everyone gets on well with everyone else
I tell off individuals who do not pull their weight

Category E

I look after the finances of the group
I direct and organise the activities of the group
I make sure that things get done

Category F

I look after the traditions of the group
I pass on knowledge and information to group members
I am keen that everyone knows about the group norms

Add up the scores in each category for Part 1 and Part 2. This gives you an overall score per category, which ranges from the minimum score of 6 points (6 × 1) to the maximum score of 42 points (6 × 7). The highest category score represents your dominant leadership role and the lowest category score represents your least prominent leadership role.

These prototypes are: (A) the Warrior, whose expertise lies in defending the group; (B) the Scout, who is adept at seeking new resources and opportunities; (C) the Diplomat, who has a natural affinity for liaising with other groups; (D) the Arbiter, who seems to be the peacekeeper within the group, keeping followers united; (E) the Manager, who is efficient at allocating resources and getting things done; and (F) the Teacher, an enthusiastic and effective transmitter of knowledge to group members.

We'll now look in turn at each of these six leader prototypes, at their accompanying psychologies and even in some cases their own unique physiologies.

A. The Warrior

The primary role of the Warrior is to defend the group against external threats. In ancestral human environments these comprised predators such as leopards and snakes and hostile out-groups roaming the savannah. Warriors are fierce and physically formidable individuals and they can be recognised by their masculine build (strong jaws, low eyebrows) – they are nearly always male. Psychologically they have a set of traits that set them apart from others: bravery, competitiveness, a dominant streak and a high pain threshold. They border on psychopathy in terms of their relentless ambition and cold-heartedness towards dissidents and defectors but they also identify strongly with their group and are extremely loyal. Modern manifestations of these Warrior types are international statesmen such as Sir Winston Churchill and Joseph Stalin, sports managers such as Sir Alex Ferguson and José Mourinho, and footballers such as Diego Maradona and Vinnie Jones. Business people operating in a very competitive, ruthless environment such as Lee Iaccoca, former CEO of Chrysler, can be considered Warriors. We can also place our hero, Rick Rescorla, here.

B. The Scout

The Scout specialises in seeking resources and opportunities for the group. In ancestral environments he would have ventured out on his own, or in a small group, to search for new waterholes or hunting grounds. He is an explorer, a discoverer.

Scouts don't need to look physically formidable; they do, however, need endless stamina and must be able to stand high levels of frustration. They are nearly always male. Their psychological hallmarks include curiosity, intelligence, impatience, risk-taking and openness to new experiences. They also tend to have individualistic personalities; they like to be solitary and do things on their own. We can class great explorers such as Roald Amundsen and Sir Ernest Shackleton as Scouts: also, scientists such as Charles Darwin, Sir Isaac Newton and DNA pioneer Craig Venter; plus entrepreneurs such as Richard Branson, Bill Gates and Steve Jobs.

C. The Diplomat

The Diplomat excels at forming and maintaining alliances with other groups. In ancestral human environments it was important for bands to have allies that they could rely upon for sharing scarce waterholes, exchanging brides, and for assistance in fighting other groups. Diplomat leaders maintained this valuable network of relationships. They are generally not physically imposing (to avoid being perceived by outsiders as threatening), and tend to be shorter and of a relatively feminine appearance. They are verbally gifted and operate with a lot of tact and manipulation. Psychologically, they can be distinguished by their charm, agreeableness and social intelligence, but also by their Machiavellianism. Modern manifestations of these types are international US diplomats such as Henry Kissinger, Condoleezza Rice and Hillary Clinton, great ambassadors for sports such as Pelé and Michel Platini, notable stateswomen such as Elizabeth I or Queen Juliana (the bicycle queen of the Netherlands), humanitarians such as Mother Teresa, and UN secretary-generals such as Kofi Annan and Ban Ki-moon.

D. The Arbiter

The Arbiter is mainly a peacekeeper, maintaining and restoring harmony within a group. Ancestral human societies were riven by conflict; men would often fight to the death over important matters, including women. Arbiters made sure that these threats were dealt with, sometimes by stepping in to ensure that group cohesion was not compromised. We draw a distinction between peacekeepers and peacemakers; they may not necessarily be the same people.

Depending on their roles, Arbiters can be physically imposing, but they wear their stature lightly. The most successful ones have a soft touch, and don't elicit aggression. That's why (older) women also generally make good police officers, and they are often used to intervene in fights between drunken men on a Saturday night. Psychologically, they display emotional stability, verbal skills, empathy and a keen sense of justice. Modern manifestations of the Arbiter types are Supreme Court judges in the USA and their UK equivalents, the Law Lords, high-ranking policemen and sports referees such as Pierluigi Collina, the widely admired, retired football official.

E. The Manager

The Manager's role was to allocate resources and organise group activities. In ancestral human environments the Manager distributed food and water, oversaw the arrangement of campsites and ensured the provision of labour for collective works. They did not stand out physically, but they tended not to be very emotionally expressive because of their lack of charismatic qualities. Managers could be described as dull but functional (although you wouldn't catch a Diplomat saying it). Their unique psychological skill set comprises a high conscientiousness, patience and good planning skills. They are also democratic and fair. Modern manifestations are technocratic nation-state leaders such as Angela Merkel and Jan-Peter Balkenende, the successful CEOs you've never heard of (Howard Schultz of Starbucks, Jim Skinner of McDonald's), and generally the kind of executive leadership we see in universities and governments. One study, by Steven Kaplan, which looked at the personalities of 316 CEOs and linked them to success, found that those at the helms of the most successful companies showed the following Manager-like attributes: attention to detail, persistence, the ability to work hard, and conscientiousness.[1]

F. The Teacher

The Teacher transmits important knowledge to children and other newcomers to groups. In ancestral human environments Teachers were experts on the natural world (which plants to eat and which medicines to use) and social relationships. They could also communicate with the 'other' world, the world of the gods. They are often referred to as shamans in hunter-gatherer groups. These shamans or teachers do not actively lead people but they pass on useful knowledge that benefits the group, such as medicinal know-how and traditions. They foster group cohesion by protecting the culture of the group. These individuals are usually not physically impressive and they may even have a handicap which makes them unsuited to physically demanding tasks. Psychologically, though, they stand out in terms of their openness to experience, intellect, empathy, communication and oratorical skills. They are usually charismatic. Today, we can think of religious figures such as the Pope and Desmond Tutu as Teachers; charismatic politicians such as Barack Obama and Tony Blair can also be counted. Bono and Oprah Winfrey are two showbusiness figures whose brands of wisdom and knowledge are eagerly sought.

Appendix B
The natural history of leadership

Stage	Society	Time period	Number of individuals
1	Pre-human	> 2 million years ago	Any number
2	Band, clan, tribe	2 million to 13,000 years ago	Dozens to hundreds
3	Chiefdom	13,000 to 250 years ago	Thousands
4	Nation, state, large business	250 years ago to the present	Thousands to millions

This table provides a short natural history of leadership, suggesting that its evolution has gone through four distinct stages, from prehuman leadership to leadership in modern complex societies.

This table has been adapted from one that was originally published in *American Psychologist* in 2008.[1]

Primary coordination problem	Leadership structure	Leader	Leader–follower relations
Group movement, peace-keeping (non-human primates)	Situational	Any individual or Dominant (non-human primates)	Situational or hierarchical (non-human primates)
Group movement, peace-keeping	Informal, expertise-based	Big Man	Egalitarian
Intergroup relations	Centralised, hereditary	Chiefs, kings, warlords	Hierarchical
Peacekeeping, intergroup relations	Centralised, democratic	Heads of state, CEOs	Hierarchical but participatory

Glossary

Adaptation: a trait or behaviour that has evolved over the course of human history, owing to the immense reproductive benefit it afforded

Ambivalence hypothesis of leadership: followers want to be led but not dominated, and it is easier for leaders to dominate than to persuade

Artificial leaders: individuals whose leadership styles clash with our ancestral psychology

Behavioural leadership theory: posits that effective leadership results from certain behaviours

Big Five personality scale: embraces what psychologists consider the five main dimensions of personality: agreeableness, extraversion, neuroticism, conscientiousness, openness to experience

Charismatic leadership theory: posits that a leader rises to a position of power not through what he does, but through what he is, and his ascent comes through unwavering self-belief (and sometimes narcissism). He is a human magnet; people feel drawn to him because of his personality and stirring rhetoric

Cognitive ancestral leader prototype (CALP): someone who closely fits the archetypal profiles of good leadership

Contingency leadership theory: maintains that there is no single successful leadership style; instead, effective leadership is contingent on a number of different factors, such as the type of organisation involved and the goal to be achieved

Dark Triad: narcissism, Machiavellianism, psychopathy

Distributed (or dispersed/emergent) leadership: suggests that leadership is most effective when it is not concentrated in one pair of hands but spread around, with people of all ranks taking up leadership roles if they have the requisite expertise

Dunbar's Number: the maximum number of people in a social network that can be held together informally and without external control, estimated to be 150

Evolutionary leadership theory (ELT): the first scientific theory of leadership consistent with evolutionary theory that attempts to integrate knowledge from across the behavioural sciences

Game theory: a mathematical approach that allows scientists to model the behaviour of individuals as agents interacting with each other over a particular time period

Great Man theory: posits that truly great leaders are born, not made

Leader: someone able to exert social influence on others in order to accomplish a common goal

Leadership creep: occurs when a leader in one domain assumes leadership in another, unrelated field

Leonardo effect: the trait in those subject to little or no positive fathering to seek to become the father they never had (after Leonardo da Vinci)

Male warrior hypothesis: the evolved propensity of men to form coalitions with other men to initiate, plan and execute attacks on other groups

Mismatch Hypothesis: contends that our relatively primitive brains, which prime us for membership of fairly small, egalitarian tribes, find it tough to cope with the mammoth corporate and civic structures of the 21st century

Natural Leaders: those who run their organisations in a way that fits our ancestral psychology – and take pains to overcome the biases inherent in them

Natural selection: the theory first elucidated by Charles Darwin in the nineteenth century which contends that certain individuals thrive better than others in their environment and that these 'fitter' individuals out-reproduce their less fit compatriots

Power inversion paradox: reflects the fact that, owing to power differentials, the most powerful party tends to be excluded from any coalition

Psychoanalytic theory: posits that the charisma of a leader arises from the strong emotional bond of love and fear linking follower to leader, mirroring the bond between father and child

Rainbow leader: a rare individual who is competent in multiple domains; a Jack-of-all-trades rather than the master of one

Reverse dominance hierarchy: in which the rank and file rise up to collectively quash their self-appointed superiors

Savannah Hypothesis: contends that we still choose our leaders as if we are appointing Big Men to protect us from aggressors and predators on the savannah, which is why we consistently favour tall, fit, strong-looking males

Selective exploitation effect: whereby managers treat subordinates who have no exit opportunities worse than subordinates who do

Servant leadership: a style of leadership characterised by humility, empathy, a sense of community, a respect for ethics and responsible stewardship of a group's resources; leaders take on their roles at some cost to themselves to serve the group

Situational leadership theory: predicated on the assumption that the type of leadership required depends on the situation

STEPs: Strategies To Enhance Power

STOPs: Strategies To Overcome the Powerful

Three S's: salary, status and sex

Trait theory: a derivative of the Great Man theory, which posits that leaders are distinguished by the traits or attributes they display, such as integrity and trustworthiness

Transactional versus transformational leadership theory: contrasts a conventional style of leadership with a more visionary, inspirational style

Notes

Prologue

1 John Mackey's letter is extracted here, along with the news of his company's UK opening: http://news.bbc.co.uk/1/hi/uk/6726969. stm

2 Lawrence Ellison, CEO of Oracle, was compensated to the tune of almost $57m in 2009, making him the world's most richly rewarded executive that year: http://people.forbes.com/profile/ larry-ellison/60466

3 For generic introductions to evolutionary psychology see Barrett, Dunbar and Lycett (2005), and Buss (2008). For introductions to human evolution and the origins of human behaviour see Boyd and Silk (2008) or Laland and Brown (2002).

4 Mismatch is a concept from evolutionary biology that refers to the fact that traits that were adaptive in ancestral environments might no longer produce adaptive behaviours in modern environments, especially when these environments dramatically differ (see Crawford and Krebs, 2008).

5 For further information on ancestral leadership roles check out www.professormarkvanvugt.com or the website of the Netherlands Institute for Management and Evolutionary Psychology, imep. wordpress.com/nimep

1: The Nature of Leadership

We have drawn for part of this chapter on van Vugt, Hogan and Kaiser (2008). There is a voluminous literature on the psychology of leadership. Two especially good recent overviews are Bass and Bass (2008) and Yukl (2009).

1   The story of Rick Rescorla is recounted in James Stewart's moving *New Yorker* article entitled 'The real heroes are dead', 11 February 2002.

2   See Brown (1991) for a description of human universals. In his enjoyable little book, anthropologist Donald Brown describes the behaviours, including leadership, that are shared worldwide by introducing a fictitious people, the Universal People.

3   See Ludwig (2004) for his investigation of political leaders around the globe to get a feel for the perks and privileges associated with political leadership.

4   See Hogan and Kaiser (2005).

5   See Ohman and Mineka (2001).

6   See Betzig (1986).

7   For a general introduction into the scientific literature on leadership, see Yukl (2009).

8   See Burns (1978).

9   See Ludwig (2004).

10   See Darwin (1859). For more books on Darwin's ideas and life, see notes for Chapter 2.

11   See Carlyle (1841).

12   See Plutarch.

13   'In praise of the decisive CEO' by Stephen Plotkin, *New York Times*, 3 February 2008, in which Plotkin reviews *Judgment: How Winning Leaders Make Great Calls* by Noel M. Tichy and Warren G. Bennis, Penguin, 2007.

14   Jack Welch's profile can be found at http://www.ge.com/company/history/bios/john_welch.html. He and his wife, Suzy Welch, boast their own website at www.welchway.com. You can learn way too much about how Jack made Suzy his third wife by reading a transcript of their interview with Dan Rather at http://www.cbsnews.com/stories/2005/03/24/60II/main682830_page2.shtml.

15   See Bass and Bass (2008).

16   See Boring (1950). Boring is, perhaps, best known for introducing the young girl–old woman perceptual illusion to a wide audience; the various depictions are now called Boring figures (you can find them at http://mathworld.wolfram.com/YoungGirl-OldWomanIllusion.html).

17   See Stodgill (1974).

18   See Bass and Bass (2008).

19   See Ilies, Gerhardt and Le (2004).

20   See Freud (1950).

21   See Piovenalli (2005).

22   See McNamara and Trumbull (2007) and Bass and Bass (2008).

23   See McGregor (1968) for more on Theory X/Theory Y leadership.

24   See Tannenbaum and Schmidt (1973).

25   See Fiedler (1967). Fiedler's analysis bears similarities with the
      Ohio State Leadership Studies, dating back to the 1940s (see
      http://en.wikipedia.org/wiki/Leadership_studies).

26   See Bass and Avolio (1994).

27   See Barry (1991).

28   See Greenleaf (2002).

2: It's all just a game

We have drawn for parts of this chapter on van Vugt (2006) and King,
Johnson and van Vugt (2009).

1   To get the full buzz on bees, try the classic book by von Frisch
     (1967).

2   See King, Johnson and van Vugt (2009).

3   For a recent overview of how game theory can be used to
     understand social behaviour, see Gintis (2007).

4   See Krause and Ruxton (2002).

5   See Franks and Richardson (2006).

6   See van Vugt and Kurzban (2007).

7   See Brosnan, Newton-Fisher and van Vugt (2009) about
     personality differences in animals.

8   See Harcourt, Sweetman, Johnstone and Manica (2009).

9   See Hogan (2006).

10   See Bass and Bass (2008).

11   See King, Johnson and van Vugt (2009).

12   See Schjelderup-Ebbe (1922) for the classic paper on pecking order
     in hens.

13   Quoted from de Waal (1996).

14   Quoted from Boehm (1999).

15 See Conradt and Roper (2003).

16 See Kummer (1968).

17 Charles Darwin revealed his ideas about evolution – without using the word itself – in *On the Origin of Species*, published in 1859. Officially, Darwin shares credit for the idea of evolution by natural selection with Alfred Russel Wallace, who was thinking similar zoological thoughts on voyages around the Malay Archipelago. The two men wrote a joint paper which was presented to the Linnean Society of London in 1858. For other books on Darwin's ideas and life, see *Darwin's Dangerous Idea* by Daniel Dennett (Simon and Schuster, 1995), Robert Wright's *The Moral Animal* (Vintage, 1994) and *Darwin's Island* (Little, Brown, 2009) by Steve Jones. *The Greatest Show on Earth* by Richard Dawkins (Bantam, 2009) is also a stylish, modern introduction to the evidence for evolution by natural selection, naturally taking aim at religiously inclined opponents.

18 For generic introductions to evolutionary psychology see Barrett, Dunbar and Lycett (2005) and Buss (2008).

19 See Dunbar (2004) and Dunbar (2010).

20 See van Vugt and Schaller (2008).

21 See Tinbergen (1963).

22 For a discussion of prisoner's dilemma and other economic games, see Kelley et al. (2003).

23 See Dunbar (2004).

24 See van Vugt (2006) and (2009).

25 See Hogan (2006).

26 See Simonton (2006).

27 See Paulhus and Williams (2002).

28 See Iredale, van Vugt and Dunbar (2008).

29 See Chagnon (1988).

30 See Meier and Dionne (2009).

3: Born to follow

We have drawn for parts of this chapter on van Vugt (2008).

1 The classic social psychology experiment that opens the chapter was first conducted by Milgram, Bickman and Berkowitz (1969). It is an illustration of social contagion – taking the behaviour of others as a guide to how we should behave.

2   See Kellerman (2008). Interestingly, typing 'leadership' into Google produced 114m search results; 'followership' produced 120,000 results.

3   See van Vugt and Kurzban (2007).

4   The internet is swimming with details about Bernard Madoff's fraud. Here's one summary from *The Times*, about the lengths rich investors went to in order to join his scheme: http://business. timesonline.co.uk/tol/business/industry_sectors/banking_and_ finance/article5349168.ece.

5   See Krause and Ruxton (2002).

6   See Darwin (1871).

7   See Chance (1967).

8   The tale of Christopher McCandless is recounted in Jon Krakauer's *Into the Wild* (Villard/Random House, 1996).

9   See Bandura (1978) on social learning theory.

10 See Schmitt and Pilcher (2004) for an excellent discussion on how to find evidence for psychological adaptations.

11 See Hains and Muir (1996).

12 See Bowlby (1969).

13 Quoted from Sigmund Freud's *Moses and Monotheism* (Hogarth Press, 1939).

14 The Princes's Trust report on teenagers and gangs can be found at: http://www.princes-trust.org.uk/news_2009/080800_youth_ communities.aspx.

15 For a discussion of the Leonardo effect, see Strenger and Burak (2006).

16 *The Fiery Chariot: A Study of British Prime Ministers and the Search for Love* by Lucille Iremonger, Secker and Warburg, 1970.

17 Few can surpass William Golding, in his 1954 book *Lord of the Flies* (Faber and Faber), when it comes to imagining a parentless world ruled by children.

18 See Sherif (1966).

19 See Bass and Bass (2008).

20 See Gillet, Cartwright and van Vugt (2010).

21 See Milgram (1974). The book contains a full account of his famous obedience experiments.

22 For the way that ZenithOptimedia, a firm that compiles

marketing information, calculated that the worldwide advertising industry was worth around $400 billion in 2005, see: http://enterpriseinnovator.com/index.php?articleID=5660andsectionID=269. The firm estimated the figure had risen to $454 billion by 2007. As a comparison, that's about the same amount that is spent each year by the US government on infrastructure (hospitals, schools, roads, emergency services, etc.).

23   See Richerson and Boyd (2005).

24   See Jenness (1932).

25   See Asch (1955). Interestingly, men are more likely to show nonconformity if they are being watched by an attractive woman, because it makes them stand out (particularly if their contrarian position cannot be shown to be wrong). So they'll go against the norm, as long as rebelling doesn't make them look like a chump. See Griskevicius et al. (2006).

26   For an account of the Heaven's Gate mass suicide, see: http://edition.cnn.com/US/9803/25/heavens.gate/. Chillingly, the website announcing the cult's intention to 'exit Earth' when Comet Hale-Bopp arrived is still up (www.heavensgate.com).

27   See Sosis (2000).

28   See *Join Me* by Danny Wallace (Ebury Press, 2003) to find out how alarmingly easy it is to get people to join something for the sake of joining. Wallace runs the group's website at www.join-me.co.uk.

29   See Chaleff (2009).

30   See Kellerman (2008).

31   A summary of Cialdini's pioneering research on social influence can be found in Cialdini and Goldstein (2004).

32   The extraordinary inside story of the Lehman Brothers – and the almost cultlike deference required of its senior employees – is covered by Vicky Ward in *The Devil's Casino* (John Wiley and Sons, 2010).

4: Status seeking on the savannah: the democratic ape

1   See Boehm (1999), Dunbar (2004), Foley (1997) and Richerson and Boyd (2005).

2   Cited in Boehm (1999). The quote comes from a book by E. Lucas Bridges, *Uttermost Part of the Earth* (Dutton, 1949). A delightful review of the book can be found at http://www.time.com/time/magazine/article/0,9171,780243,00.html.

3   See Knauft (1987).

4   See Sahlins (1963) for a discussion of Big Men societies.

5   See Mitchell (1978) and (1988).

6   Authoritative reviews of the potlatch ceremony written for the layman seem hard to source, but the Wikipedia entry on potlatch is a useful starting point for further reading. For information on modern philanthropy, including lists of top donors, try philanthropyuk.org.

7   This research is discussed in Hardy and van Vugt (2006) and van Vugt and Hardy (2010).

8   See Harcourt and de Waal (1992).

9   See de Waal (1982).

10   See Trivers (1971) and van Vugt and van Lange (2006).

11   See Brosnan and de Waal (2003).

12   See Bowles and Gintis (2002) for more on the intriguing idea of Homo reciprocans.

13   See Murnighan (1978) for a discussion of coalitional theory.

14   See Curry and van Vugt (2010).

15   The 20th anniversary of the Pan-European Picnic, so pivotal in the dismantling of the Communist bloc, was widely covered in 2009: http://news.bbc.co.uk/1/hi/8209173.stm.

16   See Ruffle (1998).

17   The experiment is discussed in van Vugt, Jepson, Hart and de Cremer (2004).

18   For the stone-throwing chimp, see Osvath (2009).

19   Schneider is quoted in Boehm (1999).

20   See Dunbar (2004) for treatment of the evolutionary origins of gossip and language.

21   Mervyn Meggitt is widely believed to have written one of the earliest ethnographic accounts of warfare, in his book *Blood Is Their Argument* (Mayfield Publishing Company, 1977).

22   See Lee (1979).

23   Appropriately enough, Beatrice K. Otto's book, *Fools Are Everywhere: The Court Jester Around the World*, was published on 1 April 2001 by University of Chicago Press.

24   For a eye-opening read on bossnapping, including the amusingly relaxed attitude the French have towards the idea of their

managers being handcuffed to the photocopier, check out 'Sure, kidnap the boss', *Newsweek*, 5 May 2009.

25 See Eisenberger, Lieberman and Williams (2003).

26 See Henrich and Gil-White (2001).

5: The birth of corruption

We have drawn for part of this chapter on van Vugt, Hogan and Kaiser (2008). There is a voluminous literature on the evolution of political institutions. Especially good overviews are by Diamond (1997) and Johnson and Earle (2000). For a Darwinian view of despotism and reproductive success in history, see Betzig (1986).

1   An extraordinary profile of Mbutu can be found in the *Time* magazine article, 'Leaving fire in his wake', by Adam Zagorin Gbadolite, 24 June 2001.

2   See Ludwig (2004)

3   See Diamond (1997).

4   See Hastorf (2009).

5   See Diamond (1997) and Johnson and Earle (2000).

6   See Richerson and Boyd (2005) and Tishkoff et al. (2006).

7   See Johnson and Earle (2000).

8   See van Vugt, Hogan and Kaiser (2008).

9   See Betzig (1986) for the link between power and reproductive success.

10 See Daniels and Bright (1996).

11 See van Vugt, Hogan and Kaiser (2008).

12 'Fears of brain drain from Scotland as Obama lifts stem-cell ban', *The Scotsman*, 10 March 2009.

13 See Wrangham and Peterson (1996).

14 See Hardy and van Vugt (2006).

15 See Galinsky, Magee, Inesi and Gruenfeld (2006).

16 See Kipnis (1972).

17 See de Cremer and van Dijk (2005).

18 See Paulhus and Williams (2002).

19 *The Prince*, Niccoló Machiavelli, Penguin Classics, 2003.

20 See Jonason, Li, Webster and Schmitt (2009).

21 The astonishing details of the scandal surrounding British MPs'

expenses are summarised in *No Expenses Spared* by Robert Winnett and Gordon Rayner (Bertrams, 2009).

22   See O'Gorman, Henrich and van Vugt (2008).

23   See Gurerk, Irlenbusch and Rockenbach (2006).

24   Cited in Diamond (1997).

25   See Curry and van Vugt, M. (2010).

26   Poll on press freedom to mark the BBC World Service's 75th anniversary in 2007: http://www.bbc.co.uk/pressoffice/ pressreleases/stories/2007/12_december/10/poll.pdf.

6: The Mismatch Hypothesis

We have drawn for parts of this chapter on van Vugt, Johnson, Kaiser and O'Gorman (2008). Discussions of the mismatch idea can be found in Barkow, Cosmides and Tooby (1992). Overviews of the influence of savannah traits on leadership can be found in Bass and Bass (2008).

1   See Hogan, Curphy and Hogan (1994).

2   See Dunbar (2004) and Foley (1997).

3   See Pinker (2002).

4   See Xue et al. (2009).

5   See Barkow, Cosmides and Tooby (1992).

6   See Ohman and Mineka (2001).

7   See Levine, Prosser, Evans and Reicher (2005).

8   See Johnson and Earle (2000).

9   One of the main publications from The GLOBE project is den Hartog et al. (1999).

10   See Henrich and Gil-White (2001).

11   See van Vugt and de Cremer (1999) and de Cremer and van Vugt (2002).

12   The statistics from the Leeds University Business School appeared in the article 'Women in the boardroom help companies succeed' by Anjana Ahuja, *The Times*, 19 March 2010. One perceived advantage of female representation at senior levels is good governance, an issue addressed in 'The new sheriffs of Wall Street', *Time*, 24 May 2010. This interesting article highlights that, in the wake of the financial meltdown, women have earned prominent roles in regulating American banking. While we're on the theme, here is a piece on the under-representation of women in British

politics: http://www.guardian.co.uk/commentisfree/2010/may/12/new-coalition-politics-diversity-women.

13 For more on the male warrior hypothesis, see van Vugt, de Cremer and Janssen (2007).

14 See Judge and Cable (2004), also *Blink* by Malcolm Gladwell (Little Brown, 2005), in which Gladwell notes the unconscious prejudice that society harbours towards short men.

15 A non-evolutionary explanation of the development of cognitive leadership prototypes is discussed by Lord, Foti and de Vader (1984).

16 In 'Sorry Gordon, but your body politic doesn't match Putin's' (*Observer*, 1 November 2009), Catherine Bennett discusses how odd it seems for voters to be concerned with the fitness of their leaders.

17 See Perryman et al. (2010).

18 At least one person has taken drastic steps in order to be taken more seriously, as this story shows: 'Australian councillor, Hajnal Ban, has legs broken to become taller', *The Times*, 1 May 2009.

19 See Pawlowski, Dunbar and Lipowicz (2000) for a study on height and reproductive success in Polish men.

20 See Judge and Cable (2004) on how tall people earn more.

21 See Spisak and van Vugt (2010).

22 See Little, Burris, Jones and Roberts (2006).

23 See Livingston and Pearce (2009). They suggest, intriguingly, that the success of black figures such as Barack Obama and the Hollywood actor Will Smith might well be down to their soft, babylike facial features, which allow them to come across as unthreatening. See Rule and Ambady (2008) for more on the chiselled jaws of CEOs.

24 See van Vugt and Spisak (2008).

26 See Weber (1947).

27 See Cohen et al. (2004).

28 *Disappearing World: Ongka's Big Moka* was a 1976 documentary on gift-giving in the Kawelka tribe of New Guinea. 'Moka' refers to a system of exchange, in this case with pigs as the currency.

29 See McNamara and Trumbull (2007).

7: From savannah to boardroom: lessons in natural leadership

1   See Ross (1977). The fundamental attribution error formed the basis for an extremely funny and popular business book, *The No Asshole Rule* by Robert Sutton (Business Plus, 2007). The book advocated a simple two-step plan for identifying if a colleague's unpleasantness was temporary and situational, or whether he was a bona fide, 'certified asshole' (first, do encounters with him always leave you feeling worse about yourself, and second, does he always target more junior colleagues?).

2   'Overrated business "superstars" ' by Alan M. Webber, *USA Today*, posted online on 25 April 2005.

3   *The 48 Laws of Power* by Robert Greene and Joost Elffers, Viking, 1998.

4   *Outliers* by Malcolm Gladwell, Little, Brown, 2008.

5   'Gore-Tex gets made without managers' by Simon Caulkin, *Observer*, 2 November 2008.

6   *Victims of Groupthink* by Irving L. Janis, Boston, Houghton Mifflin Company, 1972.

7   *The Wisdom of Crowds* by James Surowiecki, New York, Doubleday, 2004.

8   The report by the Church Investors Group into executive remuneration can be found at its website, www.churchinvestorsgroup.org.uk.

9   *Eichmann in Jerusalem* by Hannah Arendt, Penguin Classics, 1963.

10 *Do the Right Thing: How Dedicated Employees Create Loyal Customers and Large Profits* by Jim Wharton, Wharton School Publishing, 2007.

11 'The importance of grandmothers in the lives of their children', physorg.com, posted 29 October 2009. It should be noted that current data suggests the so-called Grandmother Hypothesis applies only to maternal grandmothers, and that the presence of a paternal grandmother actually seems to raise the risk of a grandchild dying.

12 The Institute for Family Business collates information on the sector, which can be accessed through its website, www.ifb.org.uk.

13 'Women's careers: The impact of sex and gender identity on career attainment', Olivia A. O'Neill and Charles A. O'Reilly III, Stanford Graduate School of Business Working Paper No. 1775, 2004.

14   'On his marks' by Nils Pratley, *Guardian*, 5 June 2004.

Appendix A: Six Natural Leaders – a questionnaire

For more on the questionnaire and research updates, please visit www. professormarkvanvugt.com.

1   See Kaplan, Klebanov and Sorensen (2008).

Appendix B: The natural history of leadership

1   See van Vugt, Hogan and Kaiser (2008).

Bibliography

Antonakis, J., and Dalgas, O. (2009). 'Predicting elections; Child play', *Science*, 323, 1183.

Asch, S. A. (1955). 'Opinions and social pressure', *Scientific American*, 193, 31–5.

Bandura, A. (1978). 'Social learning theory of aggression', *Journal of Communication*, 28, 12–29.

Barkow, Jerome H., Cosmides, Leda, and Tooby, John, eds (1992). *The Adapted Mind: Evolutionary Psychology and the Generation of Culture*, New York, NY: Oxford University Press.

Barrett, L., Dunbar, R., and Lycett, J. (2005), *Human Evolutionary Psychology*, Palgrave.

Barry, D. (1991). 'Managing the boss-less teams: lessons in distributed leadership', *Organizational Dynamics*, 22 June.

Bass, B. M., and Avolio, B. J. (1994). *Improving Organizational Effectiveness Through Transformational Leadership*, Thousand Oaks, CA, Sage Publications.

Bass, B. M., and Bass, R. (2008). *The Bass Handbook of Leadership: Theory, Research and Managerial Applications*, 4th ed., Free Press, New York.

Betzig, L. L. (1986). *Despotism and Differential Reproduction; A Darwinian View of History*, Aldine Transaction.

Boehm, C. (1999). *Hierarchy in the Forest: The Evolution of Egalitarian Behaviour*, Harvard University Press.

Boring, E. G. (1950). 'Great men and scientific progress', *Proc. of the American Philosophical Society*, 94, no. 4.

Bowlby, J. (1969). *Attachment and Loss: Volume 1: Attachment*, London, The Hogarth Press and the Institute of Psycho-Analysis.

Bowles, S., and Gintis, H. (2002). 'Behavioural science: Homo reciprocans', *Nature*, 415, 125–8.

Boyd, R., and Silk, J. (2008). *How Humans Evolved*, 5th edn, W. W. Norton.

Brosnan, S., and de Waal, F. (2003). 'Monkeys reject unequal pay', *Nature*, 425, 297–9.

Brosnan, S. F., Newton-Fisher, N. E., and van Vugt, M. (2009). 'A melding of minds: When primatology meets social psychology', *Personality and Social Psychology Review*, 13, 129–47.

Brown, D. E. (1991). *Human Universals*, McGraw-Hill.

Burns, J. M. (1978). *Leadership*, New York, Harper and Row.

Buss, D. M. (2008). *Evolutionary Psychology, The New Science of the Mind*, 3rd edn, Allyn and Bacon.

Buss, D. M., ed. (2005). *The Handbook of Evolutionary Psychology*, Wiley.

Carlyle, T. (1841). *On Heroes, Hero Worship and The Heroic in History*.

Chagnon, N. A. (1988). 'Life histories, blood revenge, and warfare in a tribal population', *Science*, 239, 985–92.

Chaleff, I. (2009). *The Courageous Follower: Standing up to and for our leaders*. Berrett-Koehler Publishers.

Chance, M. R. A. (1967). 'Attention structure as the basis of primate rank orders', *Man*, 4, 504–18.

Cialdini, R., and Goldstein, N. (2004). 'Social influence: Compliance and conformity', *Annual Review of Psychology*, 35, 591–621.

Cohen, F., et al. (2004). 'Fatal attraction: The effects of mortality salience on political preferences as a function of leadership style', *Psychological Science*, 15, 846–51

Conradt, L., and Roper, T. (2003). 'Group decision making in animals', *Nature*, 421, 155–8.

Crawford, C., and Krebs, D. L. (2008). *Foundations of Evolutionary Psychology*, New York: Lawrence Erlbaum.

Curry, O., and van Vugt, M. (2010). 'The evolution of human coalition psychology', University of Oxford: unpublished manuscript.

Daniels, P. T., and Bright, D., eds. (1996). *The World's Writing Systems*, Oxford University Press.

Darwin, C. (1859). *On the Origin of Species*, John Murray.

Darwin, C. (1871). *The Descent of Man*, John Murray.

de Cremer, D., and van Dijk, E. (2005). 'When and why do leaders put themselves first?', *European Journal of Social Psychology*, 35, 553–63.

de Cremer, D., and van Vugt, M. (2002). 'Intra- and intergroup dynamics of leadership in social dilemmas: A relational model of cooperation', *Journal of Experimental Social Psychology, 38*, 126–36.

den Hartog, D., House, R. J., Hanges, P. J., Ruiz-Quintanilla, S. A., et al. (1999). 'Culture specific and cross culturally generalizable implicit leadership theories: Are attributes of charismatic/transformational leadership universally endorsed?', *Leadership Quarterly*, 10, 219–56.

de Waal, F. (1982). *Chimpanzee Politics: Power and Sex among Apes*, Johns Hopkins University Press.

de Waal, F. (1996). *Good Natured: The Origins of Right and Wrong in Humans and Other Animals*, Harvard University Press.

Diamond, J. (1997). *Guns, Germs and Steel*, London, Vintage.

Dunbar, R. (2004). *Grooming, Gossip and the Evolution of Language*, London, Faber and Faber.

Dunbar, R. (2010). *How Many Friends Does One Person Need?*, London, Faber and Faber.

Eisenberger, N. I., Lieberman, M. D., and Williams, K. D. (2003). 'Does rejection hurt? An FMRI study of social exclusion', *Science*, 302, 290–2.

Fiedler, F. (1967). *A Theory of Leadership Effectiveness*, McGraw-Hill.

Foley, R. A. (1997). 'The adaptive legacy of human evolution: A search for the environment of evolutionary adaptedness', *Evolutionary Anthropology*, 4, 194–203.

Franks, N. R., and Richardson, T. (2006). 'Teaching in tandem-running ants', *Nature*, 439, 153.

Freud, S. (1950). *Totem and Taboo*, London, Routledge.

Galinsky, A., Magee, J. C., Inesi, E., and Gruenfeld, D. (2006). 'Power and perspectives not taken', *Psychological Science*, 17, 1068–74.

Gillet, J., Cartwright, E., and van Vugt, M. (2010). 'Selfish or servant leadership? Leadership personalities in coordination games. Personality and individual differences', in press.

Gintis, H. (2007). 'A framework for the unification of the behavioral sciences', *Behavioral and Brain Sciences*, 30, 1–16.

Greenleaf, R. K. (2002). *Servant Leadership: A journey into the nature of legitimate power and greatness*, 25th anniversary edn, Paulist Press.

Griskevicius, V., Goldstein, N. J., Mortensen, C. R., Cialdini, R. B., and Kenrick, D. T. (2006). 'Going along versus going alone: When fundamental motives facilitate strategic (non)conformity', *Journal of Personality and Social Psychology*. 91(2), 281–94.

Gurerk, O., Irlenbusch, B., and Rockenbach, B. (2006). 'The competitive advantage of sanctioning institutions', *Science*, 312, 108–11.

Hains, S., and Muir, D. (1996). 'Infant sensitivity to adult eye direction', *Child development*. 67, 1940–51.

Harcourt, A., and de Waal, F. (1992). *Coalitions and Alliances in Humans and Other Animals*, Oxford University Press.

Harcourt, J. L., Sweetman, G., Johnstone, R. A., and Manica, A. (2009). 'Personality counts: The effects of boldness on shoal choice in three-spined sticklebacks', *Animal behaviour*, 77, 1501–5.

Hardy, C. L., and van Vugt, M. (2006). 'Nice guys finish first: The competitive altruism hypothesis', *Personality and Social Psychology Bulletin*, 32, 1402–13.

Hastorf, C. A. (2009). 'Rio Balsas most likely region for maize domestication', *Proceedings of the National Academy of Sciences*, 106: 4957–8.

Henrich, J., and Gil-White, F. J. (2001). 'The evolution of prestige: Freely conferred status as a mechanism for enhancing the benefits of cultural transmission', *Evolution and human behavior*, 22:165–96.

Hogan, R. (2006). *Personality and the Fate of Organizations*, LEA Inc.

Hogan, R., Curphy, G. J., and Hogan, J. (1994). 'What we know about leadership: effectiveness and personality', *American Psychologist*, 49, 493–504.

Hogan, R., and Kaiser, R. (2005). 'What we know about leadership', *Review of General Psychology*, 9, 169–80.

Ilies, R., Gerhardt, M., and Le, H. (2004). 'Individual differences in leadership emergence: Integrating meta-analytic findings and behavior genetics estimates', *International Journal of Selection and Assessment*, 12, 207–19.

Iredale, W., van Vugt., M., and Dunbar, R. (2008). 'Showing off in humans: male generosity as mate signal', *Evolutionary Psychology*, 6, 386–92.

Jenness, A. (1932). 'The role of discussion in changing opinion regarding a matter of fact', *The Journal of Abnormal and Social Psychology*, Vol. 27(3), 279–96.

Johnson, A. W., and Earle, T. (2000). *The Evolution of Human Societies: From Foraging Groups to Agrarian States*, Stanford University Press.

Jonason, P., Li, N., Webster, G., and Schmitt, D. (2009). 'The dark triad; Facilitating a short term mating strategy in men', *European Journal of Social Psychology*, 23, 5–18.

Judge, T. A., and Cable, D. M. (2004). 'The effect of physical height on workplace success and income: preliminary testing of a theoretical model', *Journal of Applied Psychology*, 89, 428–41

Kaplan, N., Klebanov, M., and Sorensen, M. (2008). 'Which CEO characteristics and abilities matter?', Swedish Institute for Financial Research Conference on the Economics of the Private Equity Market; AFA 2008 New Orleans Meetings Paper.

Kellerman, B. (2008). *Followership: How Followers are Creating Change and Changing Leaders*, Harvard Business Press.

Kelley, H. H., et al. (2003). *An Atlas of Interpersonal Situations*, Cambridge University Press.

King, A. J., Johnson, D. D. P., and van Vugt, M. (2009). 'The origins and evolution of leadership', *Current Biology*, 19, 1591–682.

Kipnis, D. (1972). 'Does power corrupt?', *Journal of Personality and Social Psychology*, 24, 33–41.

Knauft, B. M. (1987). 'Reconsidering violence in simple human societies: homicide among the Gebusi of New Guinea', *Current Anthropology*, 28, 457–500.

Krause, J., and Ruxton, G. (2002). *Living in Groups*, Oxford, Oxford University Press.

Kummer, H. (1968). *Social Organisation of Hamadryas Baboons*, University of Chicago Press.

Laland, K. N., and Brown, G. R. (2002). *Sense and Nonsense: Evolutionary Perspectives on Human Behaviour*, Oxford University Press.

Lee, R. B. (1979). *The !Kung San: Men, Women and Work in a Foraging Society*, Cambridge University Press.

Levine, M., Prosser, A., Evans, D., and Reicher, S. (2005). 'Identity and emergency intervention', *Personality and Social Psychology Bulletin*, 31, 443–53.

Little, A. C., Burris, R. P., Jones, B., and Roberts, S. C. (2006). 'Facial appearance affects voting decisions', *Evolution and Human Behavior*, 28, 18–27.

Livingston, R. W. and Pearce, N. (2009). 'The Teddy Bear Effect: does babyfaceness benefit black CEOs?', *Psychological Science*, 20, 1229–36.

Lord, R. G., Foti, R. J., and de Vader, C. L. (1984). 'A test of leadership categorization theory: Internal structure, information processing, and leadership perceptions', *Organizational Behavior and Human Performance*, Vol. 34, pp. 343–78.

Ludwig, A. (2004). *King of the Mountain: The Nature of Political Leadership*, Kentucky University Press.

McGregor, D. (1968). *Leadership and Motivation: Essays of Douglas McGregor*, MIT Press.

McNamara, P., and Trumbull, D. (2007). *An Evolutionary Psychology of Leader-Follower Relations*, Nova Publishers.

Meier, B. P., and Dionne, S. (2009). 'Downright sexy: verticality, implicit power, and perceived physical attractiveness', *Soc. Cognition*, 27, 883–92.

Milgram, S. (1974). *Obedience to authority: An Experimental View*, New York, Harper Row

Milgram, S., Bickman, L., and Berkowitz, O. (1969). 'Note on the drawing power of crowds of different size', *Journal of Personality and Social Psychology*, 13, 79–82.

Mitchell, W. (1978). *The Bamboo Fire: An Anthropologist in New Guinea*, Norton.

Mitchell, W. (1988). 'The defeat of hierarchy: gambling as exchange in a Sepik society', *American Ethnologist*, 15:638–57.

Murnighan, K. (1978). 'Models of coalition behaviour', *Psychological Bulletin*, 85, 1130–53.

O'Gorman, R., Henrich, J., and van Vugt, M. (2008). 'Constraining free riding in public goods games: designated solitary punishers can sustain human cooperation', *Proc R Soc B* 276, 323–9.

Ohman, A., and Mineka, S. (2001). 'Fears, phobias, and preparedness. Toward an evolved module of fear and fear learning', *Psychological Review*, 108, 483–522.

Osvath, M. (2009). 'Spontaneous planning for future stone throwing by a male chimpanzee', *Current Biology*, 19 (5): R190.

Paulhus, D., and Williams, K. M. (2002). 'The dark triad of personality: narcissism, Machiavellianism, and psychopathy', *Journal of Research in Personality*, 36, 556–63.

Pawlowski, B., Dunbar, R., and Lipowicz, A. (2000). 'Evolutionary fitness: Tall men have more reproductive success', *Nature*, 403, 156.

Perryman, A. A, et al. (2010). 'When the CEO is ill: Keeping quiet or going public?', *Business Horizons*, 53, 21–9.

Pinker, S. (2002). *The Blank Slate*, London, Penguin.

Piovenalli, P. (2005). 'Jesus's charismatic authority: On the historical applicability of a sociological model', *Journal of the American Academy of Religion*, 73(2): 395–427.

Plutarch. *Parallel Lives*, Penguin Classics.

Richerson, P., and Boyd, R. (2005). *Not by Genes Alone: How Culture Transformed Human Evolution*, University of Chicago Press.

Ross, L. (1977). 'The intuitive psychologist and his shortcomings: Distortions in the attribution process', in L. Berkowitz (ed.), *Advances in Experimental Social Psychology* (vol. 10), New York, Academic Press.

Ruffle, B. (1998). 'More is better but fair is fair: Tipping in dictator versus ultimatum game', *Games and Economic Behaviour*, 23, 247–65.

Rule, N. O., and Ambadi, N. (2008). 'The face of success: Inferences of personality from CEO appearance predict company profits', *Psychological Science*, 19, 109–11.

Sahlins, M. (1963). 'Poor man, rich man, big man, chief: Political types in Melanesia and Polynesia', *Comparative Studies in Society and History*, 5, 285–303.

Schjelderup-Ebbe, T. (1922). 'Beiträge zur Sozialpsychologie des Haushuhns', in *Zeitschrift für Psychologie* 88, 225–52.

Schmitt, D. P., and Pilcher, J. J. (2004). 'Evaluating evidence of psychological adaptation: How do we know one when we see one?', *Psychological Science*, 15, 643–9.

Sherif, M. (1966). *In common predicament: Social psychology of intergroup conflict and cooperation*, Boston, Houghton-Mifflin.

Simonton, D. K. (2006). 'Presidential greatness and performance: can we predict leadership in the white house', *Journal of Personality*, 49, 306–22.

Sosis, R. (2000). 'Religion and intragroup cooperation: Preliminary results of a comparative analysis of utopian communities', *Cross-Cultural Research*, 34, 70–87.

Spisak, B., and van Vugt, M. (2010). 'What's in a face? Evidence for evolved cognitive leadership prototypes about age and masculinity/femininity in war and peace', VU University Amsterdam, unpublished manuscript.

Stodgill, R. M. (1974). *Handbook of Leadership: A Survey of Theory and Research*, New York, Free Press.

Strenger, C., and Burak, J. (2006). 'The Leonardo effect: why entrepreneurs become their own fathers', *International Journal of Applied Psycho-analytic Studies*, 2, 103–28.

Tannenbaum, R., and Schmidt, W. H. (1973). 'How to choose a leadership pattern', *Harvard Business Review*, 51, 162–4.

Tinbergen, N. (1963). 'On aims and methods in ethology', *Zeitschrift für Tierpsychologie*, 20: 410–33.

Tishkoff, S. A., et al. (2006). 'Convergent adaptation of human lactase persistence in Africa and Europe', *Nature Genetics*, 39: 31–9.

Todorov, A., et al. (2005). 'Inferences of competence from faces predict election outcomes', *Science*, 308, 1623–6.

Trivers, R. L. (1971). 'The evolution of reciprocal altruism,' *Quarterly Review of Biology*, 46, 35–57.

van Vugt, M. (2006). 'Evolutionary origins of leadership and followership,' *Personality and Social Psychology Review*, 10, 354–71.

van Vugt, M. (2008). 'Follow me: The origins of leadership', *New Scientist*, 14 June.

van Vugt, M. (2009). 'Despotism, democracy and the evolutionary dynamics of leadership and followership', *American Psychologist*, 64, 54–6.

van Vugt, M. (2010). 'Evolutionary and biological approaches to leadership', in D. Day and J. Antonakis, eds., *The Nature of Leadership*, London, Sage.

van Vugt, M., and de Cremer, D. (1999). 'Leadership in social dilemmas: The effects of group identification on collective actions to provide public goods', *Journal of Personality and Social Psychology*, 76, 587–99.

van Vugt, M., de Cremer, D., and Janssen, D. P. (2007). 'Gender differences in cooperation and competition – The male-warrior hypothesis', *Psychological Science*, 18, 19–23.

van Vugt, M., and Hardy, C. (2010). 'Cooperation for reputation: Wasteful contributions as costly signals in public goods', *Group Processes and Intergroup Relations*, 1–11.

van Vugt, M., Hogan, R., and Kaiser, R. (2008). 'Leadership, followership, and evolution: Some lessons from the past', *American Psychologist*, 63, 182–96.

van Vugt, M., Jepson, S., Hart, C., and de Cremer, D. (2004). 'Autocratic leadership in social dilemmas: A threat to group stability', *Journal of Experimental Social Psychology*, 40, 1–13.

van Vugt, M., Johnson, D. D. P., Kaiser, R. B., and O'Gorman, R. (2008). 'Evolution and the social psychology of leadership: The mismatch hypothesis', in C. L. Hoyt, G. R. Goethals and D. R. Forsyth, eds, *Leadership at the Crossroads: Psychology and Leadership* (Vol. 1), Westport CT, Praeger.

van Vugt, M., and Kurzban, R. (2007). 'Cognitive and social adaptations for leadership and followership: Evolutionary game theory and group dynamics', in J. Forgas, W. von Hippel and M. Haselton, *Sydney Symposium of Social Psychology*, Vol. 9: 'The evolution of the social mind: Evolutionary psychology and social cognition', London, Psychology Press.

van Vugt, M., and Schaller, M. (2008). 'Evolutionary perspectives on group dynamics: An introduction', *Group Dynamics*, 12, 1–6.

van Vugt, M., and Spisak, B. (2008). 'Sex differences in leadership emergence during competitions within and between groups', *Psychological Science*, 19, 854–8.

van Vugt, M., and van Lange, P. (2006). 'The altruism puzzle: Psychological adaptations for prosocial behavior', in M. Schaller, D. Kenrick and J. Simpson, eds, *Evolution and Social Psychology*, Psychology Press.

von Frisch, K. (1967). *The Dance Language and Orientation of Bees*, Belknap Press.

Weber, M. (1947). *The Theory of Social and Economic Organization*, translated by A. M. Henderson and Talcott Parsons, The Free Press.

Wrangham, R., and Peterson, D. (1996). *Demonic Males: Apes and the Origins of Human Violence*, Boston, Houghton Mifflin.

Xue, Y., et al. (2009). 'Human Y chromosome base substitution mutation rate measured by direct sequencing in a deep-rooting pedigree', *Current Biology*, 19, 1453–7.

Yukl, G. (2009). *Leadership in Organisations*, New York, Prentice Hall.

Index